Dr. C's™ Ultimate

TEXAS MPJE REVIEW 2022

MASTERING THE MPJE COMPETENCIES

GARY CACCIATORE, Pharm.D., J.D.

Published by Dr. C's Review Guides
https://www.mpjereviews.com
info@mpjereviews.com

March 2022

978-0-578-34588-8

TABLE OF CONTENTS

INTRODUCTION

Dr. C's Ultimate Texas MPJE® Review Guide 2022 is intended to serve as a study guide for the Texas Multistate Pharmacy Jurisprudence Exam (MPJE®) and is best used with the textbook, *Texas and Federal Pharmacy and Drug Law, 13th Edition.*

The review guide follows the same general order (with some exceptions) as *Texas and Federal Pharmacy and Drug Law, 13th Edition*; however, the textbook provides more detailed and thorough information on each topic. References to *Texas and Federal Pharmacy and Drug Law, 13th Edition* are indicated in this guide by the abbreviation *TFPDL.*

Texas and Federal Pharmacy and Drug Law, 13th Edition is available for purchase at *www.mpjereviews.com* or at Amazon.com.

Study Tips are provided throughout this book to note important material and clarify information that we have found is often misunderstood or causes confusion.

As you experienced when you were a pharmacy student, recent graduate, or a seasoned pharmacist who last sat for an exam more than a few years ago, your study plan and preparation are critical to your success. The Texas MPJE requires you to fully comprehend state and federal laws, regulations, and a pharmacist's responsibilities.

Dr. C's Ultimate Texas MPJE® Review Guide 2022 has been developed by a pharmacy regulatory expert with education and experience in both law and pharmacy. The review guide is designed to assist you in focusing on the elements of the exam that may appear on the Texas MPJE, although the author has no specific knowledge of questions that are on the exam.

The key to success is to allow adequate time in your study plan to review parts of the law that are least familiar to you. We believe this review guide will help in the process and support your successful exam completion.

The author would like to thank Motto Publishing Services and Kurt Wehrs for their help in the production of this review guide and Debra Smith for her contributions and help in producing previous editions of this guide.

ACKNOWLEDGEMENT

Special thanks to Fred S. Brinkley, Jr., R.Ph., M.B.A., for his contributions to the original and previous editions of this book and for serving as a mentor and friend to the author for over 25 years.

ABOUT THE AUTHOR

Gary Cacciatore, Pharm.D., J.D.

Gary Cacciatore is the founder and President of Dr. C's Review Guides. In 2021, he retired from Cardinal Health, where he served as Associate Regulatory Counsel and Vice President of Regulatory Affairs.

Prior to joining Cardinal Health, Dr. Cacciatore was an Assistant Professor at the University of Houston College of Pharmacy and the University of Houston Law Center, where he taught courses in pharmacy law and ethics, drug information, and food and drug law. He currently serves as an Adjunct Professor at the University of Houston College of Pharmacy and the University of Florida College of Pharmacy.

Dr. Cacciatore received his Doctor of Pharmacy degree with high honors from the University of Florida College of Pharmacy. He earned his Doctor of Jurisprudence degree with honors from the University of Houston Law Center.

Dr. Cacciatore is admitted to the bar in Texas and is a registered pharmacist in Texas and Florida.

ACRONYMS

Most acronyms are defined the first time they are used in this book (and often several times), but here is a list of some of the major acronyms used.

ACPE	Accreditation Council for Pharmacy Education
APRN	Advanced Practice Registered Nurse
ASC	Ambulatory Surgical Center
CE	Continuing Education
CEU	Continuing Education Unit
CFR	Code of Federal Regulations
cGMP	Current Good Manufacturing Practices
DEA	Drug Enforcement Administration
DPS	Department of Public Safety (Texas)
DTM	Drug Therapy Management
FCSA	Federal Controlled Substances Act
FDA	Food and Drug Administration
FDCA	Food, Drug, and Cosmetic Act
FQHC	Federally Qualified Health Center
HIPAA	Health Insurance Portability and Accountability Act
LTCF	Long-Term Care Facility
MPJE	Multistate Pharmacy Jurisprudence Exam
NABP	National Association of Boards of Pharmacy
NAPLEX	North American Pharmacist Licensure Examination
NDC	National Drug Code
OTC	Over-the-Counter
PA	Physician Assistant
PIC	Pharmacist-in-Charge
PMP	Prescription Monitoring Program
PPI	Patient Package Insert
PPPA	Poison Prevention Packaging Act
REMS	Risk Evaluation and Mitigation Strategies
TCSA	Texas Controlled Substances Act
TDDA	Texas Dangerous Drug Act
TDSHS	Texas Department of State Health Services
TFPDL	Texas and Federal Pharmacy and Drug Law, 13th Edition
TPA	Texas Pharmacy Act
TSBP	Texas State Board of Pharmacy
USP	United States Pharmacopeia

Information on the Multistate Pharmacy Jurisprudence Exam (MPJE®)

General Information

Registration Bulletin

Detailed information on the MPJE is available from the National Association of Boards of Pharmacy (NABP) NAPLEX/MPJE Candidate Application Bulletin, which is available for download on NABP's website. The bulletin contains detailed information on registering for the exam, scheduling testing appointments, fees, identification requirements, security, question types, and exam results. Candidates should download and read the Candidate Application Bulletin carefully as well as visit the NABP website for additional information specific to the MPJE.

Exam Content and Structure

The MPJE is a 120-item computer-based examination that uses adaptive technology. This means the computer adapts the questions you receive based on your previous responses. Of the 120 items on the exam, 100 count toward your score. You are allowed 2½ hours to complete the exam, and you must answer 107 questions for your exam to be scored. The questions not counting toward your score are being pre-tested; however, you will not know which questions count toward your score and which questions are being pre-tested. Because it is a computer-based examination, you cannot go back and review a question or change an answer once you have confirmed it and moved to the next question. You also cannot skip a question. Since there is a penalty for unanswered questions, you should answer all of the questions.

The exam content and questions are developed by board of pharmacy representatives, practitioners, and educators from around the country who serve as item writers. Each state board of pharmacy approves the questions that are used for its particular state.

Previously, results were reported on a scaled score, and candidates had to achieve a score of 75 to pass the exam. This is not 75% but a scaled score whereby your performance is measured against predetermined minimum abilities. NABP no longer reports actual scores. Scores are only reported as pass or fail, and results are generally provided seven business days after you take the exam. Candidates are allowed five attempts to pass the exam.

While you must have a good base knowledge of the laws and rules governing the practice of pharmacy in your state, memorizing the laws will not suffice. The exam is not simply questions that ask you to identify or repeat the law. There are many situational questions that will require you to apply the law to the facts provided. When approaching these types of questions, it is helpful to remember that the goal of the Texas State Board of Pharmacy is to protect the public health. Answers that address that goal are most likely to be correct. At the same time, the Board must enforce the laws, so many of the laws and rules are intended to assist the Board with this responsibility. Rules related to recordkeeping and documentation are especially important to the Board to help it identify who or what caused an error in a pharmacy that may result in patient harm. Keeping these responsibilities of the Texas State Board of Pharmacy in mind may help you choose between answers on the exam.

The MPJE consists of several types of questions including multiple choice, multiple response, and ordered response questions. Examples of each question type are provided below.

Multiple Choice Sample Question

A Texas pharmacist must obtain how many continuing education (CE) hours to renew his or her license in each renewal period?

a. 15 hours
b. 20 hours
c. 30 hours
d. 40 hours

Multiple Response Sample Question

Which are permissible ways for a pharmacist to obtain continuing education? Select all that apply.

_____ Completing an ACPE-accredited continuing education course
_____ Attending a Texas State Board of Pharmacy meeting
_____ Auditing a course at a College of Pharmacy
_____ Taking an Advanced Cardiac Life Support class

STUDY TIP: When answering multiple response questions, it is recommended that you choose more than one answer. If only one answer is correct, it is more likely to be a multiple choice question.

Ordered Response Sample Question

Place the following products in order from the least abuse potential to the greatest abuse potential. (All options must be used.) Left click the mouse to highlight, drag, and order the answer options.

Unordered Options	**Ordered Response**
Tylenol with Codeine #4	______________
Sudafed	______________
Valium	______________
Vicodin	______________

STUDY TIP: Make sure you read the ordered response question carefully and put the items in the correct order and not the reverse order. Double check the order before submitting your answer.

Federal versus State Law

It is important to understand that **no distinction is made on the exam between federal and state law questions**. You should answer each question in terms of the prevailing laws of the state in which you are seeking licensure, which for purposes of this review guide is Texas. This means that you should not see a question on the exam that starts with the words, "According to the Federal Controlled Substances Act . . ." Such a question would not be valid because it is asking you to answer the question based on federal law only. If Texas has a law that is different and stricter than the federal law, that is the law that must be followed and would be the correct answer.

Basic Study and Preparation Tips

Below are helpful study and preparation tips to consider for the MPJE:

- Read and review relevant laws, regulations, and available government resources.
- Revisit pharmacy law course materials from pharmacy school (if recent graduate) and update information.
- When completing any practice questions, make sure you understand the concept as well as why the correct answer is correct and the other options are incorrect.
- Make and memorize charts and lists (e.g., label requirements, quantities, time frames).
- Be prepared to read exam directions and questions carefully and recall applicable laws.
- Be prepared to apply knowledge and skills of relevant laws and regulations.
- Be prepared to select the best answer. Do not overanalyze the questions or focus on the very rare instances that may change the answer.
- Be prepared to use time management skills during the exam (spending an average of 1.25 minutes on each question).
- Do not rely on what your own work environment does. Your employer may have additional or stricter policies, but you must answer exam questions based on the legal and regulatory requirements.
- Do not overlook important words such as "must," "can," "should," and "may."
- Do not forget to consider federal and state laws, choosing the stricter requirement when both apply.
- Do your best to remain relaxed and focused.

Pre-MPJE Exam

NABP offers a Pre-MPJE exam that candidates can register to take online at NABP's website. This is the only practice exam that features valid questions from previous versions of the MPJE. The exam consists of 40 questions and 50 minutes is allotted to complete the exam. The Pre-MPJE can be taken only one time for each jurisdiction in which a person is seeking licensure.

The official NABP Pre-MPJE exam can only be taken on the NABP's website. There are other websites using the term "Pre-MPJE" that are not affiliated with NABP.

MPJE Competency Statements

Each question on the MPJE is tied to a specific competency statement. You must master a certain number of competencies to pass the exam. It is imperative that you read through the competency statements. The competency statements for the MPJE can be accessed on NABP's website. The Texas State Board of Pharmacy also publishes the *Candidate's Guide to the Texas Pharmacy Jurisprudence Exam* which contains Texas-specific competency objectives. We have reprinted both the MPJE® competency statements and the *Candidate's Guide to the Texas Pharmacy Jurisprudence Exam* on the following pages.

Note: At the time of publication of this book, NABP was in the process of redrafting the MPJE Competencies. Readers should check the NABP website and Candidate Application Bulletin for the current version of the MPJE Competencies.

MPJE®
Competency Statements

Area 1 | Pharmacy Practice (83%)

1.1 Legal responsibilities of the pharmacist and other pharmacy personnel

1.1.1 Unique legal responsibilities of the pharmacist-in-charge (or equivalent), pharmacists, interns, and pharmacy owners

Responsibilities for inventory, loss and/or theft of prescription drugs, the destruction/disposal of prescription drugs, and the precedence of Local, State, or Federal requirements

1.1.2 Qualifications, scope of duties, and conditions for practice relating to pharmacy technicians and all other non-pharmacist personnel

Personnel ratios, duties, tasks, roles, and functions of non-pharmacist personnel

1.2 Requirements for the acquisition and distribution of pharmaceutical products, including samples

1.2.1 Requirements and record keeping in relation to the ordering, acquiring, and maintenance of all pharmaceutical products and bulk drug substances/excipients

Legitimate suppliers, pedigrees, and the maintenance of acquisition records

1.2.2 Requirements for distributing pharmaceutical products and preparations, including the content and maintenance of distribution records

Legal possession of pharmaceutical products (including drug samples), labeling, packaging, repackaging, compounding, and sales to practitioners

1.3 Legal requirements that must be observed in the issuance of a prescription/drug order

1.3.1 Prescription/order requirements for pharmaceutical products and the limitations on their respective therapeutic uses

Products, preparations, their uses, and limitations applicable to all prescribed orders for both human and veterinary uses

1.3.2 Scope of authority, scope of practice, and valid registration of all practitioners who are authorized under law to prescribe, dispense, or administer pharmaceutical products, including controlled substances

Federal and State registrations, methadone programs, office-based opioid treatment programs, regulations related to retired or deceased prescribers, internet prescribing, and limits on jurisdictional prescribing

1.3.3 Conditions under which the pharmacist participates in the administration of pharmaceutical products or in the management of patients' drug therapy

Prescriptive authority, collaborative practice, consulting, counseling, medication administration (including immunizations and vaccines), ordering labs, medication therapy management, and disease state management

1.3.4 Requirements for issuing a prescription/order

Content and format for written, telephonic voice transmission, electronic facsimile, computer and internet, during emergency conditions, and tamper-resistant prescription forms

1.3.5 Requirements for the issuance of controlled substance prescriptions/orders

Content and format for written, telephonic voice transmission, electronic facsimile, computerized and internet, during emergency conditions, conditions for changing a prescription, time limits for dispensing initial prescriptions/drug orders, and requirements for multiple Schedule II orders

1.3.6 Limits of a practitioner's authority to authorize refills of a pharmaceutical product, including controlled substances

1.4 Procedures necessary to properly dispense a pharmaceutical product, including controlled substances, pursuant to a prescription/drug order

1.4.1 Responsibilities for determining whether prescriptions/orders were issued for a legitimate medical purpose and within all applicable legal restrictions

Corresponding responsibility, maximum quantities, restricted distribution systems, red flags/automated alerts, controlled substances, valid patient/prescriber relationship, and due diligence to ensure validity of the order

1.4.2 Requirements for the transfer of existing prescription/order information from one pharmacist to another

1.4.3 Conditions under which a prescription/order may be filled or refilled

Emergency fills or refills, partial dispensing of a controlled substance, disaster or emergency protocol, patient identification, requirement for death with dignity, medical marijuana, and conscience/moral circumstances

1.4.4 Conditions under which prospective drug use review is conducted prior to dispensing

Patient specific therapy and requirements for patient specific documentation

1.4.5 Conditions under which product selection is permitted or mandated

Consent of the patient and/or prescriber, passing-on of cost savings, and appropriate documentation

1.4.6 Requirements for the labeling of pharmaceutical products and preparations dispensed pursuant to a prescription/order

Generic and therapeutic equivalency, formulary use, auxiliary labels, patient package inserts, FDA medication guides, and written drug information

1.4.7 Packaging requirements of pharmaceutical products, preparations, and devices to be dispensed pursuant to a prescription/order

Child-resistant and customized patient medication packaging

1.4.8 Conditions under which a pharmaceutical product, preparation, or device may not be dispensed

Adulteration, misbranding, and dating

1.4.9 Requirements for compounding pharmaceutical products

Environmental controls, release checks and testing, beyond-use date (BUD), and initial and ongoing training

1.4.10 Requirements for emergency kits

Supplying, maintenance, access, security, and inventory

1.4.11 Conditions regarding the return and/or reuse of pharmaceutical products, preparations, bulk drug substances/excipients, and devices

Charitable programs, cancer or other repository programs, previously dispensed, and from "will call" areas of pharmacies

1.4.12 Procedures and requirements for systems or processes whereby a non-pharmacist may obtain pharmaceutical products, preparations, bulk drug substances/excipients, and devices

Pyxis (vending), after-hour's access, telepharmacies, and secure automated patient drug retrieval centers

1.4.13 Procedures and requirements for establishing and operating central processing and central fill pharmacies

Remote order verification

1.4.14 Requirements for reporting to PMP, accessing information in a PMP, and the maintenance of security and confidentiality of information accessed in PMPs

1.4.15 Requirements when informed consent must be obtained from the patient and/or a duty to warn must be executed

Collaborative practice and investigational drug therapy

1.5 Conditions for making an offer to counsel or counseling appropriate patients, including the requirements for documentation

1.5.1 Requirements to counsel or to make an offer to counsel

1.5.2 Required documentation necessary for counseling

1.6 Requirements for the distribution and/or dispensing of non-prescription pharmaceutical products, including controlled substances

1.6.1 Requirements for the labeling of non-prescription pharmaceutical products and devices

1.6.2 Requirements for the packaging and repackaging of non-prescription pharmaceutical products and devices

1.6.3 Requirements for the distribution and/or dispensing of poisons, restricted, non-prescription pharmaceutical products, and other restricted materials or devices

Pseudoephedrine, dextromethorphan, emergency contraception, and behind-the-counter products, as appropriate

1.7 Procedures for keeping records of information related to pharmacy practice, pharmaceutical products, and patients, including requirements for protecting patient confidentiality

1.7.1 Requirements pertaining to controlled substance inventories

1.7.2 Content, maintenance, storage, and reporting requirements for records required in the operation of a pharmacy

Prescription filing systems, computer systems and backups, and prescription monitoring programs

1.7.3 Requirements for protecting patient confidentiality and confidential health records

HIPAA requirements and conditions for access and use of information

1.8 Requirements for handling hazardous materials such as described in USP <800>

1.8.1 Requirements for appropriate disposal of hazardous materials

1.8.2 Requirements for training regarding hazardous materials

Reverse distributors, quarantine procedures, comprehensive safety programs, and Material Safety Data Sheets

1.8.3 Environmental controls addressing the proper storage, handling, and disposal of hazardous materials

Ventilation controls, personal protective equipment, work practices, and reporting

1.8.4 Methods for the compounding, dispensing, and administration of hazardous materials

All hazardous materials including sterile and non-sterile compounding

Area 2 | Licensure, Registration, Certification, and Operational Requirements (15%)

2.1 Qualifications, application procedure, necessary examinations, and internship for licensure, registration, or certification of individuals engaged in the storage, distribution, and/or dispensing of pharmaceutical products (prescription and non-prescription)

2.1.1 Requirements for special or restricted licenses, registration, authorization, or certificates

Pharmacists, pharmacist preceptors, pharmacy interns, pharmacy technicians, controlled substance registrants, and under specialty pharmacist licenses (Nuclear, Consultant, etc.)

2.1.2 Standards of practice related to the practice of pharmacy

Quality assurance programs (including peer review), changing dosage forms, therapeutic substitution, error reporting, public health reporting requirements (such as notification of potential terrorist event, physical abuse, and treatment for tuberculosis), and issues of conscience and maintaining competency

2.1.3 Requirements for classifications and processes of disciplinary actions that may be taken against a registered, licensed, certified, or permitted individual

2.1.4 Requirements for reporting to and participating in programs addressing the inability of an individual licensed, registered, or certified by the Board to engage in the practice of pharmacy with reasonable skill and safety

Impairment caused by the use of alcohol, drugs, chemicals, or other materials or mental, physical, or psychological conditions

2.2 Requirements and application procedure for the registration, licensure, certification, or permitting of a practice setting or business entity

2.2.1 Requirements for registration, license, certification, or permitting of a practice setting

In-state pharmacies, out-of-state pharmacies, specialty pharmacies, controlled substance registrants, wholesalers, distributors, manufacturers/repackagers, computer services providers, and internet pharmacies

2.2.2 Requirements for an inspection of a licensed, registered, certified, or permitted practice setting

2.2.3 Requirements for the renewal or reinstatement of a license, registration, certificate, or permit of a practice setting

2.2.4 Classifications and processes of disciplinary actions that may be taken against a registered, licensed, certified, or permitted practice setting

2.3 Operational requirements for a registered, licensed, certified, or permitted practice setting

2.3.1 Requirements for the operation of a pharmacy or practice setting that is not directly related to the dispensing of pharmaceutical products

Issues related to space, equipment, advertising and signage, security (including temporary absences of the pharmacist), policies and procedures, libraries and references (including veterinary), and the display of licenses

2.3.2 Requirements for the possession, storage, and handling of pharmaceutical products, preparations, bulk drug substances/excipients, and devices, including controlled substances

Investigational new drugs, repackaged or resold drugs, sample pharmaceuticals, recalls, and outdated pharmaceutical products

2.3.3 Requirements for delivery of pharmaceutical products, preparations, bulk drug substances/excipients, and devices, including controlled substances

Issues related to identification of the person accepting delivery of a drug, use of the mail, contract delivery, use of couriers, use of pharmacy employees, use of kiosks, secure mailboxes, script centers, use of vacuum tubes, and use of drive-up windows

Area 3 | General Regulatory Processes (2%)

3.1 Application of regulations

3.1.1 Laws and rules that regulate or affect the manufacture, storage, distribution, and dispensing of pharmaceutical products, preparations, bulk drug substances/excipients, and devices (prescription and non-prescription), including controlled substances

Food, Drug, and Cosmetic Act(s) and Regulations, the Controlled Substances Act(s) and Regulations, OBRA 90's Title IV Requirements, Practice Acts and Rules, other statutes and regulations, including but not limited to dispensing of methadone, child-resistant packaging, tamper-resistant packaging, drug paraphernalia, drug samples, pharmacist responsibilities in Medicare-certified skilled-nursing facilities, NDC numbers, and schedules of controlled substances

TEXAS STATE BOARD OF PHARMACY

CANDIDATE'S GUIDE TO THE TEXAS PHARMACY JURISPRUDENCE EXAM

As required by the Texas Pharmacy Act, the Texas State Board of Pharmacy administers a Texas Pharmacy Jurisprudence Exam to candidates for licensure in Texas.

TEXAS PHARMACY JURISPRUDENCE EXAM

The Board uses the services of the National Association of Boards of Pharmacy (NABP) and administers their Multistate Pharmacy Jurisprudence Exam (MPJE). Although the MPJE is developed for use by multiple states, all of the exam questions on the Texas version of the exam are applicable to pharmacy practice in Texas. This exam is a comprehensive exam, which includes questions on both federal and state statutes and rules pertaining to the practice of pharmacy in Texas.

The exam is designed to measure each applicant's knowledge of pharmacy law. Candidates should be aware of conflicting areas between Texas and Federal laws and rules and should answer exam questions on the basis of the more stringent statute or rule. You will be given two and one-half hours to answer 120 multiple choice questions.

Since the exam is a qualifying exam, applicants are not competing against each other for a passing score. An applicant is required to attain a score of no less than 75 on the exam. The score is calculated by first determining the candidate's ability level on the MPJE and then comparing the candidate's ability level to the predetermined minimum acceptable ability level established for the MPJE. An applicant who passes NAPLEX but fails the Texas Pharmacy Jurisprudence Exam is required to repeat only the Jurisprudence exam. If an applicant passes the Texas Pharmacy Jurisprudence Exam but fails NAPLEX, the applicant may use the passing grade on the Jurisprudence examination for licensure purposes for a period of two years from the date of passing the exam.

Rev. 03/18

COMPETENCY OBJECTIVES

The MPJE Competency Statements, found in the MPJE Registration Bulletin, serve as the blueprint for the topics covered on the Texas Pharmacy Jurisprudence Examination. The competency objectives contained in this document are a detailed supplement to the MPJE Competency Statements.

The attached list of competency objectives provides a guide to the facts and information that you should be prepared to apply to practical situations. Although the exam is a multiple-choice exam, the competency objectives are written in an essay format. Test experts believe that one of the best ways to prepare for an exam is to prepare for an essay exam.

HOW TO OBTAIN COPIES OF LAWS AND REGULATIONS

Information regarding Texas Pharmacy Rules & Laws can be obtained from the Texas State Board of Pharmacy website (www.pharmacy.texas.gov).

The Poison Prevention Packaging Act (summary publication) may be obtained from the U.S. Consumer Product Safety Commission's website (www.cpsc.gov).

The Federal Food, Drug and Cosmetic Act may be obtained from the Food and Drug Administration's website (www.fda.gov).

Please note that the Texas Food, Drug and Cosmetic Act is patterned after and tracks the federal Act very closely. The Texas Food, Drug and Cosmetic Act may be obtained at (http://www.statutes.legis.state.tx.us/).

Rev. 03/18

TEXAS STATE BOARD OF PHARMACY JURISPRUDENCE EXAM COMPETENCY OBJECTIVES

I. Texas Pharmacy Act

Objectives: The candidate should be prepared to:

1. discuss the purpose of the Board;
2. explain the definitions in the Act;
3. describe the qualifications for membership and the makeup of the Board;
4. explain the rule-making authority of the Board;
5. discuss the responsibilities of the Board;
6. discuss inspections by the Board or its representative;
7. explain unlawful practice of pharmacy;
8. discuss pharmacist-intern registration;
9. discuss the number of times a licensing exam may be retaken;
10. list qualifications for licensing by examination and by reciprocity;
11. describe requirements for display of a pharmacist's license and renewal certificate;
12. discuss renewal of a pharmacist's license;
13. describe the mandatory continuing education requirements for renewing a pharmacist license;
14. describe the procedures and effects of placing a pharmacist license on inactive status;
15. list grounds for discipline of a pharmacist's and pharmacy's license;
16. discuss disciplinary action in a Class E Pharmacy;
17. discuss temporary suspension of a pharmacist's and pharmacy's license;
18. discuss the penalties that may be imposed by the Board and methods for reinstatement of a license;
19. describe the application procedures for licensure and renewal of pharmacy licenses;
20. list and give time limits for the items that must be reported to the Board by a pharmacy and pharmacist;
21. discuss administration and provision of dangerous drugs by practitioners;
22. discuss the unlawful use of the word "Pharmacy" and the title "Registered Pharmacist";
23. discuss the requirements for drug substitution;
24. discuss the requirements for emergency refills;
25. discuss the requirements for release of confidential records; and
26. explain the requirements for operating a remote pharmacy service.

Rev. 03/18

II. Texas Pharmacy Rules of Procedure

Objectives: The candidate should be prepared to:

1. discuss the items that constitute "unprofessional conduct," "gross immorality," or "fraud, deceit or misrepresentation" in the practice of pharmacy as grounds for discipline of a pharmacist license;
2. discuss the items that constitute failure to establish and maintain effective controls against diversion of prescription drugs as grounds for discipline of a pharmacy license;
3. describe Board disciplinary procedures against a licensee;
4. discuss the application procedure for reissuance or removal of restrictions on a license;
5. discuss the goals and objectives of internship, the requirements for the Texas colleges of pharmacy internship programs, and the requirements for graduates of out-of-state colleges of pharmacy;
6. explain the extended internship program;
7. discuss the duties that a pharmacist-intern may perform;
8. describe preceptor requirements;
9. discuss examination and reciprocity requirements;
10. explain the requirements for renewal of a pharmacist's license that has expired;
11. describe procedures for change of location, name, ownership, or managing officers of a pharmacy;
12. describe the procedures for closing a pharmacy;
13. discuss the return of dispensed prescription drugs;
14. discuss the requirements for prescription pickup locations;
15. explain the registration requirements of a pharmacy that uses a pharmacy balance;
16. discuss the terms "failure to engage in the business described in the application for a license" and "ceased to engage in the business described in the application for a license";
17. describe the responsibilities of the pharmacist-in-charge of a pharmacy that experiences a fire or other disaster;
18. discuss notification of theft or loss of a controlled substance or dangerous drug;
19. discuss the Board's inventory requirements;
20. explain the requirements for, and the differences in, the requirements for personnel, operational standards, and records in a:

Rev. 03/18

- Class A (Community) Pharmacy;
- Class A-S (Community Sterile Compounding) Pharmacy;
- Class B (Nuclear) Pharmacy;
- Class C (Institutional) Pharmacy;
- Class C (Institutional) Pharmacy Located in a Freestanding Ambulatory Surgical Center;
- Class C-S (Institutional Sterile Compounding) Pharmacy;
- Class D (Clinic) Pharmacy;
- Class E (Non-Resident) Pharmacy;
- Class E-S (Non-Resident Sterile Compounding) Pharmacy;
- Class F Pharmacy Located in a Freestanding Emergency Medical Care Facility; and
- Class G (Central Prescription Drug or Medication Order Processing) Pharmacy.

21. explain the similarities and differences in the requirements for the use of pharmacy technicians and pharmacy technician trainees; their duties, ratios, and training in each class of pharmacy listed in number 20;

22. discuss the responsibilities of the pharmacist-in-charge in each of the classes of pharmacy;

23. discuss the pharmacist's responsibilities for patient counseling and the provision of drug information to patients in Class A pharmacies;

24. discuss the requirements for patient medication records in Class A and Class C pharmacies;

25. discuss drug regimen review requirements in Class A and Class C pharmacies;

26. discuss identification of pharmacy personnel in Class A and Class C pharmacies;

27. describe security requirements for each of the classes of pharmacy;

28. describe the requirements for the temporary absence (off-site and on-site) of a pharmacist in Class A (Community) pharmacies;

29. describe the three-file system for prescriptions that is required in Texas;

30. explain the requirements for written, verbal, and facsimile (FAX) prescriptions;

31. list the requirements for a prescription label;

32. explain the requirements for the use of automation in pharmacies;

33. discuss refill requirements for dangerous drugs and controlled substances;

34. explain the procedures for documenting refill authorization;

Rev. 03/18

35. relate the procedures for telephonic and electronic transfer of prescription information between pharmacies;
36. discuss the requirements for maintaining prescription records in a data processing system;
37. discuss Schedule II controlled substance official prescription requirements and exceptions to the use of Schedule II controlled substance official prescriptions;
38. discuss the requirements and restrictions for prescriptions issued by practitioners not licensed in Texas;
39. discuss the requirements and restrictions for drug therapy management and for administration of immunizations and vaccinations by a pharmacist under written protocol of a physician;
40. discuss the requirements and restrictions for prescriptions carried out or signed by advanced practice registered nurses and physician assistants;
41. discuss the requirements for a Class A Pharmacy that compounds non-sterile preparations;
42. discuss the requirements for a Class A-S Pharmacy that compounds sterile preparations;
43. describe the requirements of a pharmacy providing centralized prescription dispensing services;
44. describe the requirements for a pharmacy providing central prescription drug or medication order processing;
45. describe the requirements for inpatient records of a hospital or ambulatory surgical center;
46. discuss the absence of pharmacist records in a Class C Pharmacy;
47. discuss the requirements for maintaining records in a data processing system in a Class C Pharmacy;
48. describe the requirements for supplying drugs from the emergency room or radiology department of a hospital;
49. discuss the requirements for dispensing prescriptions to outpatients of a hospital;
50. discuss record requirements for Schedule II controlled substances and floor stock in a Class C Pharmacy;
51. describe the limitations for a Class D Pharmacy drug/device formulary and the petition process for an expanded formulary;
52. explain the requirements for pharmacist supervision in a Class D Pharmacy and the petition process for an alternative visitation schedule;

Rev. 03/18

53. discuss the requirements for Class E pharmacies mailing prescriptions to Texas patients;
54. describe the standards for the provision of pharmacy services through an automated pharmacy system;
55. describe the standards for the provision of pharmacy services through a telepharmacy system;
56. describe the standards for the provision of pharmacy services through an emergency medication kit;
57. discuss the regulations governing pharmacists;
58. explain the procedures for reporting approved continuing education and the penalties for reporting falsely;
59. discuss the procedures for placing a pharmacist's license on inactive status and for reactivating an inactive license;
60. list the requirements for destruction of dispensed drugs;
61. list the requirements for disposal of stock prescription drugs;
62. discuss the regulations concerning generic substitution;
63. discuss requirements for the use of automation in a pharmacy; and
64. describe how a pharmacist can become Board Certified.

III. Federal and State Controlled Substances Acts and Regulations

Objectives: The candidate should be prepared to:

1. discuss the terms defined in the State and Federal Controlled Substances Acts (CSA);
2. discuss who must register with the Drug Enforcement Administration (DEA);
3. describe types of registration and procedures for registering with DEA;
4. relate the procedures and limitations to distribute controlled substances from one registrant to another without obtaining a second registration;
5. discuss the storage requirements for controlled substances in pharmacies;
6. list all records that must be maintained for acquisition of controlled substances;
7. list all records that must be maintained for dispensing and disposition of controlled substances;
8. describe central recordkeeping requirements and restrictions;

Rev. 03/18

9. discuss the requirements for obtaining, executing, and storing DEA order forms;
10. describe the procedures to follow for a theft or loss of DEA order forms;
11. describe the correct procedures for the return of controlled substances to a supplier;
12. state methods for disposing of expired or contaminated controlled substances;
13. list the legal requirements of prescriptions for Schedule II, III, IV, and V controlled substances;
14. discuss the specific refill requirements for Schedule II, III, IV, and V controlled substances;
15. discuss emergency refill requirements for Schedule III, IV, and V controlled substances;
16. describe the requirements for partial dispensing of Schedule II and Schedule III, IV, and V controlled substances;
17. describe the procedure for a pharmacist accepting an emergency oral order for a Schedule II controlled substance and the pharmacist's responsibilities;
18. describe the Federal "transfer warning" statement and the requirements for its use;
19. explain the possible implications for knowingly dispensing a forged or altered prescription;
20. discuss the Texas CSA restrictions on the sale of over-the-counter (OTC) Schedule V products;
21. discuss Schedule II controlled substance official prescription requirements and exceptions to the use of Schedule II controlled substance official prescriptions;
22. discuss the criteria used to place a drug product in each of the five schedules;
23. recognize commonly used controlled substances and their schedules;
24. describe procedures for reporting a theft or loss of controlled substances to DEA and DPS;
25. briefly discuss requirements for employee screening;
26. explain the procedures for disposing of the DEA registration certificate and unused order forms upon discontinuance or transfer of business;
27. describe the legal use of methadone;
28. briefly explain the special requirements for a practitioner using methadone to treat addiction;

Rev. 03/18

29. briefly explain the special requirements for a practitioner using Subutex® or Suboxone® to treat addiction;
30. discuss a pharmacist's corresponding responsibility for controlled substance prescription orders;
31. describe requirements regarding whom a practitioner may designate as an agent for the purpose of communicating a practitioner's instructions (prescription) to a pharmacist;
32. discuss the requirements to fill a prescription for a Schedule II controlled substance issued by a practitioner not licensed in Texas; and
33. discuss the conditions and requirements which allow a pharmacist to dispense a fax prescription for a Schedule II controlled substance.

IV. Federal and State Food, Drug, and Cosmetic Acts

Objectives: The candidate should be prepared to:

1. discuss the terms defined in the State and Federal Law;
2. list conditions causing a drug or device to be deemed adulterated;
3. list the conditions causing a drug or device to be deemed misbranded;
4. state the registration requirements for "Manufacturers" and "Distributors";
5. explain the illegal acts of a pharmacist under the Durham-Humphrey Amendments;
6. describe contents of a manufacturer's label;
7. state the minimum number of years prescriptions must be kept;
8. discuss FDA's recall classification system; and
9. briefly explain the requirements of FDA's Good Manufacturing Practices.

V. Texas Dangerous Drug Act

Objectives: The candidate should be prepared to:

1. discuss the terms defined in the Texas Dangerous Drug Act;
2. list the labeling requirements for dangerous drugs dispensed by a pharmacist and by a practitioner;
3. describe the requirements of refilling a prescription;
4. list the classes of persons who may possess dangerous drugs in the performance of their official duties;
5. discuss the records a pharmacy is required to maintain under the Act;

Rev. 03/18

6. describe the primary enforcing agency and legal proceedings under the Act;
7. explain forgery under the Act; and
8. describe the requirements for designation as an agent of a practitioner for the purpose of communicating a practitioner's instructions (prescription) to a pharmacist.

VI. Miscellaneous Laws and Regulations Pertaining to Pharmacy Practice

1. Hazardous Substances:

Objectives: The candidate should be prepared to:

- summarize the Poison Prevention Packaging Act of 1970 and a pharmacist's responsibilities under the Act; and
- discuss exceptions to the child-resistant packaging requirements for specific products and patient-specific requests.

2. United States Postal Regulations:

Objectives: The candidate should be prepared to:

- state the U.S. Postal regulations for mailing controlled substances.

3. Texas Optometry Act:

Objectives: The candidate should be prepared to:

- discuss the requirements and limitations for prescribing by therapeutic optometrists. The Texas Optometry Act and rules may be viewed at the following link:

http://www.tob.state.tx.us

Rev. 03/18

CHAPTER ONE

Federal Food, Drug, and Cosmetic Act (FDCA), Poison Prevention Packaging Act (PPPA), and Other Miscellaneous Federal Laws

CHAPTER ONE

Federal Food, Drug, and Cosmetic Act (FDCA), Poison Prevention Packaging Act (PPPA), and Other Miscellaneous Federal Laws

I. Federal Food, Drug, and Cosmetic Act (FDCA) and Major Amendments

A. Food, Drug, and Cosmetic Act of 1938

1. Following deaths caused by sulfanilamide elixir in 1937, Congress passed the first legislation that required new drugs to be proven safe prior to marketing.
2. Established the FDA and is the primary federal law dealing with food, drug, cosmetic, and medical device safety today (with many amendments).

B. Durham-Humphrey Amendments of 1951

1. Established two classes of drugs: prescription and over-the-counter (OTC).

STUDY TIP: You are expected to know those pharmaceutical products that require a prescription. It is particularly important to know that certain products in the same drug class may be either prescription or nonprescription depending on the product or the strength. For example, some insulin products are nonprescription; however, certain other insulin products such as Lantus® and Humalog® are prescription-only products. Other examples—ibuprofen 400 mg, 600 mg, and 800 mg—require a prescription while ibuprofen 200 mg does not.

---

2. Authorized verbal prescriptions and prescription refills.

C. Kefauver-Harris Amendments of 1962

1. Required new drugs be proven safe and effective for their claimed use.
2. Increased safety requirements for drugs and established Good Manufacturing Practices (GMPs) for manufacturing of drugs.
3. Gave FDA jurisdiction over prescription drug advertising.

D. Prescription Drug Marketing Act of 1987 (PDMA)

1. Bans the reimportation of prescription drugs and insulin products produced in the United States (except by the manufacturer).

Note: This prohibition is on the reimportation of drugs produced in the United States and then exported. This is different than the importation of drugs manufactured in another country. Importation of drugs is generally prohibited; however, the Medicine Equity and Drug Safety (MEDS) Act of 2000 and the Medicare Prescription Drug Improvement and Modernization Act of 2003 both have provisions that allow importation of drugs under specific conditions. On September 24, 2020, FDA finalized regulations that permit states or Indian tribes (and in certain circumstances in conjunction with wholesalers and pharmacies) to serve as sponsors to import drugs from Canada with detailed requirements. A few states (but not Texas) have passed laws to allow drug importation from Canada, but as of the date of this book's publication, no state plan has been approved by FDA or implemented.

2. Bans the sale, trade, or purchase of prescription drug samples.

STUDY TIP: TSBP rules on samples are consistent with federal law and prohibit most pharmacies from selling, purchasing, trading, or possessing prescription drug samples. The only exception is for pharmacies that are owned by a charitable organization or by a city, state, or county government and that are part of a healthcare entity providing care to indigent or low-income patients at no or reduced cost. Such samples may only be provided at no charge to patients.

---

3. Mandates the storage, handling, and recordkeeping requirements for prescription drug samples.
4. Prohibits, with certain exceptions, the resale of prescription drugs purchased by hospitals or healthcare facilities.
   Note: There are some exceptions to 4. above, but this law is intended to prevent diversion of drugs due to price differentials because hospitals generally receive lower prices for drugs than community pharmacies.

E. The Drug Quality and Security Act (DQSA) of 2013—These amendments to the FDCA addressed two primary topics: large-scale compounding by pharmacies, and establishment of a framework for a uniform track and trace system for prescription drugs throughout the supply chain.

1. Drug Compounding Quality Act (DCQA).
   a. Maintains regulation of traditional compounding with states under Section 503A, but establishes Section 503B

in the FDCA that allows facilities that are compounding sterile pharmaceuticals that are not based on patient-specific prescriptions to register with the FDA as an "Outsourcing Facility."

b. Outsourcing facilities that meet the Act's requirements are exempt from the new drug provisions (FDCA Section 505), adequate directions for use (FDCA Section 502(f)(1)), and drug track and trace provisions (FDCA Section 582).

c. Outsourcing facilities, often referred to as 503B facilities, are permitted to compound sterile products without receiving patient-specific prescriptions or medication orders. They are primarily regulated by FDA and are subject to FDA's current Good Manufacturing Practices (cGMPs).

d. Compounding pharmacies that are not registered with FDA as an "outsourcing facility" are often referred to as 503A facilities or 503A pharmacies and may only compound products pursuant to an individual prescription or medication order. They are permitted to do limited anticipatory compounding, are primarily regulated by the states, and are subject to USP Chapter 797 quality standards for sterile compounding.

e. Outsourcing facilities must:

- **(1)** Have a licensed pharmacist who provides direct oversight for the drugs compounded;
- **(2)** Register as an outsourcing facility. The FDA website provides a list of the names of each outsourcing facility along with the state where the facility is located, whether the facility compounds from bulk drug substances, and whether drugs compounded from bulk are sterile or nonsterile;
- **(3)** Report to the Secretary of HHS upon registering, and every six months thereafter, the drugs sold in the previous six months;
- **(4)** Be inspected by FDA according to a risk-based inspection schedule and pay annual fees to support it;
- **(5)** Report serious adverse event experiences within 15 days and conduct a follow-up investigation and reporting similar to current drug manufacturers; and

(6) Label products with a statement identifying them as a compounded drug and other specified information about the drug.

f. Outsourcing facilities may not compound a drug product that includes a bulk drug substance unless:

(1) The bulk drug substance appears on a list identifying bulk drug substances for which there is a clinical need (the 503B bulks list); or

(2) The drug product compounded from such bulk drug substance appears on FDA's drug shortage list at the time of compounding, distribution, and dispensing.

Note: Bulk drug substances must be accompanied by a valid certificate of analysis and must have been manufactured by an establishment registered with FDA. In addition, if an applicable United States Pharmacopeia (USP) or National Formulary monograph exists, bulk drug substances must comply with the monograph. FDA issued an Interim Policy on Compounding Using Bulk Drug Substances under Section 503B of FDCA, which is in place while FDA develops the 503B bulks list. The guidance describes conditions under which the agency does not intend to take action against outsourcing facilities that compound drug products from bulk drug substances that cannot otherwise be used in compounding under Section 503B. See the compounding section of FDA's website for more information.

g. Interstate distribution of compounded drugs from a 503A pharmacy.

(1) Section 503A also limits interstate distribution of compounded drugs to 5% unless the compounder is located in a state that has entered into a memorandum of understanding (MOU) with FDA addressing inordinate amounts of compounded drugs in interstate commerce and providing for appropriate investigation of complaints by a state.

(2) In states that have entered into an MOU with FDA, a pharmacy is considered to have distributed an inordinate amount of compounded drug products in interstate commerce if the number of prescription

orders for compounded human drug products that the pharmacy distributed interstate during any calendar year is greater than 50% of the sum of:

(i) the number of prescription orders for compounded human drug products that the pharmacy sent out of (or caused to be sent out of) the facility in which the drug products were compounded during that same calendar year; plus

(ii) the number of prescription orders for compounded human drug products that were dispensed (e.g., picked up by a patient) at the pharmacy during that same calendar year.

Note: All of the compounded drugs must still be prepared based on an individually identified patient. Details on how these calculations are made can be found on the compounding page of FDA's website and in FDA's Standard MOU.

(3) In states that have not entered into an MOU with FDA, a pharmacy may not distribute (or cause to be distributed) compounded drug products out of the state in which they are compounded in quantities that exceed 5% of the total prescription orders dispensed or distributed by such pharmacy.

Note: FDA has announced that it is extending the period for states to decide whether to sign the MOU and before FDA begins enforcing the 5% rule. The new deadline for states to sign the MOU and comply with the 5% rule is October 22, 2022.

(4) As of this book's publication date, Texas has not entered into an MOU with FDA addressing inordinate amounts of compounded drugs in interstate commerce. This means that beginning October 22, 2022, Texas pharmacies may not distribute (or cause to be distributed) compounded drug products out of state in quantities that exceed 5% of the total prescription orders dispensed or distributed by such pharmacy.

Note: Readers should search for the latest information on this topic, as there is ongoing litigation that may impact these requirements and deadlines.

STUDY TIP: FDA has issued several additional guidance documents to implement the Compounding Quality Act that are beyond the scope of this review guide. Detailed information may be found on FDA's website.

2. Drug Supply Chain Security Act (DSCSA) (Track and Trace).
   a. Provides for a uniform national framework for an electronic track and trace system for prescription drugs as they move through the supply chain and sets national standards for states to license drug wholesaler distributors.
   b. Applies to prescription drugs for human use in finished dosage form, but certain products are exempted including blood and blood components, radioactive drugs, imaging drugs, certain intravenous products for fluid replacement, dialysis solutions, medical gases, compounded drugs, medical convenience kits containing drugs, certain combination products, sterile water, and products for irrigation.
   c. Manufacturers are required to provide "Transaction Data" for each product sold. Wholesalers are required to receive transaction data upon purchase and subsequently provide transaction data to buyer (pharmacies or other wholesalers), and pharmacies are required to receive transaction data and pass this information along if they further distribute the product.
   d. "Transaction Data" includes Transaction Information, Transaction History, and a Transaction Statement.
      (1) Transaction Information includes the product's name, strength, and dosage form; NDC number; container size and number of containers; date of transaction; and name and address of the person from whom ownership is being transferred and to whom ownership is being transferred. A unique product identifier or serialized numerical identifier (SNI) will also be required that identifies an individual bottle or unit of sale.
      (2) Transaction History is a paper or electronic statement that includes prior transaction information for each prior transaction back to the manufacturer.
      (3) Transaction Statement is a paper or electronic statement by the seller that the seller is authorized (licensed), received the product from an authorized

(licensed) person, received the transaction information and transaction history from the prior owner if required, did not knowingly ship a suspect or illegitimate product, has systems and processes to comply with verification requirements, and did not knowingly provide false transaction information.

STUDY TIP: Transaction data must be maintained for 6 years by each supply chain partner.

e. Pharmacies may only receive drugs with product identifiers. Pharmacies are not yet required to authenticate (scan) those product identifiers.
Note: A product identifier is a standardized graphic with three elements: the product's standardized numerical identifier (SNI), which comprises the National Drug Code plus a unique alphanumeric serial number; a lot number; and an expiration date. Product identifiers must be in human- and machine-readable formats.

f. Pharmacies must investigate and properly handle suspect and illegitimate products.

(1) Suspect products are products that one has reason to believe are potentially counterfeit, diverted, stolen, subject of a fraudulent transaction, intentionally adulterated, or appear otherwise unfit for distribution such that they would result in serious adverse health consequences or death to humans.

(2) Illegitimate products are products for which credible evidence shows that the product is counterfeit, diverted, stolen, subject of a fraudulent transaction, intentionally adulterated, or appears otherwise unfit for distribution such that it would result in serious adverse health consequences or death to humans.

(3) Pharmacies must investigate any suspect or illegitimate product. As part of the investigation, a pharmacy must verify the product identifier of at least 3 products or 10% of the suspect product, whichever is greater, or all of the packages if there are fewer than 3. Pharmacies must also verify any illegitimate product in response to a notification of illegitimate product from FDA or a trading partner.

Note: This requirement was scheduled to go into effect on November 27, 2020, but FDA has delayed enforcement until November 27, 2023.

(4) If a product is illegitimate, pharmacies must notify FDA using Form FDA 3911 and notify trading partners within 24 hours. Pharmacies should also work with the manufacturer to prevent illegitimate products from reaching patients.

g. Pharmacies that are "distributing" (distributing is defined as providing a drug to anyone other than the consumer/patient, as compared to dispensing which is providing a drug to the patient/consumer) must have a wholesale distribution license and must pass DSCSA transaction data with that distribution. The only exceptions to having a distribution license and passing transaction data are as follows:

(1) When the distribution is between two entities that are affiliated or under common ownership;

(2) When a dispenser is providing product to another dispenser on a patient-specific basis;

(3) When a dispenser is distributing under emergency medical reasons; or

(4) When a dispenser is distributing "minimal quantities" to a licensed practitioner for office use.

h. The DSCSA will be fully implemented by 2023 with enhanced electronic tracking and tracing of products at the individual package level using the unique product identifiers on each package.

II. Prohibited Acts Under the FDCA

Nearly all violations of the FDCA cause the products to be adulterated and/or misbranded. It is important to understand the difference between these two concepts. Although drug manufacturers are more likely to violate the FDCA, actions taken by pharmacists (e.g., a dispensing error) could also cause a product to be adulterated or misbranded. It is likely these are the types of situations that may be covered on the MPJE.

A. Adulteration—A drug is adulterated if:

1. It contains any filthy, putrid, or decomposed substance.

2. It has been prepared or held under unsanitary conditions where it may have been contaminated.

3. The methods of manufacture do not conform to current Good Manufacturing Practices (cGMPs).
4. It has been manufactured, processed, packed, or held in any factory, warehouse, or establishment and the owner, operator, or agent of such factory, warehouse, or establishment delays, denies, or limits an inspection, or refuses to permit entry or inspection.
5. The container is composed of any poisonous or deleterious substance which may contaminate the drug.
6. It contains an unsafe color additive.
7. It purports to be a drug in an official compendium, and its strength differs from or its quality or purity falls below the compendium standard, unless the difference is clearly stated on the label.
   Note: This means if the product claims to meet USP standards but its strength or quality does not meet those standards, it is adulterated.
8. It is not in a compendium, and its strength differs from or its quality falls below what it represents (i.e., what is on its label).
9. It is mixed or packed with any substance which reduces its strength or quality or the drug has been substituted in whole or in part.

STUDY TIP: If a product's strength differs from what is represented on its label, it could be both misbranded and adulterated.

B. Misbranding—A drug is misbranded if:

1. The labeling is false or misleading in any particular way.
2. It is a prescription drug and the manufacturer's label fails to contain the following information:
   a. The name and address of the manufacturer, packer, or distributor.
   b. Brand and/or generic name of the drug or drug product.
   c. The net quantity (weight, quantity, or dosage units).
   d. The weight of active ingredient per dosage unit.
   e. The federal legend, "Rx only."
   f. If not taken orally, the specific routes of administration (e.g., for IM injection).
   g. Special storage instructions if appropriate.
   h. Manufacturer's control number (lot number).
   i. Expiration date.

j. Adequate information for use (package insert and medication guide or patient package insert if required). This includes other information required (e.g., certain products, including opioids and benzodiazepines, require "black boxed warnings" to alert healthcare professionals about essential information regarding the product).

STUDY TIP: These labeling requirements are for the manufacturer's container. When a pharmacist dispenses a drug to a patient pursuant to a valid prescription, the label does not have to contain all these elements except requirements for patient package inserts and medication guides. State prescription drug labeling requirements would dictate what is required on the label.

3. It is an OTC drug and fails to contain the following:

a. A principal display panel, including a statement of identity of the product.

b. The name and address of the manufacturer, packer, or distributor.

c. Net quantity of contents.

d. Cautions and warnings needed to protect user.

e. Adequate directions for safe and effective use (for layperson).
*Note: OTC products must have adequate **directions** for safe and effective use while prescription products must have adequate **information** for use (i.e., the package insert).*

f. Content and format of OTC product labeling in "Drug Facts" panel format including:

(1) Active Ingredients.
(2) Purpose.
(3) Use(s)—indications.
(4) Warnings.
(5) Directions.
(6) Other Information.
(7) Inactive Ingredients (in alphabetical order).
(8) Questions? (optional) followed by telephone number.

STUDY TIP: Pharmacists don't usually concern themselves with these labeling requirements as it is expected that manufacturers will label their products appropriately, but you should know the labeling requirements for OTC drugs.

4. It is a drug liable to deterioration unless it is packaged or labeled accordingly.
5. The container is made, formed, or filled as to be misleading.
6. The drug is an exact imitation of another drug or offered for sale under the name of another drug.
7. It is dangerous to health when used in the dosage or manner suggested in the labeling.
8. It is packaged or labeled in violation of the Poison Prevention Packaging Act.

STUDY TIP: The FDCA specifically states that a drug that is not packaged in a child-resistant container (if required) is misbranded. This may not be as obvious because it is about the packaging and not the label or labeling.

C. Adulteration and Misbranding as Applied to Pharmacies
   1. Dispensing a prescription without authorization causes the drug to be misbranded even if it is labeled correctly by the pharmacist. This is because a prescription drug product is only exempt from the manufacturer's labeling requirements in B.2. above when it is dispensed pursuant to a valid prescription.

STUDY TIP: There are a number of drug products that are currently approved and sold for both prescription and OTC use. For example, Prilosec and Prilosec OTC contain the same active ingredient (omeprazole), but the indications for the prescription product require a diagnosis (e.g., GERD) and supervision by a doctor, while the OTC version is indicated for heartburn. Readers should be aware of the common medications that may be sold both as a prescription and OTC, and that their labeling and indications will not be the same. Pharmacists must also have a prescription in order to dispense the prescription product, or the product would be misbranded.

---

   2. Misfilling a prescription with the wrong drug, strength, or directions for use will always cause the drug to be misbranded.
   3. If a misfilled prescription involves the wrong strength of the drug prescribed, it would also be adulterated. This is because the definition of adulteration includes when the strength differs from or quality falls below that which it represents.
   4. If a drug is subject to a Risk Evaluation and Mitigation Strategy (REMS) and it is prescribed or dispensed without

meeting the requirements of the REMS, it is misbranded because the REMS program is part of the official labeling of the drug.

5. The advertising or promotion of a compounded drug that is false or misleading would be misbranding.
6. An expired drug product in a manufacturer's bottle is adulterated because after the expiration date, the strength cannot be assured. If a prescription is filled using an expired product, it may also be misbranded if the pharmacist placed a beyond-use date that is after the expiration date of the drug.
7. If a pharmacist counts a medication on a tray that has residue from another medication, the product would be adulterated.
8. If a pharmacist stores inventory in a room or refrigerator where the temperature is not adequately controlled, the products would be adulterated.
9. If a pharmacist stores a specific product incorrectly, such as stocking a medication on a pharmacy shelf instead of in the refrigerator as required, this will lead to the product being adulterated.
10. If a pharmacist fails to dispense a medication in a child-resistant container when required, this would be misbranding.

STUDY TIP: You are more likely to encounter questions related to adulteration and misbranding based on scenarios in a pharmacy.

III. Other Provisions of the FDCA and Federal Regulations

A. Special Warning Requirements for OTC Products in the FDCA

STUDY TIP: These are special labeling requirements under federal regulations for products containing the following ingredients. Normally the manufacturer's label would include these warnings, but you should be familiar with these requirements.

---

1. FD&C Yellow No. 5 (tartrazine) and No. 6 (21 CFR 201.20)—Must disclose presence and provide warning in "precautions" section of label that may cause allergic reaction in certain susceptible persons.
2. Aspartame (21 CFR 201.21)—Must contain warning in "precautions" section of labeling to the following effect:

Phenylketonurics: Contains phenylalanine ___ mg per ___ (dosage unit).

3. Sulfites (21 CFR 201.22)—Prescription drugs containing sulfites (often used as a preservative) must contain an allergy warning in the "warnings" section of the labeling.
4. Mineral Oil (21 CFR 201.302)—Requires warning to only be taken at bedtime and not be used in infants unless under advice of a physician. Label also cannot encourage use during pregnancy.
5. Wintergreen Oil (methyl salicylate) (21 CFR 201.303 and 201.314(g)(1))—Any drug containing more than 5% methyl salicylate (often used as flavoring agent) must include warning that use other than directed may be dangerous and that article should be kept out of reach of children.
6. Sodium Phosphates (21 CFR 201.307)—Limits the amount of sodium phosphates oral solution to no more than 90 ml per OTC container. Also requires specific warnings.
7. Isoproterenol Inhalation Preparations (21 CFR 201.305)—Requires warning not to exceed dose prescribed and to contact physician if difficulty in breathing persists.
8. Potassium Salt Preparations for Oral Ingestions (21 CFR 201.306)—Requires warning regarding nonspecific small-bowel lesions consisting of stenosis, with or without ulceration, associated with the administration of enteric-coated thiazides with potassium salts.
9. Ipecac Syrup (21 CFR 201.308)
    a. The following statement (boxed and in red letters) must appear: "For emergency use to cause vomiting in poisoning. Before using, call physician, the poison prevention center, or hospital emergency room immediately for advice."
    b. The following warning must appear: "Warning: Keep out of reach of children. Do not use in unconscious persons."
    c. The dosage of the medication must appear. The usual dosage is 1 tablespoon (15 ml) in individuals over one year of age.
    d. May only be sold in 1 oz. (30 ml) containers.
10. Phenacetin (acetophenetidin) (21 CFR 201.309)—Must contain warning about possible kidney damage when taken in large amounts or for a long period of time.

11. Salicylates (21 CFR 201.314)—Aspirin and other salicylate drugs must have special warnings for use in children including warning regarding Reye's syndrome. Retail containers of 1¼ grain (pediatric) aspirin cannot be sold in containers holding more than 36 tablets.
12. OTC Drugs for Minor Sore Throats (21 CFR 201.315)—Any OTC product that states "For the temporary relief of minor sore throats" must include this warning:
"Warning—Severe or persistent sore throat or sore throat accompanied by high fever, headache, nausea, and vomiting may be serious. Consult physician promptly. Do not use more than 2 days or administer to children under 3 years of age unless directed by physician."
13. Alcohol Warning (21 CFR 201.322)—Internal analgesics and antipyretics including acetaminophen, aspirin, ibuprofen, naproxen, ketoprofen, etc., are required to have a warning for persons consuming 3 or more alcoholic beverages per day and to consult with a doctor before taking.
14. Over-the-Counter Drugs for Vaginal Contraceptive and Spermicide Use Containing Nonoxynol 9 as the Active Ingredient (21 CFR 301.325)—These are subject to several warning requirements including one that states "Sexually transmitted diseases (STDs) alert: This product does not protect against HIV/AIDS or other STDs and may increase the risk of getting HIV from an infected partner."
15. OTC Pain Relievers (21 CFR 301.326)
    a. Acetaminophen.
        (1) Must have "acetaminophen" prominently displayed.
        (2) Must warn about liver toxicity.
        (3) Must warn not to use with other products containing acetaminophen and to talk to a doctor or pharmacist before taking with warfarin.
    b. Nonsteroidal Anti-Inflammatory Drugs (NSAIDs).
        (1) Must include term "NSAID" prominently on label.
        (2) Must contain "stomach bleeding" warning.
16. OTC Products Containing Iron in Solid Oral Dosage Form (21 CFR 310.518(a))
    a. Must provide the following warning: "Accidental overdose of iron-containing products is a leading cause of fatal poisoning in children under 6. Keep this product

out of reach of children. In case of accidental overdose, call a doctor or poison control center immediately."

   b. This warning requirement also applies to dietary supplements containing iron as indicated in 21 CFR 101.17(e).

B. Additional OTC Requirements

   1. Tamper-Evident Packaging—Manufacturers and packagers of OTC drugs (except dermatological, dentifrice, insulin, or lozenge products) for sale at retail must package products in a tamper-evident package. OTC products not packaged properly would be considered misbranded and adulterated.

   2. Repackaging of OTC Products—A pharmacist that repackages OTC products would be subject to cGMP requirements and would have to meet all additional requirements including the manufacturer labeling and tamper-evident packaging if offered for sale to the public.

STUDY TIP: If a patient wishes to purchase an OTC drug in a smaller package size than what is commercially available, a pharmacist cannot break open a commercial OTC product and sell the lesser quantity by placing it in a vial and labeling it. The only way this can be done is if the patient has a prescription for the smaller quantity and the OTC drug is filled as a prescription as discussed in 3. below.

---

   3. When an OTC product is prescribed and filled as a prescription, the OTC labeling requirements do not have to be followed. The prescription drug labeling requirements would apply and would include the prescriber's directions for use. If an OTC drug is filled as a prescription, any instructions for refills would apply, as would beyond-use dates (valid for one year).

C. FDA Drug and Device Recall Classifications

   1. Class I—Reasonable probability product will cause either serious adverse effects on health or death.

   2. Class II—May cause temporary or medically reversible adverse effects on health or where probability of serious adverse effects is remote.

   3. Class III—Not likely to cause adverse health consequences.

D. Advertising and Promotion of Prescription Drugs

   1. Prescription drug advertising is regulated by FDA.

   2. Over-the-counter (OTC) drug advertising is regulated by the Federal Trade Commission (FTC).

3. Advertising of Prescription Drug Prices (including by pharmacists)—The advertising of prescription drug prices is considered reminder advertising under FDA regulations (21 CFR 200.200). However, such advertising is exempt from FDA advertising regulations provided that the following conditions are met:
   a. The only purpose of the advertising is to provide information on price, not information on the drug's safety, efficacy, or indications for use.
   b. The advertising contains the proprietary name of the drug (if any), the generic name of the drug, the drug's strength, the dosage form, and the price charged for a specific quantity of the drug.
   c. The advertising may include other information, such as the availability of professional or other types of services, as long as it is not misleading.
   d. The price stated in the advertising shall include all charges to the consumer; mailing and delivery fees, if any, may be stated separately.
4. A pharmacy that compounds products may advertise that it provides compounding services, including that it compounds specific products. However, if a pharmacy makes any therapeutic claims regarding those products, it would be subject to FDA's rules on advertising, which are complex and beyond the scope of this book.

E. Patient Package Inserts (PPIs)
1. Supplied by the manufacturer and written for a layperson.
2. Required to be given to patients in the community setting when new and refill prescriptions for certain products are dispensed.
3. Currently required for:
   a. Oral contraceptives (21 CFR 310.501).
   b. Estrogen-containing products (21 CFR 310.515).
4. Hospitalized or Institutionalized Patients—A PPI must be provided to a patient prior to the first administration of the drug and every 30 days thereafter.

STUDY TIP: This may not happen in practice, but you need to know it is legally required.

---

5. Failure to provide a PPI for these drugs would cause them to be misbranded.

F. Medication Guides (MedGuides)
1. Similar to PPI program but with amended requirements for institutionalized patients.
2. FDA requires Medication Guides for all new and refill prescriptions dispensed in the community setting when:
   a. Patient labeling could prevent serious adverse effects.
   b. Product has serious risks relative to benefits.
   c. Patient adherence to directions is crucial.
3. Medication Guides must be written in a standard format and in language suitable for patients.
4. Manufacturers must obtain FDA approval before distributing Medication Guides and are responsible for ensuring that a sufficient number of Medication Guides are provided to pharmacies. Many manufacturers include the Medication Guide at the bottom of the package insert, but most pharmacy computer systems also print Medication Guides for the products that need them at the time of dispensing.
5. FDA maintains a searchable Medication Guide database on its website, and there are over 1000 products that now require a Medication Guide. Some of the drugs, drug classes, and biologicals requiring Medication Guides include:
   a. Accutane® (isotretinoin)
   b. Antidepressants in children and teenagers
   c. Coumadin® (warfarin sodium)
   d. Epogen® (epoetin alfa)
   e. Forteo® (teriparatide, rDNA origin)
   f. Lindane® shampoo and lotion
   g. Lotronex® (alosetron hydrochloride)
   h. Nolvadex® (tamoxifen)
   i. Non-Steroidal Anti-Inflammatory Drugs (NSAIDs)
   j. Remicade® (infliximab)
   k. Trizivar® (abacavir sulfate, lamivudine, and zidovudine)
   l. Opioid analgesics and cough products
   m. Benzodiazepines
6. Failure to provide a Medication Guide when dispensing a drug that requires one would cause the drug to be misbranded.

STUDY TIP: Consumer Medication Information (CMI), which is often provided to community pharmacy patients for all new and refill prescriptions dispensed, is written patient information that is not equivalent to or substitutable for FDA-regulated and mandated PPIs and MedGuides.

G. Prescription Drugs: Side Effects Statement

1. To enable consumers to report side effects of prescription drugs to FDA, pharmacies and pharmacists are required to distribute a side effects statement to patients when dispensing all new and refill prescriptions in the outpatient setting.
2. The side effects statement provided with each prescription drug must read "Call your doctor for medical advice about side effects. You may report side effects to FDA at 1-800-FDA-1088."
3. The side effects statement can be distributed on a sticker attached to the pharmacy container, on a preprinted pharmacy prescription vial cap, on a separate sheet of paper, or found within CMI or MedGuides.

H. Risk Evaluation and Mitigation Strategies (REMS)

1. REMS are strategies to manage a known or potential serious risk associated with a drug, drug class, or biological product. FDA requires a REMS if FDA finds that it is necessary to ensure that the benefits of the drug, drug class, or biological product outweigh the risks of the product. A REMS can include a Medication Guide, Patient Package Insert, a communication plan, elements to assure safe use, and an implementation system. It must also include a timetable for assessment of the REMS.
2. Elements to assure safe use may include:
    - **a.** Special training, experience, or certification of healthcare practitioners prescribing the drugs;
    - **b.** Special certification for pharmacies, practitioners, or healthcare settings that dispense the drug;
    - **c.** Dispensing drugs to patients only in certain healthcare settings such as hospitals;
    - **d.** Dispensing drugs to patients with evidence or other documentation of safe use conditions such as laboratory test results;
    - **e.** Monitoring patients using the drug; or
    - **f.** Enrolling each patient using the drug in a registry.

3. A complete list of products with approved REMS can be found on the FDA's website and may include an entire drug class such as the Opioid Analgesic REMS.
4. Example of a REMS—Isotretinoin (Accutane) iPLEDGE Program.
    a. Only doctors registered in iPLEDGE can prescribe isotretinoin. Doctors registered with iPLEDGE must agree to assume the responsibility for pregnancy counseling of female patients of childbearing potential. Prescribers must obtain and enter into the iPLEDGE system negative test results for those female patients of childbearing potential prior to prescribing isotretinoin.
    b. Only patients registered in iPLEDGE can be prescribed isotretinoin. In addition to registering with iPLEDGE, patients must comply with a number of key requirements that include completing an informed consent form, obtaining counseling about the risks and requirements for safe use of the drug, and, for women of childbearing potential, complying with required pregnancy testing and use of contraception.
    c. Only pharmacies registered in iPLEDGE can dispense isotretinoin. To register in iPLEDGE, a pharmacy must select a Responsible Site Pharmacist who must obtain iPLEDGE program information and registration materials via the internet (*www.ipledgeprogram.com*) or telephone (1-866-495-0654) and sign and return the completed registration form. To activate registration, the Responsible Site Pharmacist must access the iPLEDGE program via the internet (*www.ipledgeprogram.com*) or telephone (1-866-495-0654) and attest to the following points:
        (1) I know the risk and severity of fetal injury/birth defects from isotretinoin.
        (2) I will train all pharmacists on the iPLEDGE program requirements.
        (3) I will comply and seek to ensure that all pharmacists comply with iPLEDGE program requirements.
        (4) I will obtain isotretinoin from iPLEDGE registered wholesalers.
        (5) I will return to the manufacturer (or delegate) any unused product.

(6) I will not fill isotretinoin for any party other than a qualified patient.

d. To dispense isotretinoin, pharmacists must obtain authorization from iPLEDGE via the internet (*www.ipledgeprogram.com*) or telephone (1-866-495-0654) signifying the patient is registered, has received counseling and education, and is not pregnant.

e. Product is dispensed in blister packages which cannot be broken, and a 30-day supply is the maximum quantity that can be dispensed.

f. No refills are allowed.

5. Example REMS—Thalomid (Thalidomide) REMS

a. Prescriber Requirements

(1) The prescriber enrolls and becomes certified with Celgene for the Thalomid REMS program.

(2) The prescriber counsels patient on the benefits and risks of Thalomid.

(3) The prescriber provides contraception and emergency contraception counseling.

(4) The prescriber verifies negative pregnancy test for all female patients of reproductive potential.

(5) The prescriber completes a Thalomid Patient-Physician Agreement Form with each patient and sends to Celgene.

(6) The prescriber/patient completes applicable mandatory confidential survey.

(7) The prescriber obtains an authorization number from Celgene and writes it on every prescription along with patient risk category.

(8) The prescriber writes no more than a 4-week (28-day) supply, with no automatic refills or telephone prescriptions.

(9) The prescriber sends Thalomid prescription to certified pharmacy.

b. Pharmacy Requirements

(1) Pharmacy must be certified in the Thalomid REMs program with Celgene.

(2) Prescriptions can only be accepted with an authorization number and patient risk category.

(3) Authorization numbers are valid for 7 days from the date of the last pregnancy test for females of reproductive potential and 30 days from the date issued for other patients.
(4) Pharmacy must obtain a confirmation number prior to dispensing via toll free number or online. The confirmation number is valid for 24 hours and must be entered on the prescription. This means the prescription must be dispensed within 24 hours of obtaining the confirmation number.
(5) No automatic refills or telephone prescriptions are permitted.
(6) Prescription must be written for 4-week (28-day) supply or less.
(7) No refills are allowed and subsequent prescriptions may be dispensed only if there are 7 days or less remaining on the existing prescription.
(8) A certified Thalomid REMS counselor must counsel the patient, and counseling must be documented.
(9) Prescription must be dispensed with a medication guide.
(10) Prescriptions cannot be transferred to another pharmacy without prior authorization from Celgene.

I. National Drug Code (NDC) Number

1. A unique 10-character number that identifies a particular drug by manufacturer or packager (labeler), product, and package size. NDC numbers will have one of the following configurations: 4-4-2, 5-3-2, or 5-4-1.
   a. First 4 to 5 digits = labeler code.
   b. Next 3 to 4 digits = specific drug, strength, and dosage form.
   c. Last 1 to 2 digits = package size.
2. NDC numbers are required for a drug manufacturer to list its product with FDA. Although FDA suggests NDC numbers be included on the drug's label, they are not technically required. Nearly all drug manufacturers include NDC numbers because they facilitate automated processing of drug data by government agencies, third-party payers, wholesalers, and manufacturers.

STUDY TIP: NDC numbers should not appear on nondrug products. If a dietary supplement or medical device has an NDC number on its label, it would be misbranded. Medical devices have unique device identifiers (UDIs) instead of NDC numbers. Any product that implies it is an FDA-approved drug and it is not would also be misbranded.

3. While nearly all drug products have an NDC number, an NDC code does not indicate a drug is approved by FDA.
4. FDA has proposed to standardize the NDC format and move to an 11-digit code, but that proposed change has not yet been adopted.
   Note: Although the NDC is 10 digits, the standard for billing and claims submissions is an 11-digit NDC. This is accomplished by inserting a leading zero into one of the segments: first segment if it is four numbers, second segment if it is three numbers, or added to the beginning of the third segment if it only has one number.

J. FDA Orange Book

1. Official name is *Approved Drug Products with Therapeutic Equivalence Evaluations.*
2. Available on FDA's website.
3. The primary source for determining the generic equivalency of drugs. To be considered generically equivalent, a drug must be both pharmaceutically equivalent and therapeutically equivalent to the reference drug product (normally the brand-name drug).
4. Definitions:
   - **a.** "Pharmaceutical equivalents" are drug products in identical dosage forms and route(s) of administration that contain identical amounts of the identical active drug ingredient.
   - **b.** "Therapeutic equivalents" are approved drug products that are pharmaceutical equivalents for which bioequivalence has been demonstrated, and they can be expected to have the same clinical effect and safety profile when administered to patients under the conditions specified in the labeling.
     Note: This means the drug is bioequivalent to the reference drug product.
5. Uses 2-letter coding system to indicate equivalency with first letter being the key:

   a. A = Drug products that the FDA considers to be pharmaceutically equivalent and therapeutically equivalent.
   b. B = Drug products that the FDA considers NOT to be pharmaceutically equivalent and therapeutically equivalent.

STUDY TIP: The first letter of the 2-letter code tells you if the product is considered equivalent. It is recommended that the reader look up an Orange Book listing in the FDA Orange Book database online and be familiar with its format.

6. Products with no known or suspected bioequivalence issues:
   a. AA—conventional dosage forms.
   b. AN—solutions and powders for aerosolization.
   c. AO—injectable oil solutions.
   d. AP—injectable aqueous solutions.
   e. AT—topical products.
7. Products with actual or potential bioequivalence problems, but for which adequate scientific evidence has established bioequivalence for those products, are given a rating of AB.
8. There are situations where there may be multiple pharmaceutically equivalent reference drugs that have not been determined to be bioequivalent to each other. For these products, the FDA implemented a three-character code such as AB1, AB2, and AB3. If a generic drug product establishes bioequivalence to one of the reference drugs, it will receive the same three-character code as the reference drug. An example includes Adalat CC (AB1) and Procardia XL (AB2), which are both reference drugs with the same dosage form and active ingredients, but they are not rated as bioequivalent to one another.

K. FDA Purple Book
   1. Official name is *Lists of Licensed Biological Products with Reference Product Exclusivity and Biosimilarity or Interchangeability Evaluations.*
   2. Lists biological products that are considered biosimilars and provides interchangeability evaluations for these products.
   3. Biosimilar or biosimilarity means that the biological product is highly similar to the reference product notwithstanding minor differences in clinically inactive components, and

there are no clinically meaningful differences between the biological product and the reference product in terms of the safety, purity, and potency of the product.

4. An interchangeable product is a product that has been shown to be biosimilar to the reference product and can be expected to produce the same clinical result as the reference product in any given patient.
5. Only biological products that have been designated "interchangeable" may be substituted for the original reference product by a pharmacist in Texas. Biosimilar products would require prescriber intervention in order to substitute.
   Note: While there are several biosimilar products on the market (e.g., adalimumab, bevacizumab, and epoetin alfa), as of the date of this book's publication, FDA has only designated one product as interchangeable. Semglee (insulin glargine-yfgn) is approved by FDA as interchangeable with (and can be substituted at the pharmacy level for) its reference product, Lantus® (insulin glargine).

L. Medical Devices

1. The FDA regulates companies that manufacture and repackage medical devices.
2. A medical device includes instruments, apparatuses, machines, implants, or other related articles intended to treat or prevent disease but, unlike drugs, does not achieve its primary purpose through chemical action within or on the body and does not depend on being metabolized.
3. The FDA classifies medical devices based on the risk associated with the device.
   a. Class I devices are deemed to be low risk and are therefore subject to the least regulatory controls. Dental floss is an example.
   b. Class II devices are higher risk and require greater regulatory controls. Syringes are an example.
   c. Class III devices are generally the highest risk devices and are subject to the highest level of regulatory control, and those that pose a significant risk of illness or injury require premarket approval by the FDA. Replacement heart valves are an example.
4. Not all medical devices require a prescription, but many do (e.g., contact lenses).

5. Certain Class I and Class II devices are exempt from premarket approval and GMPs, but typically must still comply with other regulatory requirements unless they are exempt.

M. Animal Drugs

1. The FDA regulates drugs intended to be used by animals.
2. Animal drugs have to be approved by the FDA as safe and effective.
3. The FDA determines if an animal drug must be sold as a prescription or OTC drug.
4. Animal prescription products can be dispensed only by or upon the lawful written order of a licensed veterinarian.
5. The manufacturer's label of an animal prescription drug product must bear the legend "Caution: Federal law restricts this drug to use by or on the order of a licensed veterinarian."
6. Veterinarians can legally prescribe approved human drugs for animals in certain circumstances (this is called extra-label or off-label use). Therefore, pharmacies and pharmacists may receive and dispense such prescriptions.
7. The FDA has released guidance regarding the compounding of animal drugs, which allows pharmacies to compound animal drugs under specific circumstances.

IV. Poison Prevention Packaging Act of 1970 (PPPA)

A. Administered by Consumer Product Safety Commission (CPSC).

B. Requires child-resistant containers for all prescription drugs and for the following nonprescription drugs, drug classes, preparations, or dietary supplements:

1. Aspirin—Any aspirin-containing preparation for human use in dosage form intended for oral administration.
2. Methyl Salicylate (oil of wintergreen)—Liquid preparations containing more than 5% by weight of methyl salicylate unless packaged in pressurized spray containers.
3. Controlled Drugs
   Note: There are some Schedule V controlled substances available without a prescription under federal law, but this doesn't apply in Texas. See Chapter Three in this book.
4. Methyl Alcohol (methanol)—Household substances in liquid form containing 4% or more by weight of methyl alcohol unless packaged in a pressurized spray container.
5. Iron-Containing Drugs—With the exception of animal feeds used as vehicles for the administration of drugs,

noninjectable animal and human drugs providing iron for therapeutic or prophylactic purposes, which contain a total amount of elemental iron equivalent to 250 mg.

6. Dietary Supplements Containing Iron—With the exception of those preparations in which iron is present solely as a colorant, dietary supplements that contain an equivalent of 250 mg or more of elemental iron in a single package.
7. Acetaminophen—Preparations for human use in a dosage form intended for oral administration and containing more than 1 g of acetaminophen in a single package.
   Exemptions:
   a. Acetaminophen-containing effervescent tablets or granules containing less than 10% acetaminophen with a median lethal dose greater than 5 g/kg of body weight and that release at least 85 ml of carbon dioxide per grain of acetaminophen when placed in water.
   b. Unflavored acetaminophen-containing preparations in powder form, other than those intended for pediatric use, that are packaged in unit doses with no more than 13 grains of acetaminophen per unit dose and that contain no other substance subject to the special packaging requirements.
8. Diphenhydramine HCl—Preparations for human use in oral dosage forms containing more than the equivalent of 66 mg of diphenhydramine base in a single package.
9. Ibuprofen—Preparations for human use in oral dosage forms containing 1 gram or more of ibuprofen in a single package.
10. Loperamide—Preparations for human use in oral dosage forms containing more than 0.045 mg of loperamide in a single package.
11. Lidocaine—Products containing more than 5 mg of lidocaine in a single package (includes all dosage forms including creams, sprays, and transdermal patches).
12. Dibucaine—Products containing more than 0.5 mg of dibucaine in a single package (includes all dosage forms including creams, sprays, and transdermal patches).
13. Naproxen—Preparations for human use in oral dosage forms containing 250 mg or more of naproxen in a single package.
14. Ketoprofen—Preparations for human use in oral dosage forms containing more than 50 mg of ketoprofen in a single package.

15. Fluoride—Products containing more than 50 mg of elemental fluoride and more than 0.5% fluoride in a single package.
16. Minoxidil—Preparations for human use containing more than 14 mg of minoxidil in a single package (includes topical products that must continue to meet requirements once applicator is installed by consumer).
17. Imidazolines—Products containing 0.08 mg or more in a single package. Imidazoline is a drug class that includes tetrahydrozoline, naphazoline, oxymetazoline, and xylometazoline often found in ophthalmic and nasal products.
18. Any drug switched from Rx to OTC status.

C. Exemptions:
   1. Request of patient or physician.

STUDY TIP: Only the patient can provide a blanket request for all future prescriptions. The prescriber can only request a non-child-resistant container on an individual prescription. The request is not required to be in writing, although it is good practice to have it in writing.

   2. Bulk containers not intended for household use.
   3. Drugs distributed to institutionalized patients.
   4. Prescription drugs packaged for residents of LTCFs and other institutional settings if the facility personnel will administer the medications to the patients.
   5. One package size of OTC drugs designed for the elderly.
   6. Specific prescription and nonprescription drug exemptions include:
      a. Oral contraceptives, conjugated estrogens, and northindrone acetate in manufacturer's dispenser package.
      b. Medroxyprogesterone acetate tablets.
      c. Sublingual nitroglycerin and sublingual and chewable isosorbide dinitrate of 10 mg or less.
      d. Aspirin and acetaminophen in effervescent tablets or granules.
      e. Potassium supplements in unit-dose packaging.
      f. Sodium fluoride containing no more than 264 mg of sodium fluoride per package.
      g. Anhydrous cholestyramine and colestipol packets.
      h. Erythromycin ethylsuccinate granules for oral suspension and oral suspensions in packages containing no more than 8 g of erythromycin.

i. Erythromycin ethylsuccinate tablets in packages containing no more than 16 g erythromycin.
j. Prednisone tablets containing no more than 105 mg per package.
k. Methylprednisolone tablets containing no more than 84 mg per package.
l. Mebendazole tablets containing no more than 600 mg per package.
m. Betamethasone tablets containing no more than 12.6 mg per package.
n. Preparations in aerosol containers intended for inhalation.
o. Pancrelipase preparations.
p. Sucrose preparations in a solution of glycerol and water.
q. Hormone replacement therapy products that rely solely upon the activity of one or more progestogen or estrogen substances.

STUDY TIP: It is important to know all of the products that are exempt from the Poison Prevention Packaging Act including details as to strengths and dosage forms.

BONUS STUDY TIP: For pharmacies, the law requires the dispensing of medications in a new vial/bottle and safety cap with each prescription filled. A pharmacy is permitted to reuse a glass container if a new safety cap is provided with each fill.

EXTRA BONUS STUDY TIP: When a pharmacist does not comply with PPPA, in addition to violating PPPA (CPSC enforces), it is also a misbranding violation of FDCA (FDA enforces).

V. Other Federal Laws and Regulations

A. Federal Hazardous Substances Act of 1966

1. The Consumer Product Safety Commission administers and enforces this act which is intended to protect consumers from hazardous and toxic substances.
2. Requires the label on the immediate package of a hazardous product and any outer wrapping or container that might

cover up the label on the package to have the following information in English:

  a. The name and business address of the manufacturer, packer, distributor, or seller;
  b. The common or usual or chemical name of each hazardous ingredient;
  c. The signal word "Danger" for products that are corrosive, extremely flammable, or highly toxic;
  d. The signal word "Caution" or "Warning" for all other hazardous products;
  e. An affirmative statement of the principal hazard or hazards that the product presents (e.g., "Flammable," "Harmful if Swallowed," "Causes Burns," "Vapor Harmful," etc.);
  f. Precautionary statements telling users what they must do or what actions they must avoid to protect themselves;
  g. Where it is appropriate, instructions for first aid treatment if the product injures someone;
  h. The word "Poison" for a product that is highly toxic, in addition to the signal word "Danger";
  i. If a product requires special care in handling or storage, instructions for consumers to follow to protect themselves; and
  j. The statement "Keep out of the reach of children." If a hazardous product such as a plant does not have a package, it still must have a hang tag that contains the required precautionary information. That information must also be printed in any literature that accompanies the product and that contains instructions for use.

3. The act does not apply to drugs regulated by FDA but may apply to other products sold in a pharmacy such as bleach, cleaning fluids, antifreeze, etc.

B. Federal Hazard Communication Standard

1. The Occupational and Safety Health Administration (OSHA) administers and enforces this regulation which requires employers (including pharmacies) that deal with hazardous materials to meet the Hazard Communication Standard. *See 29 CFR 1910.1200.*
2. The standard requires chemical manufacturers and importers to classify the hazards of chemicals they produce or import and to prepare appropriate labels and Safety Data

Sheets (SDS), which were formerly known as Material Safety Data Sheets (MSDS).

3. Drugs in solid, final dosage form for administration to patients (such as tablets or capsules) are exempt from these requirements. However, hazardous drugs such as those subject to USP 800, chemicals, or products not in solid, final dosage form for administration (such as liquid products used in compounding) may be covered. Generally, a pharmacy may rely on the manufacturer to determine if a product is considered hazardous and will supply an SDS for that product. If a pharmacy has any such products, it is required to have a written Hazard Communication Plan.
4. The plan must include a list of hazardous chemicals in the workplace, must ensure all such products are appropriately labeled and have a Safety Data Sheet, and must include training for all workers on the hazards of chemicals, appropriate protective measures, and where and how to obtain additional information.

   Note: Additional details can be found in OSHA's publication "Small Entity Compliance Guide for Employers that Use Hazardous Chemicals."

C. Centers for Medicare and Medicaid Services (CMS) Requirements

1. Tamper-Resistant Prescriptions—CMS requires that all written prescriptions meet certain tamper-resistant requirements to prevent unauthorized copying and to prevent counterfeiting (with some exceptions). The tamper-evident features must include:
   - **a.** One or more industry-recognized features designed to prevent unauthorized copying of a completed or blank prescription form;
   - **b.** One or more industry-recognized features designed to prevent the erasure or modification of information written on the prescription pad by the prescriber; and
   - **c.** One or more industry-recognized features designed to prevent the use of counterfeit prescription forms.
2. Pharmacy Services at Long-Term Care Facilities
   - **a.** Medication Regimen Reviews—CMS regulations require a consultant pharmacist to perform a Medication Regimen Review for all long-term care patients every 30 days. The pharmacist must report any irregularities to the attending physician, the facility's medical director, and

the facility's director of nursing, and these reports must be acted upon.

b. Each resident's drug therapy must be free of unnecessary drugs. This includes avoiding drugs at excessive doses or durations and limiting psychotropic drugs to diagnosed and documented conditions.

c. When used PRN, psychotropic drugs must be limited to 14 days unless the practitioner documents the rationale for extending an order beyond 14 days. PRN orders for psychotropic drugs cannot be renewed unless the attending physician evaluates the patient for appropriateness of that drug.

d. To reduce medication waste, pharmacies may not dispense more than a 14-day cycle of medications to LTCF residents, with limited exceptions.

e. Pharmacies must ensure routine and emergency drugs are provided in a timely manner to all residents. The use of emergency medication kits is permissible to help meet this requirement.

D. Delivering Prescriptions by U.S. Mail or Common Carrier

1. Delivery by Mail (postal regulations administered by the U.S. Postal Service)—General postal regulations do not allow dangerous substances to be mailed; however, there are exceptions for prescription drugs.

   a. Noncontrolled—Prescriptions containing noncontrolled substances (Dangerous Drugs) may be mailed by a pharmacy to the ultimate user provided that the medications are not alcoholic beverages, poisons, or flammable substances.

   b. Controlled substances may be mailed to patients under the following requirements:

      (1) The prescription container must be labeled in compliance with prescription labeling rules;

      (2) The outer wrapper or container in which the prescription is placed must be free of markings that would indicate the nature of the contents (including the name of the pharmacy as part of the return address on the mailing package as that may alert individuals that drugs may be in the package); and

      (3) No markings of any kind may be placed on the package to indicate the nature of contents.

c. Controlled substances may be mailed to other DEA registrants (practitioners, other pharmacies, distributors, or drug disposal firms) provided they are placed in a plain outer container or securely overwrapped in plain paper and all recordkeeping requirements are met.

2. Delivery by Common Carrier—Any prescription drug may be delivered from a pharmacy to a patient by common carrier such as UPS or FedEx. This delivery includes all schedules of controlled substances and dangerous drugs. Common carriers are not subject to postal regulations.

E. Federal Tax-Free Alcohol Regulations

1. Pharmacies sometimes use 95% ethanol (190 proof) for compounding purposes.
2. When used for scientific, medicinal, or mechanical purposes or to treat patients, such alcohol is considered "tax free."
3. The Alcohol and Tobacco Tax and Trade Bureau (TTB) regulates tax-free alcohol with the federal Bureau of Alcohol, Tobacco, Firearms, and Explosives (ATF). ATF is responsible for enforcement.
4. A user permit must be acquired from TTB, and specific recordkeeping requirements must be met.
5. Tax-free alcohol cannot be resold or used in any beverage product.

VI. Privacy—HIPAA, HITECH, and "Texas HIPAA"

A. Most pharmacies are a "covered entity" under HIPAA and must be in compliance with these requirements.

B. Notice and Acknowledgement

1. Pharmacies must provide patients with a "Notice of Privacy Practices" and make a good faith effort to obtain a written acknowledgement of receipt of the Notice from the patient.
2. The Notice must be provided upon first service delivery to the patient.
3. The HIPAA privacy rule requires mandatory provisions in the Notice.

C. Use and Disclosure of Protected Health Information (PHI)

1. Protected Health Information (PHI) is the HIPAA term for patient-identifiable information.
2. Pharmacies may use and disclose PHI to provide treatment for payment and for healthcare operations without authorization from the patient.

3. Pharmacies may also use and disclose PHI for certain governmental functions without authorization from the patient. This includes uses and disclosures for public health activities such as reporting adverse events to FDA, to health oversight agencies such as boards of pharmacies or state drug monitoring programs, and to law enforcement agencies.
4. Other uses and disclosures, such as for marketing purposes, require a signed authorization from the patient. If the covered entity receives remuneration for the marketing, the authorization form must expressly inform the patient of such.
5. Face-to-face communications about alternative drugs or health products are considered part of treatment and not marketing.
6. Refill reminders for a currently prescribed drug (or one that has lapsed for no more than 90 days) are not considered marketing as long as any payment made to the pharmacy in exchange for making the communication is reasonable and related to the pharmacy's cost of making the communication.

D. Business Associates (BAs)
   1. BAs are persons or entities, other than members of a pharmacy's workforce, who perform a function or service on behalf of the pharmacy that requires the use or disclosure of PHI (e.g., collection agencies and external auditors).
   2. Pharmacies are required to enter into business associate contracts with these BAs, which require the BAs to meet many of the same requirements for protecting PHI as a covered entity under HIPAA.

E. Patient Rights and Administrative Requirements
   1. Patients have a right to access and obtain a copy of their PHI. Covered entities including pharmacies must comply with a request within 30 days, but may extend time by no more than 30 additional days if they notify the individual of the reason for the delay.

STUDY TIP: TSBP Rule 291.28 requires pharmacies to reply to a request from a patient for a copy of his or her confidential information within 15 days, which is stricter than HIPAA.

   2. Patients have a right to amend their PHI records and request an accounting of disclosures of their PHI made by

a pharmacy under certain circumstances. Pharmacies must comply with a request to amend or request for an accounting of disclosures within 60 days, but may extend by no more than 30 additional days if they notify the individual of the reason for the delay.

3. Pharmacies must establish policies and procedures to protect from accidental or intentional uses and disclosures of PHI through the use of appropriate administrative, technical, and physical safeguards to protect the privacy of PHI.
4. Pharmacies must train all employees on privacy policies and impose sanctions on employees for any violations of privacy policies.
5. Pharmacies must designate a Privacy Official who is responsible for development and implementation of HIPAA-related policies and procedures and compliance.
6. Pharmacies must also designate a contact person to receive complaints. This person may also be the Privacy Official.
7. Minimum Necessary Standard.
    a. When using and disclosing PHI, a pharmacy must make reasonable efforts to limit PHI to the minimum necessary to accomplish the intended purpose.
    b. The minimum necessary standard does not apply to disclosures to healthcare providers for treatment purposes. These disclosures would include prescription transfers or providing prescription information to physicians.
    c. The minimum necessary standard does not apply to disclosures for which the patient has signed an authorization.
    d. The minimum necessary standard does apply to disclosures for payment.
8. Incidental Disclosures.
    a. Unintended "incidental" disclosures are not a violation of the Privacy Rule as long as reasonable safeguards are in place.
    b. Examples: Sales representatives or janitorial service members accidentally see PHI during the normal course of their jobs; a customer overhears counseling that is performed discreetly in a private area.

Note: PHI must be properly disposed of by pharmacies. Pharmacies have been fined for improperly disposing PHI (such as labeled pharmacy vials and paper records) into dumpsters accessible to the public and unauthorized individuals.

F. HITECH Act—The HITECH Act amended HIPAA to strengthen many of its provisions.

1. Among other things, the HITECH Act added a breach notification requirement that requires:
    a. Covered entities, including pharmacies, to notify individuals of a breach of their "unsecured" PHI within 60 calendar days after the breach is discovered.
    b. BAs to report any breaches of unsecured PHI to the covered entity and provide the identities of each affected individual.
2. A "breach" is defined as unauthorized acquisition, access, use, or disclosure of PHI that compromises its security or privacy. It does not include instances in which there has been an inadvertent disclosure from an authorized individual to another person authorized to access PHI within the same organization. A breach also does not include instances in which the covered entity or BA has a good faith belief that the PHI is not further acquired, accessed, retained, used, or disclosed.
3. For breaches affecting fewer than 500 individuals, covered entities must maintain a log of these breaches and notify HHS of these breaches annually.
4. If more than 500 individuals are affected, the Secretary of HHS and prominent local media must be notified in addition to the affected individuals within 60 days after the breach is discovered.

G. Texas "HIPAA"—Texas privacy laws, among other requirements, have a broader definition of a covered entity and more stringent training requirements. *See TFPDL pages A.41–43.* The Texas State Board of Pharmacy also has specific rules on "Confidentiality" and "Patient Access to Confidential Records" that are generally consistent with HIPAA. One difference, however, is that TSBP rules require a pharmacy to respond to a request for confidential records by a patient within 15 days which is stricter than HIPAA's 30-day timeline. *See TSBP Rules 291.27 and 291.28 or TFPDL pages E.18–20.*

CHAPTER TWO

Federal and Texas Controlled Substances Acts

CHAPTER TWO

Federal and Texas Controlled Substances Acts

Note: Throughout this chapter, unless otherwise noted, requirements listed as part of the FCSA are the same under the TCSA.

I. Drug Classifications

A. Schedule I (C-I) Drugs

1. High potential for abuse and severe potential for dependence (addiction).
2. No currently accepted medical use in treatment in the U.S.
3. Lack of accepted information on the safety of their use under medical supervision.
4. Include opiates and derivatives such as heroin and dihydromorphine; hallucinogens such as marijuana, lysergic acid diethylamide (LSD), peyote, and mescaline; and depressants such as methaqualone.

STUDY TIP: Texas has not legalized medical or recreational use of marijuana. While many states have "legalized" marijuana, it is still a Schedule I controlled substance under federal law, has no accepted medical use, and is technically illegal. Whether or not the federal government enforces the law is a different issue and beyond the scope of this book.

B. Schedule II (C-II) Drugs

1. High potential for abuse.
2. Have currently accepted medical use in treatment in the U.S. or currently accepted medical use with severe restrictions.
3. Abuse of the drug or other substances may lead to severe physical or psychological dependence (addiction).
4. Include opium and other narcotics such as morphine, codeine, dihydrocodeine, oxycodone, acetaminophen with hydrocodone (Vicodin®), methadone, meperidine, hydromorphone, fentanyl, and cocaine; stimulants such as amphetamine, methamphetamine, phenmetrazine, and methylphenidate; and depressants such as pentobarbital, secobarbital, amobarbital, glutethimide, and phencyclidine.

STUDY TIP: The term "narcotic" refers to drugs that are derivatives of opium, poppy straw, cocaine, or ecgonine. While all narcotics are controlled substances, not all controlled substances are narcotics.

C. Schedule III (C-III) Drugs

1. Potential for abuse less than Schedules I and II.
2. Have currently accepted medical use in treatment in the U.S.
3. Abuse of the drug or other substance may lead to moderate or low physical dependence (addiction) or high psychological dependence (addiction).
4. Include some narcotic Schedule II drugs, but in combination with another ingredient such as aspirin with codeine or acetaminophen with codeine (e.g., Tylenol #3). Also include some nonnarcotic drugs including suppository forms of amobarbital, secobarbital, or pentobarbital; stimulants such as chlorphentermine, phendimetrazine, and benzphetamine; anabolic steroids including testosterone; and ketamine and paregoric.

STUDY TIP: Note that the suppository forms of amobarbital, secobarbital, and pentobarbital are Schedule III, but other dosage forms are Schedule II.

D. Schedule IV (C-IV) Drugs

1. Low potential for abuse relative to Schedule III.
2. Have currently accepted medical use in treatment in the U.S.
3. Abuse may lead to limited physical or psychological dependence (addiction) relative to Schedule III.
4. Include narcotics such as dextropropoxyphene and products with no more than 1 mg of difenoxin and no less than 25 micrograms of atropine sulfate per dosage unit; depressants such as alprazolam, chloral hydrate, diazepam, lorazepam, and phenobarbital; stimulants such as diethylpropion and phentermine; and other drugs such as carisoprodol, tramadol, pentazocine, and butorphanol.

STUDY TIP: Be careful with drugs that have similar names but are in different schedules, such as phenmetrazine (C-II), phendimetrazine (C-III), and phentermine (C-IV).

E. Schedule V (C-V) Drugs

1. Low potential for abuse relative to Schedule IV.
2. Have currently accepted medical use in treatment in the U.S.

3. Abuse of the drug or other substance may lead to limited physical or psychological dependence (addiction) relative to Schedule IV.
4. Include pregabalin (Lyrica®), antitussive products containing codeine, antidiarrheal products containing opium, and certain antiseizure drugs such as brivaracetam (Brivact®) and lacosamide (Vimpat®).
Note: Hemp derivatives, including cannabidiol (CBD), were formerly considered Schedule I controlled substances, but those containing no more than 0.3% tetrahydrocannabinol (THC) were removed from the FCSA in 2018. There is also an FDA-approved prescription cannabidiol drug derived from cannabis (not from hemp), Epidiolex®, that was originally placed in Schedule V of the FCSA and TCSA. In late 2020, both DEA and Texas Department of State Health Services (TDSHS) removed Epidiolex® from Schedule V so it is no longer a controlled substance.

F. Exempted Prescription Drug Products
1. Manufacturers may apply to DEA to exempt a product or chemical from certain provisions of the Controlled Substances Act (labeling and inventory) if the product or chemical is not likely to be abused. These products may still be considered controlled substances for certain criminal violations even though they are not labeled as controlled substances.
2. Exempted prescription drug preparations include nonnarcotic products containing small amounts of phenobarbital, butalbital, chlordiazepoxide, or meprobamate. A common example is Fioricet® (butalbital, acetaminophen, and caffeine).
3. The DEA Exempt Prescription Product List can be found on DEA's website.

G. Listed Chemicals
1. Listed Chemicals are chemicals that, in addition to legitimate uses, are used in manufacturing a controlled substance.
2. In addition to specific chemicals, OTC products containing ephedrine, pseudoephedrine, or phenylpropanolamine are considered Listed Chemicals.
Note: Ephedrine and phenylpropanolamine products have been removed from the market by FDA for safety reasons.
3. These products are not controlled substances under federal law but are subject to certain sales limitations and other restrictions. See Section X.D. below.

H. Scheduling Authority for Controlled Substances

1. Federal—U.S. Attorney General, as head of the Department of Justice (which DEA is under), may add, delete, or reschedule substances but must obtain a scientific and medical recommendation from FDA.
2. State—The Commissioner of the Texas Department of State Health Services may add, delete, or reschedule substances but cannot override actions by the legislature.

II. Scheduling of Compounded Controlled Substances

STUDY TIP: You should know the concentration limits below and be able to calculate which schedule a particular compounded product would be classified under. However, first be sure that the codeine or opium is being compounded with another nonnarcotic therapeutic agent. Any straight narcotic, regardless of concentration, will always be in Schedule II. For example, if codeine or opium is only being mixed with water or simple syrup, it is still a Schedule II regardless of the concentration.

A. A pharmacy may compound narcotic controlled substances pursuant to a prescription. However, DEA limits the compounding of "aqueous or oleaginous solutions or solid dosage forms" to no more than a 20% concentration. DEA considers compounding of these types of products with a narcotic ingredient greater than 20% to be manufacturing even if the pharmacist has a prescription to compound the product.

B. The narcotic substance must be compounded with one or more nonnarcotic therapeutic ingredients.

C. Concentration Limits

1. Codeine
   - **a.** C-V limit = 200 mg/100 ml.
   - **b.** C-III limit = 1.8 g/100 ml and 90 mg/dosage unit.

STUDY TIP: Although concentration limits are the same under Texas law and federal law, Texas requires all codeine and dihydrocodeine products to be dispensed pursuant to a prescription. Products such as Cheracol® and Robitussin AC® are Schedule V, but they require a prescription in Texas. These products contain the maximum amount of codeine allowed for Schedule V. If you add even 1 mg of codeine to these products, they would then be a Schedule III.

2. Dihydrocodeine
    a. C-V limit = 100 mg/100 ml.
    b. C-III limit = 1.8 g/100 ml and 90 mg/dosage unit.
       Note: Anything above this limit would be Schedule II.
3. Opium
    a. Federal C-V limit = 100 mg/100 ml.
    b. Texas C-V limit = 50 mg/100 ml.

STUDY TIP: The Schedule V opium limit under Texas law is 50 mg/100 ml or half the concentration under federal law. This stricter requirement means that most of the commercially available Schedule V products containing opium cannot be purchased without a prescription in Texas. These products are Schedule III controlled substances under Texas law and require a prescription.

---

    c. C-III limit = 500 mg/100 ml and 25 mg/dosage unit.
4. Morphine
    a. C-V limit = None (no morphine products are C-V; they are either C-II or C-III).
    b. C-III limit = 50 mg/100 ml.

STUDY TIP: A compounded narcotic prescription will never be a Schedule IV.

III. Registration

A. General Information

1. Every person or firm that manufactures, distributes, or dispenses any controlled substances or proposes to engage in any of these activities must register with DEA.
2. There is no state controlled substance registration in Texas.
3. Dispensers (pharmacies and practitioners) register every 3 years with DEA.
4. Practitioner registrations start with the letters "A," "B," or "F" (or "G" for Department of Defense contractors).
5. The second letter of the prefix will normally be the first letter of the practitioner's last name for individual practitioners or the first letter of a pharmacy's or hospital's name.

B. Mid-Level Practitioners

1. Practitioners, other than physicians, dentists, veterinarians, or podiatrists, who are licensed, registered, or otherwise authorized under state law to dispense (including

prescribing) controlled substances in the course of professional practice.

2. Registration begins with the letter "M."
3. May include advanced practice registered nurses and physician assistants if the state allows them to prescribe controlled substances. Other mid-level practitioners may include ambulance services, animal shelters, and veterinary euthanasia technicians.

C. Activities Requiring Separate Registrations

1. Manufacturing (C-I—C-V).
2. Distributing (C-I—C-V).
3. Reverse Distributing (C-I—C-V).
4. Dispensing (C-II—C-V)—Includes prescribing and administration by practitioners and dispensing by pharmacies.
5. Conducting research (C-I).
6. Conducting research (C-II—C-V).
7. Conducting narcotic treatment program (C-II—C-V).
8. Conducting chemical analysis (C-I—C-V).
9. Importing (C-I—C-V).
10. Exporting (C-I—C-V).

Note: On October 5, 2020, DEA issued a notice of proposed rulemaking that includes a new category of registration for an Emergency Medical Services Agency. At the time of this book's publication, this rule had not been finalized.

D. Verifying a DEA Registration (Number)

1. Step 1—Add 1st, 3rd, and 5th digits.
2. Step 2—Add 2nd, 4th, and 6th digits and multiply sum by 2.
3. Step 3—Add the sum of steps 1 and 2, and the last digit of the sum should correspond to the last digit of the DEA number.
4. Example: DEA #AB1234563.
   a. $1 + 3 + 5 = 9$.
   b. $(2 + 4 + 6) \times 2 = 24$.
   c. Total $= 33$.

E. Separate registration is required for separate locations.

1. Individual practitioners including physicians who register at one location but practice at other locations in the same state are not required to register at another site if they only prescribe controlled substances at that site. If they maintain a supply of controlled substances at that site or if the site is in another state, they would have to register at that site.

2. Each pharmacy must have a separate DEA registration.
3. DEA will sometimes issue a campus registration that may include multiple buildings, but approval for a campus registration is done on a case-by-case basis.

F. Application for Registration

1. DEA Form 224 for dispensers (practitioners and pharmacies).
2. Application must be signed (or electronically signed) by the applicant if it is for an individual, by a partner if it is for a partnership, or by an officer if it is for a corporation.
3. An applicant can authorize another individual to sign the application and renewals by filling out a Power of Attorney (POA) granting that individual the authority and filing that POA with the DEA Registration Unit.

G. Exemptions (Who does not have to register with DEA)

1. An agent or employee of any registered manufacturer, distributor, or dispenser if acting in the usual course of business or employment.

STUDY TIP: Exempted persons would include pharmacists working in a pharmacy and nurses working in a hospital or physician's office.

---

2. A common or contract carrier or warehouseman or an employee thereof whose possession is in the usual course of business or employment.
3. An ultimate user (patient) who possesses a controlled substance for a lawful purpose.
4. Officials of the U.S. Armed Services, Public Health Service, or Bureau of Prisons acting in the course of their official duties.

STUDY TIP: In Texas, these "federal" practitioners in 4. above can issue electronic Schedule II prescriptions. However, they can't issue written Schedule II prescriptions to be filled off base or out of the facility where they practice when one of the exemptions to electronic controlled substance prescriptions applies. This is because they would not be written on a Texas Official Prescription Form. TSBP only issues official prescription forms to DEA registered practitioners. When an exemption from electronic prescriptions applies for Schedule III–V controlled substances from these practitioners, written prescriptions can be filled off base.

H. Practitioner's Use of Hospital DEA Number

1. Interns, residents, staff physicians, and mid-level practitioners who are agents or employees of a hospital or other institution may administer, dispense, or prescribe controlled substances under the registration of the hospital or other institution when acting in the usual course of business or employment.
2. The hospital must assign a specific internal code for each practitioner authorized to use the hospital's DEA number, and this must be available at all times to other registrants and law enforcement agencies. This internal code shall be a suffix to the hospital's DEA number (e.g., AP1234563-10 or AP1234563-A12).
3. Controlled substance prescriptions written by these practitioners are valid and can be filled by any pharmacy, not just the hospital pharmacy where they are employed.

I. Temporary Use of Registration Upon Sale of a Pharmacy

If the new owner has not yet obtained a DEA registration, DEA permits the new owner to continue the business of the pharmacy under the previous owner's registration provided the following requirements are met:

1. The new owner must expeditiously apply for an appropriate DEA registration and state licensure.
2. The previous owner grants a Power of Attorney to the new owner that provides for the following:
    - **a.** The previous owner agrees to allow the controlled substance activities of the pharmacy to be carried out under his or her DEA registration;
    - **b.** The previous owner agrees to allow the new owner to carry out the controlled substance activities of the pharmacy, including the ordering of controlled substances, as an agent of the previous owner;
    - **c.** The previous owner acknowledges, as the registrant, that he or she will be held accountable for any violations of controlled substance laws which may occur; and
    - **d.** The previous owner agrees that the controlled substance activities of the pharmacy may be carried out under his or her DEA registration and shall remain in effect for no more than 45 days after the purchase date.

STUDY TIP: This temporary use procedure is not in a DEA rule. It was authorized many years ago in a policy letter from DEA. It is a practical policy as it makes sense to allow the new owner time to obtain a DEA registration after a change in ownership while still allowing patients to obtain refills and have prescriptions filled. An owner cannot apply for a DEA registration until the owner has received a state pharmacy license and state controlled substance license if applicable. The 45-day limitation was in the original guidance from DEA, but some DEA offices may permit a longer time period if needed.

IV. Ordering and Transferring Controlled Substances

A. Ordering Schedule II Controlled Substances—DEA Form 222

1. Required for each sale or transfer of C-II drugs (except dispensing to ultimate user).
2. Only one item may be ordered on each numbered line.
3. Orders for etorphine hydrochloride and diprenorphine must contain only orders for these substances.
4. The number of lines completed must be noted on the form.
5. Name and address of supplier from whom the controlled substances are being ordered must be entered.
6. Must be signed (or electronically signed) by the registrant (individual, partner, or officer) and by the person being authorized to execute DEA Form 222.
7. Registrant may authorize other individuals to execute forms by creating a Power of Attorney (POA). This Power of Attorney does not need to be sent to DEA but must be maintained in the pharmacy. A sample DEA Power of Attorney can be found in Chapter B of TFPDL and in the *DEA Pharmacist's Manual.*

STUDY TIP: Previously, DEA allowed the person who signed the last application or renewal to issue a POA to allow other individuals to sign DEA Form 222. Remember, that person may have signed the renewal application based on a POA from the registrant. That provision was removed effective October 30, 2019. This means that only the actual registrant may grant a POA for signing DEA Form 222.

8. Forms that are not complete, legible, properly prepared, or signed will not be accepted.
9. Forms that show any alteration, erasure, or changes will not be accepted.

10. Single Copy DEA Form 222

a. Effective October 30, 2019, DEA finalized rules to transition from a triplicate (3 copy) DEA Form 222 to a single copy DEA Form 222 with additional security features. There was a two-year transition period during which existing triplicate DEA Forms 222 could have been used, but as of October 30, 2021, only the single copy DEA Form 222 may be used.

b. The new single forms contain 20 order lines per form rather than 10 order lines on the triplicate forms.

c. The purchaser filling out a single copy DEA Form 222 must make a copy of the original form for its records and submit the original form to the supplier. The copy may be retained in paper or electronic form.
Note: If kept electronically, the copy of DEA Form 222 does not need to be stored on a different server or system from the purchaser's other records. Also, electronic copies of DEA Form 222 may also be stored on a system at a location different from the registered location. However, at all times, the forms must be readily retrievable at the registered location.

d. The supplier may only fill an order from the original form and not from a copy. The supplier must record on the original form the number of containers furnished for each ordered item and the date the products are shipped to the purchaser.
Note: There was some confusion as to whether the purchaser or the supplier had to fill out the DEA number of the supplier on the single-copy form because the instructions for that part of the form state that it is to be entered by the purchaser. This was different from the previous triplicate DEA Form 222, which required the supplier to fill out that section. DEA clarified that the purchaser should enter that information, but if it is omitted, the supplier may complete that part of the form. See 86 Fed. Reg. 38230 (July 20, 2021).

e. Most suppliers (e.g., wholesalers) are required to report the acquisition and disposition of Schedule II and certain Schedule III and IV controlled substances to DEA's Automation of Reports and Consolidated Orders System (ARCOS). A supplier who reports transactions to

ARCOS is not required to send a copy of the original DEA Form 222 to the DEA because this information is already reported to ARCOS. However, if a supplier is not required to report transactions to ARCOS (e.g., a pharmacy or practitioner acting as a supplier under the 5% rule), it must submit a copy of the original DEA Form 222 to DEA either by mail or by email to *DEA.Orderforms@usdoj.gov* when acting as a supplier.
Note: When a pharmacy acts as a supplier, in addition to submitting a copy of DEA Form 222 to DEA by mail or email, the pharmacy must have a system to identify any suspicious orders, which, when identified, must be reported online to DEA's Suspicious Orders Report System (SORS).

f. When the product has been received, the purchaser must record the number of containers received and the date received for each item on the copy of the DEA Form 222 it made when ordering the product.

g. Texas rules also require a pharmacist to verify that controlled substances listed on a supplier's invoice were actually received by recording on the invoice his or her initials and the actual date of receipt.

STUDY TIP: The purchaser or the person obtaining the product always provides the original DEA Form 222 to the supplier and makes a copy for their records to record the products received.

---

11. If a completed order form is lost or stolen, the purchaser must prepare another DEA Form 222 along with a statement containing the serial number and date of the lost form and stating that the goods covered by the first order were not received because the form was lost.

12. If an order cannot be filled in its entirety, the supplier may fill the order in part and supply the balance within 60 days.

13. A pharmacy may fax a completed DEA Form 222 to a supplier in order for the supplier to prepare the order; however, the supplier may not ship the product until the original DEA Form 222 is received and verified.

14. Electronic Ordering Through the Controlled Substance Ordering System (CSOS).

a. Each pharmacy must appoint a CSOS coordinator who will serve as that pharmacy's recognized agent regarding issues pertaining to issuance of, revocation of, and changes to digital certificates issued under that registrant's DEA registration.

b. The CSOS allows electronic orders based on digital certificates issued by the DEA Certification Authority that are valid until the expiration of the DEA registration for the facility (3 years).

c. Even though each CSOS Certificate expires when the DEA registration of the facility expires, it is issued to *individual subscribers*. Certificates must never be used by anyone other than the individual subscriber (a person, not a location) to whom the certificate was issued.

d. There are two types of CSOS Certificates:

(1) CSOS Administrative Certificates are used to digitally sign communications with DEA as well as with other participants in the CSOS community. Administrative Certificates are issued only to CSOS Coordinators and are not valid for electronic ordering.

(2) CSOS Signing Certificates are used for digitally signing controlled substance orders. Signing Certificates are issued to approved Registrant and Power of Attorney applicants. Approved Coordinator applicants will only be issued a Signing Certificate if he or she holds a valid Power of Attorney for controlled substance ordering and has requested a Signing Certificate on his or her CSOS Certificate Application.

e. All CSOS applications must be audited by an independent third-party auditor prior to use and whenever changes are made to the software to ensure that the software is in compliance with DEA regulations.

f. An electronic order for controlled substances may not be filled if any of the following occurs:

(1) The required data fields have not been completed.

(2) The order is not signed using a digital certificate issued by DEA.

(3) The digital certificate used has expired or been revoked prior to signature.

(4) The purchaser's public key will not validate the digital certificate.

(5) The validation of the order shows that the order is invalid for any reason.

g. If an order cannot be filled, the supplier must notify the purchaser and provide a statement as to the reason (e.g., improperly prepared or altered). A supplier may, for any reason, refuse to accept any order. If a supplier refuses, a statement that the order is not accepted is sufficient.
h. When a purchaser receives an unaccepted electronic order from the supplier, the purchaser must electronically link the statement of nonacceptance to the original order. The original statement must be retained for two years. Neither a purchaser nor a supplier may correct a defective order. The purchaser must issue a new order for the order to be filled.

B. Ordering Schedule III–V Controlled Substances

1. Schedule III–V controlled substances can be ordered through normal ordering processes from a wholesaler or manufacturer but must be documented by a pharmacy with an invoice provided by the wholesaler or manufacturer.
2. The invoice must contain:
    a. Name of controlled substance.
    b. Dosage form and strength.
    c. Number of units per container (e.g., 100-tablet bottle).
    d. Quantity received (containers).
    e. Date of receipt.
    f. Name, address, and DEA number of registrant from where controlled substance was received.
3. All invoices for controlled substances must be initialed by the receiving pharmacist in Texas (except in Class C-ASC and Class F pharmacies, where they must be signed by the person receiving who does not have to be a pharmacist).

C. Transfers of Controlled Substances Between Registrants—The 5% Rule

1. A pharmacy does not have to register with DEA as a distributor as long as total quantities of controlled substances distributed during a 12-month period in which the pharmacy is registered do not exceed 5% of the total quantity of all controlled substances dispensed and distributed during that same 12-month period.
2. Example: A pharmacy dispenses and distributes a total of 10,000 doses (i.e., tablets, capsules, teaspoons, etc.) of all controlled substances (not just CII drugs). This pharmacy would

be allowed to transfer 500 doses without being registered with DEA as a distributor.

3. If the transfer is for a Schedule II controlled substance, a DEA Form 222 is required. For Schedule III–V controlled substances, an invoice provided by the supplier is required with all of the required elements listed in B.2. above.
4. Transfers can only be made to the address listed on a DEA registration. This requirement applies to all controlled substances, not just Schedule II controlled substances.

STUDY TIP: Notice that for Schedule II controlled substances, the person (purchaser) receiving the product initiates and fills out the DEA Form 222, which is sent to the supplier or seller. However, for Schedule III–V controlled substances, an invoice is provided by the supplier or seller to the purchaser.

V. Additional Requirements for Controlled Substances

A. Storage and Security

1. Pharmacies may store controlled substances in a secure cabinet that is locked.
2. Pharmacies may store controlled substances by dispersal throughout the noncontrolled stock to deter theft.
3. Pharmacies may not store all controlled substances on one unsecured shelf.

STUDY TIP: While many pharmacies keep some or all of their controlled substances in locked storage, it is only required in Texas for Schedule II controlled substances in Class C (Institutional) and Class F (Freestanding Emergency Medical Care Facility) pharmacies.

B. Theft or Significant Loss of Controlled Substances

1. A theft or significant loss of controlled substances must be reported in writing to DEA within one business day of discovery of the theft or significant loss. DEA also recommends notifying local police.
2. TSBP also requires notification to the Board of a theft or significant loss of controlled substances immediately upon discovery.

STUDY TIP: Any theft must be reported but only "significant" losses.

3. Complete DEA Form 106 (Theft or Loss of Controlled Substances). This form can be filled out online at DEA's website.
4. Submitting the DEA Form 106 immediately is not necessary if the pharmacy needs time to investigate the facts, but an initial notification must be provided in writing to DEA within one business day of discovery.
Note: At the time of this book's publication, DEA had proposed revising this rule to require that DEA Form 106 be filed within 15 days of discovery. The proposed changes would also require the form to be filled out online which most pharmacies already do.

C. Reporting Losses of Listed Chemicals (Primarily Pseudoephedrine Products in a Pharmacy)
1. DEA requires any unusual or excessive loss or disappearance (this would include a theft) of a listed chemical to be reported to DEA at the earliest practicable opportunity.
2. A written report must be provided within 15 days and must include a description of the circumstances of the loss (in-transit, theft from premises, etc.).
3. DEA Form 107 is used to report the loss.

D. Miscellaneous DEA Rules and Policies
1. Convicted Felon Rule—A pharmacy cannot employ someone who has access to controlled substances if the person has been convicted of a felony involving controlled substances unless a waiver is granted by DEA.
2. Employee Screening Procedures—DEA requires pharmacies to screen potential employees with specific questions regarding criminal history and use of controlled substances.
3. Employee Responsibility to Report Drug Diversion—Individual employees are required to report any diversion by other employees to a responsible security official of the employer.
4. Patients Bringing Controlled Substances from Home (Residence) to the Hospital
According to the DEA Pharmacist's Manual, if a patient is admitted to a hospital via ambulance/emergency medical services (EMS) and there is no family present and the patient has in his or her possession dispensed medications, including controlled substances, it is DEA's position that:
    a. If the treating practitioner deems that it is medically appropriate for the patient to continue to take any

controlled substance medications brought from the patient's residence to the DEA-registered hospital, the hospital could secure the controlled substances with the patient's effects in his or her hospital room (e.g., in a small safe or secured lockbox). Thus, the hospital has not taken possession of the controlled substances, and it would not be considered an unlawful distribution by the ultimate user under 21 U.S.C. § 841(a).

b. If the treating practitioner deems that it would be medically inappropriate for the patient to continue taking any controlled substance medication(s) brought from the patient's residence to the DEA-registered hospital, or it is the hospital's policy not to permit patients to bring already dispensed controlled medications into the hospital, then the hospital has the following options:

(1) If a member of the patient's household arrives at the hospital, the hospital can turn over the patient's medications, including controlled substances, to him or her. The member of the patient's household can take the controlled medications back to the household and/or dispose of them in a manner that is in accordance with federal, state, local, and tribal laws and regulations.

(2) If a hospital has modified its DEA registration to become an authorized collector and has placed a collection receptacle at its registered location, then a member of the patient's household may dispose of the patient's medications, including controlled substances, in the hospital's collection receptacle.

(3) If a hospital has empty mail-back packages (no modification of the DEA registration is required), then the hospital may provide one or more of the mail-back packages to a member of the patient's household to place the medications, including controlled substances, into the mail-back package(s) and seal the package(s) for mailing to the authorized DEA-registered reverse distributor for disposal purposes.

(4) If there is no member of the patient's household present, DEA understands that there may be circumstances where there is no authorized person to dispose of the controlled substances, such as when controlled substances are abandoned and return to the ultimate user is not feasible. In such instances, the affected entities should contact local law enforcement or their local DEA Diversion Field Office for guidance on proper disposal procedures.

5. Federal Transfer Warning (21 CFR 209.5)—The following warning is required to be on the label of Schedule II–IV controlled substances when dispensed to a patient: "Caution: Federal law prohibits the transfer of this drug to any person other than the patient for whom it was prescribed." The only exception would be for a controlled substance dispensed in a "blinded" clinical study.

STUDY TIP: Most pharmacies comply with this requirement by including this language in small print on every prescription label, but it is legally only required for Schedule II–IV controlled substances. It is not required on labels for Schedule V controlled substances or dangerous drugs (noncontrolled substances).

E. Disposal and Destruction of Controlled Substances

1. Onsite destruction of controlled substances in a pharmacy must be done using DEA Form 41 which requires the name and NDC number of the drug, the strength, the dosage form, the package size, and the quantity of the controlled substances destroyed. It also requires recording the method by which the drugs were destroyed and two signatures of employees who witnessed the destruction. Because it is difficult to comply with all other laws including EPA requirements, most pharmacies do not use this method of destruction.
   Note: DEA Form 41 is also used to document destruction of controlled substances that a pharmacy received as an authorized collector even though these drugs are not "stock" controlled substances because they are not part of the pharmacy's inventory. See 3. below.
2. Transfer to an Authorized (Registered) Reverse Distributor—This is the preferred method of destruction and is simply a transfer from one DEA registrant (the pharmacy) to another (the reverse distributor). Because this is a transfer, a DEA Form 41 is not required. The transfer must be documented

with an invoice for Schedule III–V controlled substances and a DEA Form 222 for Schedule II controlled substances.

STUDY TIP: Be sure to understand the difference between use of a DEA Form 41 which is used to destroy controlled substances on the premises of a pharmacy (even though this is rarely done) and transferring controlled substances to a DEA registered reverse distributor for destruction, which requires a DEA Form 222 (CII) or an invoice (CIII–V).

---

3. Disposal of Controlled Substances Collected From Ultimate Users and Other Non-Registrants.
   a. DEA rules allow pharmacies to modify their DEA registrations to serve as a collector of controlled substances from ultimate users including patients, the personal representative of the patient in the event of the patient's death, and long-term care facilities.
   b. A pharmacy or hospital is not required to serve as a collector.
   c. A pharmacy that serves as a collector must meet specific requirements for collection receptacles and may also provide a mail-back program. *See DEA Rule 21 CFR 1304.22(f) or TFPDL pages B.26–27 for details.*

STUDY TIP: A collector that conducts a mail-back program may only accept packages that the collector made available. If the collector receives a package that they did not make available, the collector must notify DEA within three business days of receipt.

---

   d. Drugs collected in receptacles may either be destroyed onsite or sent to a DEA registered reverse distributor for destruction. If destroyed onsite, DEA Form 41 would be used. DEA Form 41 has a separate section for "collected substances." Instead of indicating the specific controlled substances being destroyed, it requires the unique identification number of the inner liner from the collection receptacle or the mail-back package.
   e. DEA also conducts Drug Take Back Days to collect controlled substances (and other drugs) from ultimate users.
4. Disposal of Controlled Substances of a Hospice Patient by Employees of the Hospice—The SUPPORT Act, a comprehensive opioid bill passed by Congress in late 2018,

authorized an employee of a qualified hospice program to handle controlled substances for the purpose of destruction that were lawfully dispensed to a person receiving hospice care. DEA has yet to adopt regulations to implement this law and practice.

F. Inventories

1. An initial inventory is required on the first day the pharmacy is open for business.
2. Newly scheduled drugs or drugs moved from one schedule to another must be inventoried on the day scheduled or moved to a new schedule. DEA requires a biennial (every 2 years) inventory that must be maintained in the pharmacy for 2 years. However, TSBP rules require an annual inventory, so pharmacies in Texas must conduct an annual inventory.

STUDY TIP: It is important to note where Texas law is stricter than federal law, such as this requirement for an annual inventory of controlled substances.

---

3. Inventory Counts.
   - **a.** An exact count is required for all Schedule IIs.
   - **b.** An estimated count is allowed for Schedule III–V products unless the container holds more than 1000 tablets or capsules.
4. Although many pharmacies maintain a perpetual inventory of Schedule II controlled substances or even for all controlled substances, a perpetual inventory is only required in Texas for:
   - **a.** Schedule II controlled substances in Class C (Institutional) pharmacies.
   - **b.** All controlled substances stored at a remote location under the remote pharmacy rules.
   - **c.** All controlled substances in Class C Ambulatory Surgical Centers (ASCs).
   - **d.** All controlled substances in Class F (Freestanding Emergency Medical Facility) pharmacies.
5. TSBP rules require that inventories (other than initial and change of pharmacist-in-charge inventories) be signed by the person(s) taking the inventory and the pharmacist-in-charge, and that the signature of the pharmacist-in-charge be notarized within 3 days of the day the inventory is completed, excluding Saturdays, Sundays, and federal holidays.

G. Records

1. Records of controlled substances must be maintained for 2 years under federal and Texas law.
2. DEA requires that records and inventories of Schedule II controlled substances be kept separately from all other records. Records and inventories of Schedule III–V controlled substances must be maintained separately or be "readily retrievable" from other records. "Readily retrievable" means the record is kept or maintained in such a manner that it can be separated from all other records in a reasonable time or that it is identified by an asterisk, a redline, or some other identifiable manner such that it is easily distinguishable from all other records.
3. Records of Receipt of Controlled Substances.
   a. C-II—Copy of DEA Form 222 (with the number of containers and date received filled in).
   b. C-III—C-V—Supplier's invoice.

STUDY TIP: TSBP rules require the initials of the receiving pharmacist on invoices for controlled substances except in Class C-ASC and Freestanding Class F pharmacies. In these pharmacies, a pharmacist's initials are not required because there may not be a pharmacist present. Instead, the person receiving all prescription drugs (not just controlled substances) is required to sign for his or her receipt in Class C-ASC and Freestanding Class F pharmacies.

---

4. Records of Disbursement of Controlled Substances.
   a. Dispensing records—Although most pharmacies maintain electronic dispensing records, there are still specific storage requirements for the hard copies of all controlled substance prescriptions. TSBP rules require a 3-file storage system:
      (1) File 1 = Schedule II.
      (2) File 2 = Schedules III, IV, and V.
      (3) File 3 = Nonscheduled (Dangerous drugs and OTC drugs filled as a prescription).

STUDY TIP: The 3-file storage system only applies to written prescriptions and verbal prescriptions that are reduced to writing by a pharmacist. If a controlled substance prescription is transmitted electronically, DEA requires that those electronic prescriptions be maintained electronically.

---

b. Other records of disbursement (i.e., controlled substances that leave a pharmacy) include DEA Form 106 (Theft or Significant Loss), DEA Form 41 (Destruction), DEA Form 222 for any Schedule II distributions made under the 5% rule, and invoices for Schedule III–V distributions made under the 5% rule.

H. Central Recordkeeping

1. A pharmacy wishing to maintain shipping and financial records at a central location other than the registered location must notify the nearest DEA Diversion Field Office.
2. Unless the pharmacy is notified by the DEA that permission to keep the central records is denied, the pharmacy may begin maintaining central records 14 days after notifying the DEA.
3. Central records shall not include executed DEA order forms (Copy of DEA Form 222), prescriptions, or inventories. These must be kept at the pharmacy.

STUDY TIP: Be sure to know the records that cannot be kept at a central location.

VI. Dispensing Controlled Substance Prescriptions

A. Corresponding Responsibility

1. For a prescription for a controlled substance to be valid, it must be issued for a legitimate medical purpose by an individual practitioner acting in the usual scope of his or her professional practice.
2. The responsibility for the proper prescribing and dispensing of a controlled substance is upon the prescribing practitioner, but a corresponding responsibility rests with the pharmacist who fills the prescription. This means a pharmacist cannot simply rely on the fact that a physician has a valid DEA registration to determine if a controlled substance prescription is valid.
3. Through enforcement actions, DEA and TSBP have identified a number of "red flags" that may require a pharmacist to do further investigation as to the legitimacy of controlled substance prescriptions.

STUDY TIP: You should familiarize yourself with the most common "red flags" and how to resolve them. Common red flags can be found in Chapters B and E of TFPDL and from various sources online such as the TSBP website.

B. Prescriptive Authority

1. Who can prescribe controlled substance prescriptions is determined by state law. Texas law authorizes the following practitioners to prescribe controlled substances:
    a. Physicians (MD or DO).
    b. Dentists.
    c. Podiatrists.
    d. Veterinarians.
    e. Therapeutic Optometrists and Optometric Glaucoma Specialists (with some limitations; *see Chapter Three in this book*).
    f. Advanced Practice Registered Nurses and Physician Assistants practicing in Texas. In-state advanced practice registered nurses and physician assistants may prescribe controlled substances in Schedules III–V (and in certain practice settings, Schedule II controlled substances) with some restrictions. *See Chapter Three in this book.*
2. Designated Agents.
    a. Can communicate a prescription for a C-III—C-V controlled substance when an electronic prescription is not required, but cannot authorize or prescribe.
    b. An authorized agent of the prescriber (employee or non-employee) may not verbally communicate emergency C-II prescriptions to a pharmacist. This task cannot be delegated.
    Note: The TCSA permits an agent to verbally communicate a Schedule II prescription for a prescriber in an emergency. However, DEA does not permit this practice, so the stricter federal law must be followed.
    c. DEA requires that for a non-employee of the prescriber to qualify as an agent of the prescriber, there must be a formal written appointment of the agent by the prescriber. This is important for facilities such as nursing homes, where the nurses may not be employees of the physician but may wish to call in a prescription to a pharmacy on behalf of a physician.

C. Quantity Limits for Opioids for Acute Pain

1. Prescriptions for opioid drugs in Texas for the treatment of acute pain may not exceed a 10-day supply, and no refills may be issued on such a prescription.

STUDY TIP: These limitations are for opioid drugs and only for acute pain. Not all opioid drugs are Schedule II controlled substances, and not all Schedule II controlled substances are opioids.

2. "Acute pain" means the normal, predicted, physiological response to a stimulus such as trauma, disease, and operative procedures. Acute pain is time limited. The term does not include:
   - **a.** Chronic pain;
   - **b.** Pain being treated as part of cancer care;
   - **c.** Pain being treated as part of hospice or other end-of-life care; or
   - **d.** Pain being treated as part of palliative care.
3. The quantity and refill limits above do not apply to a prescription for an opioid approved by the FDA for the treatment of substance addiction that is issued by an authorized practitioner for the treatment of substance addiction.
4. Because it may be difficult for a pharmacist to know if a prescription for more than a 10-day supply or with refills is for acute pain, the law provides that a dispenser is not subject to criminal, civil, or administrative penalties for dispensing or refusing to dispense a controlled substance under a prescription that exceeds the limits provided above.

STUDY TIP: The Texas Medical Board has interpreted this law to mean a practitioner may write an opioid prescription for acute pain for up to 10 days without a refill. However, the patient may see the practitioner in a follow-up appointment and receive another opioid prescription for up to 10 days. The law does not limit how many times this may occur. *See guidance issued by the Texas Medical Board on August 30, 2019.*

D. Changing Information or Information Omitted

Note: These DEA guidelines were issued about written controlled substance prescriptions. However, in the commentary to the DEA rule allowing electronic prescriptions, DEA made it clear that pharmacy changes to electronic prescriptions for controlled substances are governed by the same statutory and regulatory limitations that apply to paper prescriptions. The only difference is the documentation would be required to be made in the electronic record.

1. A pharmacist may not change the following items on a controlled substance prescription:
   a. Name of the patient.
   b. Name of the drug.
   c. Name of the prescribing physician.
   d. Date of the prescription.
2. Any other item such as drug strength, dosage form, quantity, or directions for use may be changed provided the pharmacist:
   a. Contacts the prescribing practitioner and receives verbal permission for the change; and
   b. Documents on the prescription (or electronic record) that the change was authorized, the name or initials of the individual granting the authorization, and the pharmacist's initials.

E. Mandatory Electronic Prescriptions for Controlled Substances

1. Texas made it mandatory that all prescriptions for controlled substances be issued electronically starting January 1, 2021, unless a specific exemption applies or in case of an emergency.
2. Exemptions—A prescription for a controlled substance is not required to be issued electronically and may be issued in writing (not verbally) for the following:
   a. Prescriptions written by veterinarians;
   b. In circumstances where electronic prescribing is not available due to temporary technological or electronic failure;
   c. By a practitioner to be dispensed by a pharmacy located outside of Texas;
   d. When the prescriber and dispenser are in the same location or under the same license;
   e. In circumstances where necessary elements are not supported by the most recently implemented national data standard that facilitates electronic prescribing;
   f. For a drug which DEA requires additional information in the prescription that is not possible with electronic prescribing;

g. For a non-patient-specific prescription pursuant to a standing order, approved protocol for drug therapy, collaborative drug management, or comprehensive medication management, in response to a public health emergency or in other circumstances in which the practitioner may issue a non-patient-specific prescription;
h. For a drug under a research protocol;
i. By a practitioner who has received a waiver from the requirement to use electronic prescribing;
Note: Waivers must be issued by the agency that licenses the practitioner and are valid for one year but can be renewed.
j. Under circumstances where the practitioner has the ability to submit an electronic prescription, but reasonably determines that it would be impractical for the patient to obtain the drugs prescribed under the provisions for electronic prescriptions in a timely manner and that a delay would adversely impact the patient's medical condition; and
k. A medication order written for a patient who is admitted to a hospital at the time the order is written and filled.

F. Electronic Prescriptions for Controlled Substances (EPCS)
1. EPCS (including for Schedule II drugs) are valid if both the prescriber's computer and the pharmacy's computer meet all DEA security requirements.
2. Prescriber requirements include:
a. Third-party certification of system.
b. Credentialing to verify a provider has the authorization to prescribe controlled substances.
c. Two-factor authentication for providers who sign an EPCS prescription.
3. Pharmacy requirements include:
a. Third-party certification of system.
b. Ability to sign and archive the controlled substance prescription.
c. The system must electronically accept and store all the information that DEA requires to document the dispensing of a prescription.
d. The system must allow the pharmacy to limit access for the annotation, alteration, or deletion of controlled substance prescriptions to specific individuals or roles.

e. The system must have an internal audit trail that documents whenever a prescription is received, altered, annotated, or deleted.
f. The pharmacy must conduct an internal audit daily that identifies any potential security problems, and the system must generate a report for review by the pharmacy if a problem is identified.
g. Pharmacy systems must be backed up daily.
h. Electronic prescription records must be kept electronically. No hard copy is required to be kept.

G. Written Controlled Substance Prescriptions

Note: Because there are many exceptions to the mandatory electronic prescription requirements, it is still important to know the requirements for written controlled substance prescriptions.

1. Must be manually signed by the practitioner and dated on the date issued.
2. Must contain:
    a. The full name and address of the patient.
    b. The drug name, strength, and dosage form.
    c. The quantity prescribed.
    d. The name, address, and DEA number of the practitioner.
    e. If written for a Schedule II prescription to be filled at a later date, the earliest date on which a pharmacy may fill a prescription.
    f. Additional requirements for controlled substance prescriptions in Texas:
        (1) The quantity prescribed must be written numerically and as a word (e.g., "Vicodin #20 (twenty)"). If the quantity is not written as a word, the pharmacist should call to verify the quantity.
        Note: This requirement is no longer in the TCSA, but it is still in the TSBP rules.
        (2) Date of birth or age of the patient.
        (3) The practitioner's telephone number at the practitioner's usual place of business.
        (4) The intended use of the drug unless the practitioner determines the furnishing of this information is not in the best interest of the patient.

    Note: (2)–(4) above are required for all prescriptions in Texas, not just for controlled substances.

(5) Written Schedule II prescriptions must be written on an Official Texas Prescription Form. *See VII.E. below.*

3. DEA does not allow pharmacists to pre-populate a controlled substance prescription with all required information and then fax or electronically send the prescription to a practitioner to be signed.

H. Verbal and Fax Controlled Substance Prescriptions

1. DEA has specific requirements for emergency verbal prescriptions for Schedule II controlled substances that include obtaining a valid electronic or written prescription within 7 days. *See Section VII. C. below.*
2. DEA permits prescriptions for Schedule III, IV, or V controlled substances to be communicated verbally to a pharmacist by a practitioner or his or her agent.
3. The TCSA technically only allows prescriptions for Schedule III, IV, and V controlled substances to be communicated verbally in an emergency (similar to the DEA rule for Schedule II prescriptions).
4. Fortunately, TSBP has indicated that pharmacists may dispense a Schedule III–V controlled substance pursuant to an otherwise valid verbal prescription. *See Section VIII. B. below and the Quick Reference Guide Chart at the end of Chapter Three in this book.*
5. Because the TCSA technically requires an emergency for Schedule III, IV, and V verbal prescriptions to be valid, the statute also requires that within seven days of issuing an emergency verbal prescription, the prescriber must provide an electronic prescription to the pharmacy.
   Note: The TCSA does not address what practitioners should do if they are exempt from the mandatory electronic prescription requirements, but logically in this situation they should send a written prescription within 7 days. In addition, although this requirement to obtain an electronic (or perhaps written) prescription following a verbal prescription for a Schedule III, IV, or V drug is in the TCSA, it may not be done in practice as it is not required by DEA. TSBP has indicated that a pharmacist may fill a verbal prescription for a Schedule III, IV, or V controlled substance pursuant to an otherwise valid verbal prescription.
6. Faxed prescriptions for controlled substances are generally treated the same as verbal prescriptions. This means faxes for

Schedule II controlled substances are only allowed in limited circumstances. *See Section VII. B. below.* Fax prescriptions are valid for Schedule III–V controlled substances under federal law, but they technically must meet the emergency requirement under the TCSA. *See 3. and 4. above.* Faxed prescriptions must have the prescriber's original signature.

VII. Schedule II Prescriptions

A. General

1. When one of the exceptions to the use of electronic prescriptions applies as listed in Section VI.E.2. above, a controlled substance prescription, including a Schedule II prescription, may be issued in writing.
2. When issued in writing, a Schedule II prescription must be issued on a Texas Official Prescription Form signed by the practitioner.
3. Verbal prescriptions for Schedule II drugs are not permitted except in an emergency. *See C. Emergency Dispensing of a Schedule II Controlled Substance Pursuant to a Verbal Prescription below.*
4. Schedule II prescriptions cannot be refilled.
5. There is no time limit under federal law as to when a Schedule II prescription must be filled after being issued by the practitioner. However, under Texas law, a prescription for a Schedule II controlled substance must be filled within 30 days after the date issued or the first date authorized to fill.

STUDY TIP: The date issued or the first date authorized to fill would be considered day zero.

---

6. Multiple Prescriptions for Schedule II Drugs.
   - **a.** DEA and Texas law permit an individual practitioner to issue multiple Schedule II prescriptions on the same day, authorizing the patient to receive a total of no more than a 90-day supply of a Schedule II controlled substance. Instructions indicating the earliest fill date on which the prescriptions can be filled must be on each prescription.

STUDY TIP: These prescriptions must be dispensed within 30 days after the earliest fill date indicated. They do not have to be presented to the pharmacy within 30 days after the date issued.

---

b. This 90-day supply limit only applies when the prescriber is issuing multiple prescriptions for a Schedule II controlled substance on the same day with instructions that some of the prescriptions are not to be filled until a later date. Except for opioid drugs for treatment of acute pain, there is legally no quantity limit on a single controlled substance prescription in Texas. However, insurance plans may limit the amount that may be filled on a single prescription, and pharmacists should exercise their corresponding responsibility on every prescription to ensure it is legitimate.

STUDY TIP: The rules for issuing multiple Schedule II prescriptions seem to cause much confusion with pharmacy students and pharmacists. Be sure you understand this concept.

B. Facsimile Prescriptions for Schedule II Controlled Substances

1. Facsimiles are generally treated the same as verbal prescriptions and are not valid for Schedule II prescriptions.
2. DEA permits faxed prescriptions to serve as the original prescription in three limited situations:
   a. Prescriptions faxed by a practitioner or practitioner's agent for a Schedule II narcotic controlled substance to be compounded for the direct administration to a patient by parenteral, intravenous, intramuscular, subcutaneous, or intraspinal infusion. *See 21 CFR 1306.11(e). Note: This provision is only for narcotic Schedule II controlled substances.*
   b. Prescriptions faxed by a practitioner or practitioner's agent for a Schedule II controlled substance for a resident of a long-term care facility. *See 21 CFR 1306.11(f).*
   c. Prescriptions faxed by a practitioner or practitioner's agent for a Schedule II narcotic controlled substance for a patient enrolled in a hospice care program certified and/or paid for by Medicare or licensed by the state. *See 21 CFR 1306.11(g).*
   Note: This provision is only for narcotic Schedule II controlled substances.
      (1) The practitioner or practitioner's agent must note on the prescription that the patient is a hospice patient.

(2) The patient need not be in a hospice facility and may be in a home-based program as long as he or she is enrolled in a hospice program.

3. The section of the TCSA that also permitted faxed prescriptions to serve as the original in the same limited circumstances was inadvertently removed, but TSBP had indicated that pharmacists may follow the federal law in these situations. The faxed prescription would need to contain the Texas Official Prescription form, however.

C. Emergency Dispensing of a Schedule II Controlled Substance Pursuant to a Verbal Prescription

1. In an emergency situation, a practitioner may telephone (or fax) a Schedule II prescription to a pharmacy.

STUDY TIP: Communication must be from the prescriber and not a designated agent.

---

2. Emergency means that the immediate administration of the drug is necessary for the proper treatment of the ultimate user, no alternative treatment is available, and it is not possible for the prescribing practitioner to provide a written prescription.
3. The quantity prescribed and dispensed must be limited to the amount needed to treat the patient during the emergency period.
4. The prescription order must be immediately reduced to writing by the pharmacist and contain all information except the practitioner's signature.
5. If the prescriber is not known to the pharmacist, the pharmacist must make a reasonable effort to determine that the phone authorization came from a valid practitioner.
6. Within 7 days after authorizing an emergency telephone prescription, the prescribing practitioner must furnish the pharmacist a valid electronic prescription for the controlled substance prescribed.

STUDY TIP: DEA permits the practitioner to provide either a written or electronic prescription within 7 days after authorizing an emergency verbal prescription for a Schedule II drug. Texas law specifies an electronic prescription must be provided, but if the practitioner has a waiver, it makes sense that he or she would need to send a written prescription.

---

7. If the prescriber fails to deliver an electronic (or written) prescription, the pharmacist must notify the nearest DEA office.

STUDY TIP: Remember the quantity that may be prescribed verbally in an emergency is not limited to a specific day's supply (e.g., 48 hours, 72 hours, 7 days). It is the amount needed to treat the patient during the emergency period. The only time limit is the 7 days required when the prescriber must send an electronic prescription to the pharmacy.

D. Partial Dispensing of a Schedule II Controlled Substance Prescription

1. 72-Hour Rule
    - **a.** If a pharmacist is unable to fill the entire quantity on a Schedule II controlled substance prescription, a partial quantity may be provided so long as the remaining quantity is provided within 72 hours.
    - **b.** If the remaining quantity cannot be provided, the pharmacist must notify the prescriber.
    - **c.** This rule also applies to an emergency verbal prescription for a Schedule II controlled substance.

    Note: It is the position of DEA that the pharmacy must have the balance of the prescription ready for dispensing prior to the 72-hour limit, but the patient is not required to pick up the balance of the prescription within that 72-hour limit.
2. 30-Day Rule
    - **a.** If requested by the patient or the prescriber, a pharmacist can provide a partial quantity of a Schedule II controlled substance prescription, and the patient may obtain additional quantities for up to 30 days.
    - **b.** The total quantity dispensed may not exceed the original quantity prescribed.
    - **c.** This rule applies to written and electronic prescriptions but not to emergency verbal Schedule II controlled substance prescriptions.
3. 60-Day Rule
    - **a.** For terminally ill and LTCF patients, both federal and Texas law allow partial fills of Schedule II prescriptions as many times as needed as long as the partial fillings are recorded on the prescription or maintained in the pharmacy's computer system.

b. All partial fills for terminally ill and LTCF patients must be completed within 60 days.

STUDY TIP: Be sure to understand the difference between a partial fill and a refill. Partial fills are not considered a full refill. Remember, there are no refills allowed on a Schedule II controlled substance prescription.

E. Official Prescriptions for Schedule II Controlled Substances

1. Written prescriptions for Schedule II controlled substances in Texas must be written on a Texas Official Prescription Form.
2. Official Prescription Forms are issued to prescribers by TSBP and contain security features including:
   a. A unique control number;
   b. A pantograph that reveals the word "VOID" when the form is copied;
   c. Thermochromic ink on the front with the symbol "Rx" that disappears briefly when rubbed; and
   d. A watermark of the Seal of Texas that is visible from either side in regular light.
3. Exemptions to the Use of an Official Prescription Form.
   a. Hospital inpatient medication orders.
   b. Hospital inpatients requiring an emergency quantity of a Schedule II drug upon discharge (limited to a 7-day supply and must be dispensed by the hospital pharmacy).
   c. Persons receiving treatment from a life flight helicopter medical team, emergency medical ambulance crew, or paramedic emergency medical technician.
   d. Persons receiving treatment while an inmate in a correctional facility operated by the Texas Department of Criminal Justice.
   e. Animals admitted to animal hospitals or in wildlife parks, exotic game ranches, wildlife management programs, or state or federal research facilities.
   f. Therapeutic optometrists administering topical cocaine as permitted under the Texas Optometry Act.
   g. Prescriptions from out-of-state practitioners if the pharmacy has a plan approved by TSBP.
   h. Electronic prescriptions.
4. If a Schedule II controlled substance and another drug are written together on an Official Prescription Form, the

prescription for each drug is valid. Due to prescription filing requirements, a direct image must be maintained separately for each category of prescription in the pharmacy's prescription records.

VIII. Schedule III–V Prescriptions

A. General Rules

1. May not be dispensed after six months from the date of issuance.
2. Schedule III, IV, and V prescriptions must be transmitted electronically unless one of the exceptions to the mandatory electronic prescription requirements listed in VI.E.2. above is met or the prescriber has obtained a waiver.
3. If one of the exceptions to the mandatory electronic prescription requirements listed in VI.E.2. above is met or a waiver applies, the TCSA states that a Schedule III, IV, or V prescription may be written.
4. Schedule III, IV, and V prescriptions may be refilled as indicated on the original prescription up to 5 times or 6 months unless it is for an opioid for acute pain.

STUDY TIP: There is no limit on the number of partial fills that can be provided so long as the total amount dispensed does not exceed the total number of dosage units authorized and it is within the 6-month time period. Some pharmacy computer systems count each partial fill as a refill and invalidate the prescription after 5 partial fills, but this is not legally accurate. These prescriptions are still valid if the full quantities for all refills authorized have not been dispensed within 6 months.

---

5. Texas laws and rules permit emergency refills of controlled substances in Schedules III–V under specific circumstances. *See Chapter Four, Section IV.B in this book.*
6. TSBP rules permit pharmacies to implement automatic refill programs for controlled substance prescriptions in Schedules IV and V but not those in Schedule III. *See Chapter Four, Section IV.C in this book.*

B. Verbal and Faxed Prescriptions

1. DEA permits prescriptions for Schedule III, IV, or V controlled substances to be communicated verbally to a pharmacist by a practitioner or his or her agent. However, the TCSA technically only allows prescriptions for Schedule III, IV,

and V controlled substances to be communicated verbally in an emergency (similar to the federal rule for Schedule II prescriptions).

2. Fortunately, the TCSA also provides that a pharmacist who receives a controlled substance prescription in a manner other than electronically is not required to verify that the prescription is exempt from the requirement that it be submitted electronically.
3. TSBP has indicated that this means pharmacists may dispense a Schedule III–V controlled substance pursuant to an otherwise valid verbal prescription. *See Quick Reference Guide Chart in Chapter Three in this book.*
4. Because the TCSA technically requires an emergency for Schedule III, IV, and V verbal prescriptions to be valid, the statute also requires that, within seven days of issuing an emergency verbal prescription, the prescriber must provide an electronic prescription to the pharmacy.
   Note: The TCSA does not address what practitioners should do if they are exempt from the mandatory electronic prescription requirements, but logically in this situation they should send a written prescription within 7 days. In addition, although this requirement to obtain an electronic (or perhaps written) prescription following a verbal prescription for a Schedule III, IV, or V drug is in the TCSA, it may not be done in practice as it is not required by DEA. TSBP has indicated that a pharmacist may fill a verbal prescription for a Schedule III, IV, or V controlled substance based on the language in 2.
5. Fax prescriptions are valid for Schedule III–V controlled substances under federal law, but they technically must meet the emergency requirement under the TCSA. *See 1. above.* Faxed prescriptions must have the prescriber's original signature.

C. Transfers

1. Refills of Schedule III–V controlled substances may be transferred to another pharmacy on a one-time basis.
2. If pharmacies share an electronic, real-time, online database of prescriptions, they may transfer up to the maximum number of refills permitted by law and the prescriber's authorization.
3. Only refills may be transferred. DEA and TSBP rules do not permit a pharmacy to transfer an original controlled

substance prescription that has been received at a pharmacy but not yet filled to another pharmacy. An exception to this is permitted by both DEA and TSBP policy that allows an original electronic prescription for a controlled substance (EPCS), including a Schedule II prescription, to be transferred to another pharmacy if both pharmacies have the capability to forward and receive the EPCS using an electronic sharing program.

Note: Although the procedure in 3. above is allowed by DEA and TSBP policy, some pharmacies may choose not to follow or allow this policy, and some pharmacy computer systems may not have this capability.

D. OTC Sale of Schedule V Products (Exempt narcotics)

1. The FCSA (and some state laws) allow certain Schedule V products to be purchased from a pharmacy without a prescription.
2. These products are mainly cough suppressant products containing small amounts of codeine such as Robitussin AC and products for diarrhea containing small amounts of opium.
3. While the same laws can be found in the TCSA, because all codeine products require a prescription under Texas law (even Schedule V products) and there are stricter concentration limits for opium products, there are no commercially available Schedule V products that can be purchased without a prescription in Texas. Therefore, these laws are not applicable in Texas.

   Note: By policy, TSBP is not enforcing this part of the law since all commercially available Schedule V products in Texas require a prescription.

IX. Texas Prescription Monitoring Program, Treatment of Opiate Dependence, and Methamphetamine Controls

A. Prescription Monitoring Program (PMP)

1. The Texas PMP is administered by the Texas State Board of Pharmacy and collects prescription dispensing data on all Schedule II, III, IV, and V controlled substances dispensed by a pharmacy in Texas or to a Texas resident from an out-of-state pharmacy.
2. The PMP is designed to assist pharmacists and physicians in identifying patients who may be getting prescriptions for controlled substances from multiple physicians or having prescriptions filled by multiple pharmacies.

3. Authorized users of the PMP, including pharmacists (and pharmacist interns, pharmacy technicians, and pharmacy technician trainees acting at the direction of a pharmacist), may access the PMP through the PMP AWARxE portal which can be found at the TSBP website.
4. Users of the PMP may only access the records of their own patients. Unauthorized access of PMP information is a violation of the TCSA, the Texas Pharmacy Act, and TSBP rules.
5. Mandatory Use of PMP.
    a. Practitioners (other than veterinarians) and pharmacists must check the PMP before prescribing or dispensing opioids, benzodiazepines, barbiturates, or carisoprodol.
    b. This check is not required if the patient has been diagnosed with cancer or sickle cell disease, or is receiving hospice care and that information is clearly indicated on the prescription, or if the practitioner or pharmacist is unable to access the PMP after making and documenting a good faith effort to do so.
    c. The dispensing pharmacist is responsible for review of the PMP unless the pharmacy has designated another pharmacist whose identity has been recorded in the pharmacy's computer system.
    d. If a pharmacist uses a pharmacy management system that integrates data from the PMP, a review of the pharmacy management system with the integrated data meets this requirement.
6. Electronically Transmitting Controlled Substance Prescription Information From the Pharmacy to TSBP.
    a. Dispensing information for controlled substances must be transmitted to TSBP no later than the next business day after the date the prescription was filled. If a prescription is partially filled, the information must be transmitted no later than the next business day after the prescription is completely filled.
    b. A pharmacy that does not dispense any controlled substances during a period of seven consecutive days must send a report to TSBP indicating that the pharmacy did not dispense any controlled substances during that period unless the pharmacy has obtained a waiver from reporting to the Board.

c. A pharmacy must electronically correct dispensing data submitted to the PMP within seven days of identifying an omission, error, or inaccuracy.

d. The pharmacist is responsible for making sure that the following prescription information is transmitted to TSBP:
   (1) The official prescription control number.
   (2) The prescriber's DEA registration number.
   (3) The patient's (or the animal owner's) name, age (or date of birth), and address (including city, state, and zip code).
   (4) The date the prescription was issued and filled.
   (5) The NDC number of the controlled substance dispensed.
   (6) The quantity of controlled substance dispensed.
   (7) The pharmacy's prescription number.
   (8) The pharmacy's DEA registration number.

STUDY TIP: This prescription information is the type of information that your pharmacy computer system transmits automatically, but you are expected to know what information is required to be transmitted and when it is required to be transmitted.

B. Prescribing and Dispensing of Certain Narcotic Drugs

1. Methadone is used both for the treatment of severe pain and in the detoxification and maintenance of narcotic addicts in registered narcotic treatment programs.
2. While any pharmacy can stock methadone, it can only legally be dispensed as an analgesic (for pain treatment).
3. DEA has requested manufacturers and wholesalers to voluntarily restrict sales of methadone 40 mg to hospitals and narcotic treatment clinics only; no sales to retail pharmacies are allowed.
4. Methadone (or any other drug) cannot be dispensed for the maintenance or detoxification of addicts unless it is provided through a registered narcotic treatment center.
5. Narcotic Treatment Centers must be registered with the DEA and also must be certified by the Center for Substance Abuse Treatment (CSAT) within the Substance Abuse and Mental Health Services Administration (SAMHSA) of the U.S. Department of Health and Human Services (HHS). In

Texas, these programs must also obtain a license issued by the Texas Department of Health and Human Services.

6. Narcotic treatment facilities may administer and dispense (but not prescribe) narcotic drugs to a narcotic dependent person for detoxification or maintenance treatment.
   a. Short-term detoxification means dispensing of a narcotic drug in decreasing doses for a period not to exceed 30 days.
   b. Long-term detoxification means dispensing of a narcotic drug to a narcotic dependent person in decreasing doses in excess of 30 days but not in excess of 180 days.

STUDY TIP: Make sure you understand that a narcotic treatment program is a specific type of DEA registration that permits the administration and dispensing of methadone. However, practitioners working at a registered narcotic treatment program may not write prescriptions for narcotics such as methadone for treating addiction that can be filled at a pharmacy. Pharmacies may only dispense prescriptions for methadone for pain. It is acceptable to dispense a prescription for methadone as part of a formal pain management program in which a patient is switched to methadone to control or gradually reduce the dosage of other narcotics. However, methadone cannot be dispensed from a pharmacy solely as a treatment for opioid dependency.

---

7. A physician who is not part of a narcotic treatment program may administer (not prescribe) narcotic drugs (e.g., methadone) to an addicted individual for no more than a 3-day period until the individual can be enrolled in a narcotic treatment program.
8. A hospital that is not part of a narcotic treatment program may administer narcotics to a drug-dependent person for either detoxification or maintenance therapy if the patient is being treated in the hospital for a condition other than addiction.

C. Medication-Assisted Treatment (MAT) for Opiate Dependence
   1. The Drug Addiction Treatment Act of 2000 (DATA 2000) allows office-based, specially trained practitioners to prescribe certain narcotic Schedule III–V drugs to treat opiate dependence through a risk management program outside of a narcotic treatment program. Use of these medications along with counseling and behavioral therapies to treat opioid use disorder is known as Medication-Assisted Therapy (MAT).

2. A practitioner authorized to prescribe under the Act, called a "Qualified Practitioner" (or DATA-waived practitioner), can apply for a waiver if they meet certain criteria. The waiver is provided by the Substance Abuse and Mental Health Services Administration (SAMHSA), and the practitioner is provided an identification or "X" code that must be included with the prescriber's DEA number. Pharmacists can verify a practitioner's DATA waiver at the SAMHSA website's Buprenorphine Pharmacy Lookup.
3. The only drugs that may be dispensed under this program are Subutex® (buprenorphine) and Suboxone® (buprenorphine/naloxone combination). These drugs, both Schedule III controlled substances, are available in sublingual form and may be dispensed by a pharmacy upon a prescription from a qualified practitioner.
4. A Qualified Practitioner may be allowed to treat up to 30, 100, or 275 patients, depending on his or her authorization.
5. A pharmacy can deliver a controlled substance to a DATA-waived practitioner to administer the medication by injection or implantation to a patient for purposes of maintenance or detoxification. The controlled substance must be administered to the patient within 14 days of delivery.
6. In order to encourage more practitioners to seek a DATA waiver, under practice guidelines issued by HHS on April 28, 2021, practitioners who limit their treatment to no more than 30 patients may apply for a waiver without having to meet certain DEA certification requirements related to training, counseling, and other ancillary services (e.g., psychosocial services) that are normally required.

STUDY TIP: A DATA-waived practitioner can treat opioid addiction and prescribe MAT drugs (buprenorphine and buprenorphine/naloxone) from his or her office. These practitioners do not need to work at or be registered as a narcotic treatment program. Likewise, a practitioner that is part of a narcotic treatment program cannot automatically prescribe MAT drugs to be filled at a pharmacy. He or she would also need to be a DATA-waived practitioner.

7. The Texas Board of Nursing and the Texas Medical Board have agreed that the supervising physician for any DATA-waived APRN or PA that prescribes these products for opioid dependence must also be a DATA-waived physician.

STUDY TIP: Prescribing or dispensing of certain buprenorphine products for pain may be considered "off-label" use. In these circumstances, the "X" code is not required by the prescriber.

D. The Combat Methamphetamine Epidemic Act of 2005—This law was passed by Congress to further control the sale of OTC products containing precursor chemicals used in the illicit manufacturing of methamphetamine. The law classifies all products (including multiple ingredient products) containing ephedrine, pseudoephedrine, and phenylpropanolamine as "listed chemical products."

Note: Since this law was passed, ephedrine and phenylpropanolamine products have all been removed from the market by FDA, so the law only impacts pseudoephedrine products.

Products containing a "listed chemical" are subject to the following requirements:

1. Display Restrictions—Although the products may be sold by any retailer, covered products must be placed behind a counter (not necessarily a pharmacy counter) or, if located on the selling floor, in a locked cabinet. Texas law specifies that the locked cabinet be within 30 feet and in the direct line of sight of the pharmacy counter.
2. Retail Sales Limits—Sales of covered products to an individual are limited to 3.6 grams of the base product per day and 9 grams of the base product per 30 days. Many states have sales limits per transaction.
3. For pseudoephedrine HCL, the daily limit of 3.6 grams of base product equals:
   a. 146 of the 30 mg tablets.
   b. 73 of the 60 mg tablets.
   c. 36 of the 120 mg tablets.

STUDY TIP: Texas law has different sales limits, but the federal limits in 2. and 3. above are stricter and must be followed.

4. Texas law requires the purchaser to be at least 16 years old.
5. Product Packaging—Covered products (other than liquids including gel caps) must either be in blister or unit-dose packaging.

6. Logbook Requirements.
    a. Retailer must maintain an electronic or written logbook that identifies the products by name, quantity sold, names and addresses of purchasers, and dates and times of sales.
    b. There is an exception for the logbook requirement for individual sales of a single "convenience" package of less than 60 mg of pseudoephedrine.
    c. Purchaser must present a photo identification issued by a state or federal government, must sign the logbook, and enter his or her name, address, and date and time of sale.
    d. Retailer must verify that the name entered in the logbook corresponds to the customer identification.
7. Employee Training.
    a. Employers certify that employees who deal directly with customers have undergone training to ensure they understand the requirements of the law.
    b. DEA requirements for self-certification and training can be found at *www.deadiversion.usdoj.gov/meth/index.html*.
    c. Mail Service Limitations.
        (1) Mail service companies must confirm the identity of purchasers.
        (2) Sales are limited to 7.5 grams per 30-day period.
    d. Mobile Retail Vendors ("flea markets").
        (1) Product must be placed in a locked cabinet.
        (2) Sales are limited to no more than 7.5 grams of base product per customer per 30 days.

X. Summary of Major Differences Between Texas and Federal Law Related to Controlled Substances

A. Codeine and Opium Products
1. Codeine-Containing Products.
    a. FCSA—Allows OTC "exempt" sales of Schedule V products containing codeine.
    b. TCSA—Does not allow OTC "exempt" sales of Schedule V products containing codeine. Any codeine-containing product sold in Texas requires a prescription.
2. Opium-Containing Products.
    a. FCSA—Maximum amount for Schedule V = 100 mg/100 ml.

b. TCSA—Maximum amount for Schedule V = 50 mg/100 ml.
c. Any product containing more than 50 mg/100 ml of opium in Texas would be Schedule III or Schedule II (depending on the amount).

B. Schedule V Controlled Substance Prescriptions

1. FCSA—Refills not limited to 5 refills/6 months.
2. TCSA—Refills limited to 5 refills/6 months.

C. Schedule II Controlled Substances

1. Electronic prescriptions.
   - a. FCSA—Allowed but not mandated.
   - b. TCSA—Mandatory unless exception applies.
2. Special official prescription form required in Texas for written Schedule II prescriptions.
3. Time limit for filling Schedule II prescriptions.
   - a. FCSA—No time limit.
   - b. TCSA—30 days from the date issued or the first date authorized to be filled if multiple prescriptions are issued on the same day with instruction not to fill until a later date.

D. Automatic Refills

1. FCSA—Not addressed.
2. TSCA—Not addressed.
3. TSBP—Allows pharmacies to implement automatic refill programs for controlled substances in Schedules IV and V but not Schedule III. *See Chapter Four, IV.C. in this book.*

E. Emergency Refills

1. Schedules III–V.
   - a. FCSA—Not addressed.
   - b. TCSA and TSBP—Allow emergency refills using pharmacist's professional judgment. *See Chapter Four, IV.B. in this book.*
2. Schedule II—Not allowed by FCSA or TCSA.

F. Inventories

1. FCSA—Required biennially (every 2 years).
2. TCSA—Required biennially (every 2 years).
3. TSBP—Required annually (every year) and includes a requirement that most inventories be signed by the pharmacist-in-charge and notarized within 3 days of the day the inventory is taken, excluding Saturdays, Sundays, and federal holidays.

4. Perpetual Inventory Requirements.
    a. Required for Schedule II controlled substances in Class C (Institutional) pharmacies.
    b. Required for all controlled substances in remote pharmacies. *See Board Rule 291.121.*
    c. Required for all controlled substances in Class C Ambulatory Surgical Centers (ASCs).
    d. Required for all controlled substances in Class F (Freestanding Emergency Medical Facility) pharmacies.

G. Security
1. FCSA—To deter theft, controlled substances may be stored in a secure cabinet that is locked or by dispersal throughout the noncontrolled drug stock.
2. TCSA—Same requirements, but TSBP rules specifically require Class C (Institutional), Class C-S, Class C-Ambulatory Surgical Centers (ASC), and Class F (Freestanding Emergency Medical Facility) pharmacies to have locked storage for Schedule II controlled substances.

H. Records
1. Prescription Records.
    a. Federal—Permits either a two-file or three-file system for storage of controlled substance prescriptions.
    b. Texas—TSBP requires three separate files for storage of controlled substance prescriptions.
        (1) File 1—Schedule II prescriptions.
        (2) File 2—Schedule III–V prescriptions.
        (3) File 3—Dangerous drugs and other noncontrolled prescriptions (OTC).
2. Invoices—Texas.
    Invoices of controlled substances received by a pharmacy in Texas must have the initials of the pharmacist and actual date of receipt recorded on the invoice.
    Note: In Class C Ambulatory Surgical Center (ASC) pharmacies and Class F (Freestanding Emergency Medical Facility) pharmacies, invoices of dangerous drugs and controlled substances must be initialed by the person actually receiving the drug since a pharmacist may not be present to initial the invoice.

I. Prescription Requirements
1. Restrictions on Opioid Prescriptions for Acute Pain.
    a. FCSA—No specific restrictions.

        - **b.** TCSA— No refills and 10-day supply limit for opioid prescriptions for acute pain.
    - **2.** Mandatory Electronic Prescriptions for Controlled Substances.
        - **a.** FCSA—Not required.
        - **b.** TCSA—Required (with exceptions).
    - **3.** Written Prescriptions.
        - **a.** FCSA—Allowed for Schedules III–V and required for Schedule II.
        - **b.** TCSA—Only allowed if exception to electronic prescription applies or prescriber has a waiver.
    - **4.** Verbal Prescriptions.
        - **a.** FCSA—Allowed for Schedules III–V and allowed in an emergency for Schedule II.
        - **b.** TCSA—Allowed only in an emergency for all controlled substances (Schedules II–V), but pharmacist is not responsible for determining if all requirements for verbal prescription are met.
    - **5.** Delivered prescriptions must record name of authorized delivery person; person known to pharmacist, intern, or delivery person; or address if mailed.
    - **6.** For written prescriptions, TSBP rules require the quantity to be written as a figure and spelled as a word—e.g., "#20 (twenty)."
    - **7.** Intended use required on prescriptions in Texas (required on all prescriptions); however, prescriber can opt out.
    - **8.** Name and quantity of drug and practitioner's telephone number are required on all prescriptions in Texas.
    - **9.** Age or date of birth required on controlled substance prescriptions in Texas.
- **J.** Methamphetamine Controls (e.g., pseudoephedrine)
    - **1.** Display Restrictions.
        - **a.** Federal law requires locked cabinet.
        - **b.** Texas law specifies locked cabinet within 30 feet of and in a direct line of sight from a pharmacy counter staffed by an employee of the establishment.
    - **2.** Age.
        - **a.** Federal law—No age requirement.
        - **b.** Texas law—Requires purchaser to be 16 years or older.
    - **3.** Texas law requires nonpharmacy retailers to obtain a Certificate of Authority from the Texas Department of State Health Services.

4. Texas law requires confirming legality of sale through a real-time electronic logging system.

K. Inspections

1. DEA cannot inspect financial, sales, and pricing data without a pharmacist's consent.
2. TSBP may inspect a pharmacy's financial records in the course of an investigation of a specific complaint without the pharmacist's consent.

CHAPTER THREE

Texas Dangerous Drug Act (TDDA) and Related Texas Laws and Rules

CHAPTER THREE

Texas Dangerous Drug Act (TDDA) and Related Texas Laws and Rules

I. Definitions

A. Dangerous Drugs—These include prescription medical devices and prescription drugs that are not controlled substances.

B. Designated Agent

1. An authorized person designated by a practitioner to communicate prescription drug orders to a pharmacist.
2. May be a licensed nurse, physician assistant, pharmacist, or any other individual the practitioner designates.
3. Practitioner can also authorize a licensed vocational nurse to serve as a designated agent to call in prescriptions for nurse practitioners and physician assistants.
4. Practitioners must designate in writing each agent authorized to verbally communicate prescriptions, and a pharmacist may request a list of these agents from the practitioner.

STUDY TIP: A designated agent does not have prescriptive authority and cannot authorize prescriptions. As an agent of the prescriber, he or she is allowed to communicate a prescription to the pharmacist.

II. Practitioners, Prescriptive Authority, and Valid Prescriptions

A. Independent Prescriptive Authority—These practitioners can independently prescribe under their own license.

1. Physicians (MD and DO).
2. Dentists (DDS and DMD).
3. Podiatrists (DPM).
4. Veterinarians (DVM).
5. Optometrists (OD)—Therapeutic Optometrists and Optometric Glaucoma Specialists. *See V. below.*

B. Dependent Authority

1. Physician Assistants (PA)—Dependent authority. *See IV. below.*
2. Advanced Practice Registered Nurses (APRN)—Dependent authority. *See IV. below.*

STUDY TIP: In certain practice settings, some Texas pharmacists can "sign" prescription drug orders , but they are not included in the definition of "Practitioner" under the TDDA. *See Drug Therapy Management Under Protocol in Chapter Four in this book.*

C. Out-of-State and Canadian/Mexican Practitioners

1. The Texas definition of "practitioner" includes persons licensed in other states, Canada, and Mexico in a healthcare field who can legally prescribe dangerous drugs under Texas law.
2. This means that the pharmacist can fill a prescription (written, verbal, or electronic) for a dangerous drug from a physician, dentist, podiatrist, veterinarian, or optometrist from another state. However, for Canadian and Mexican practitioners, the prescription must be written.
3. Pharmacists can also fill prescriptions for dangerous drugs from out-of-state advanced practice registered nurses and physician assistants (written, verbal, or electronic), but cannot fill prescriptions for controlled substances from out-of-state advanced practice registered nurses and physician assistants. *See IV. below.*
4. Charts of Valid Prescriptions in Texas. *See next three pages.*

STUDY TIP: It would be easy to generate questions based on these charts. Be sure you understand which types of prescriptions are valid.

TSBP QUICK REFERENCE GUIDE—PRESCRIPTIONS FOR DANGEROUS DRUGS (NON-CONTROLLED) THAT MAY BE DISPENSED IN TEXAS

Prescription (Rx) Drug Order Format & Refill Info.: / Prescriber Type:	Electronic (Electronic Data File) Rx[1]	Written (Paper) Rx	Facsimile (Faxed) Rx[1]	Oral (Verbal/Telephonic) Rx[1]
Texas Physician, Dentist, Veterinarian, or Podiatrist	Yes	Yes Manual signature or electronic replica of manual signature printed on secured paper required	Yes	Yes
Authorized Texas Advanced Practice Registered Nurse (APRN) or Physician Assistant (PA)	Yes Delegating physician information required	Yes • Manual signature or electronic replica of the manual signature printed on secured paper • Delegating physician information required	Yes Delegating physician information required	Yes Delegating physician information & DEA# required
Physician-Delegated Texas Pharmacist Performing Drug Therapy Management (DTM)	Yes • RPh practices at federally qualified health center (FQHC), hospital, hospital-based clinic, or academic healthcare institution • Delegating physician information required	Yes • Signature required • RPh practices at a FQHC, hospital, hospital-based clinic, or academic healthcare institution • Delegating physician information required	Yes • Signature required • RPh practices at a FQHC, hospital, hospital-based clinic, or academic healthcare institution • Delegating physician information required	No (Note: DTM RPh may orally communicate new Rx as designated agent of the prescribing DTM-delegating physician)
Texas Therapeutic Optometrist (T) (Topical & Oral Drugs for Health Conditions of the Eye, Excluding Glaucoma)[2]	Yes License # plus "T" designation	Yes • Manual signature or electronic replica of the manual signature printed on secured paper • License # plus "T" designation	Yes License # plus "T" designation	Yes License # plus "T" designation
Texas Therapeutic Optometrist-Optometric Glaucoma Specialist (TG) (Topical & Oral Drugs for Health Conditions of the Eye)[2]	Yes License # plus "TG" designation	Yes • Manual signature or electronic replica of the manual signature printed on secured paper • License # plus "TG" designation	Yes License # plus "TG" designation	Yes License # plus "TG" designation
Out-of-State[3] Physician, Dentist, Veterinarian, or Podiatrist	Yes	Yes Manual signature or electronic replica of the manual signature printed on secured paper	Yes	Yes
Out-of-State[3] Nurse Practitioner or Physician Assistant (Supervising Physician Required)	Yes Delegating physician information required	Yes • Manual signature or electronic replica of the manual signature printed on secured paper • Delegating physician information required	Yes Delegating physician information required	Yes Delegating physician information required
Canadian or Mexican Physician, Dentist, Veterinarian, or Podiatrist	No	Yes Manual signature or electronic replica of the manual signature printed on secured paper	No	No

[1] Name of designated agent required on electronic, faxed, and oral Rxs, if applicable. Statement indicating Rx has been "faxed" required for faxed Rxs.

[2] Therapeutic Optometrists (T) may prescribe topical or oral medications to treat the eye but must obtain (TG) certification to treat glaucoma.

[3] Includes United States (excluding TX) and U.S. Territories (Puerto Rico, U.S. Virgin Islands, American Samoa, Guam, Northern Mariana Islands).

TSBP QUICK REFERENCE GUIDE—PRESCRIPTIONS FOR CONTROLLED SUBSTANCES IN SCHEDULES III, IV, & V THAT MAY BE DISPENSED IN TEXAS

Prescription (Rx) Drug Order Format & Refill Info.: / Prescriber Type:	Electronic Prescriptions for Controlled Substances (EPCS) Rx[1,4]	Consistent with EPCS Exemptions and Other Requirements Listed in TCSA 481.0755[5]		
		Written (Paper) Rx[5]	Facsimile (Faxed) Rx[4,5]	Oral (Verbal or Telephonic) Rx[4,5]
Texas Physician, Dentist, Veterinarian, or Podiatrist	Yes	Yes Manual signature	Yes Facsimile of a manually signed written (paper) Rx	Yes
Authorized Texas Advanced Practice Registered Nurse (APRN) or Physician Assistant (PA)	Yes • For a period not to exceed 90 days • Delegating physician information & DEA# required	Yes • Manual signature • For a period not to exceed 90 days • Delegating physician information & DEA# required	Yes • Facsimile of a manually signed written (paper) Rx • For a period not to exceed 90 days • Delegating physician information & DEA# required	Yes Delegating physician information & DEA# required
Physician-Delegated Texas Pharmacist Performing Drug Therapy Management (DTM)	No	No	No	No (Note: DTM RPh may orally communicate new Rx as designated agent of the prescribing DTM-delegating physician)
Texas Therapeutic Optometrist (T) (Topical & Oral Rx Drugs for Health Conditions of the Eye, Excluding Glaucoma)[2]	Yes • Limited to one 3-day supply of any drug in Schedule III, IV, or V (No Refills) • License # plus "T" designation	Yes • Limited to one 3-day supply of any drug in Schedule III, IV, or V (No Refills) • License # plus "T" designation • Manual signature	Yes • Limited to one 3-day supply of any drug in Schedule III, IV, or V (No Refills) • License # plus "T" designation • Facsimile of a manually signed written (paper) Rx	Yes • Limited to one 3-day supply of any drug in Schedule III, IV, or V (No Refills) • License # plus "T" designation
Texas Therapeutic Optometrist-Optometric Glaucoma Specialist (TG) (Topical & Oral Drugs for Health Conditions of the Eye)[2]	Yes • Limited to one 3-day supply of any drug in Schedule III, IV, or V (No Refills) • License # plus "TG" designation	Yes • Limited to one 3-day supply of any drug in Schedule III, IV, or V (No Refills) • License # plus "TG" designation • Manual signature	Yes • Limited to one 3-day supply of any drug in Schedule III, IV, or V (No Refills) • License # plus "TG" designation • Facsimile of a manually signed written (paper) Rx	Yes • Limited to one 3-day supply of any drug in Schedule III, IV, or V (No Refills) • License # plus "TG" designation
Out-of-State[3] Physician, Dentist, Veterinarian, or Podiatrist	Yes	Yes Manual signature or electronic replica of the manual signature printed on secured paper	Yes Facsimile of a manually signed written (paper) Rx	Yes
Out-of-State[3] Nurse Practitioner or Physician Assistant	No	No	No	No
Canadian or Mexican Practitioner	No	No	No	No

[1] EPCS prescribing and pharmacy applications must meet the requirements of Title 21 Code of Federal Regulations (CFR) Chapter II Part 1311.
[2] Therapeutic Optometrists (T) may prescribe topical or oral medications to treat the eye but must obtain (TG) certification to treat glaucoma.
[3] Includes United States (excluding TX) and U.S. Territories (Puerto Rico, U.S. Virgin Islands, American Samoa, Guam, Northern Mariana Islands).
[4] Name of designated agent required on EPCS, faxed, and oral Rxs, if applicable. Statement indicating Rx has been "faxed" required for faxed Rxs.
[5] A pharmacist who receives a controlled substance prescription in a manner other than electronically is not required to verify that the prescription is exempt from the requirements for electronic transmission. A pharmacist may dispense a controlled substance pursuant to an otherwise valid written, oral, or telephonically communicated prescription consistent with the requirements in the Texas and Federal Controlled Substances Acts.

TSBP QUICK REFERENCE GUIDE—PRESCRIPTIONS FOR CONTROLLED SUBSTANCES IN SCHEDULE II THAT MAY BE DISPENSED IN TEXAS

Prescription (Rx) Drug Order Format & Refill Info.: / Prescriber Type:	Electronic Prescriptions for Controlled Substances (EPCS) Rx[1,3]	Consistent with EPCS Exemptions and Other Requirements Listed in TCSA 481.0755 & Federal CSA[4]		
		Written (Paper) Rx[4]	Facsimile (Faxed) Rx[3,4]	Oral ("Emergency Situation" Verbal & Telephonic) Rx[3,4,5]
Texas Physician, Dentist, Veterinarian, or Podiatrist	Yes	Yes Manual signature written on a TSBP "Official Form"	Yes • Facsimile of a manually signed written (paper) Rx written on a TSBP "Official Form" • Only in 3 situations described in 21 CFR §1306.11(e), (f), (g)	Yes Only for "emergency situations" in accordance with 21 CFR §1306.11(d)
Authorized Texas Advanced Practice Registered Nurse (APRN) or Physician Assistant (PA)	Yes • Delegating physician information & DEA# required • Only in specific situations	Yes • Manual signature • Written on a TSBP "Official Form" • Delegating physician information & DEA# required • Only in specific situations	Yes • Facsimile of a manually signed written (paper) Rx written on a TSBP "Official Form" • Only in 3 situations described in 21 CFR §1306.11(e), (f), (g) • Delegating physician information & DEA# required • Only in specific situations	Yes • Only for "emergency situations" in accordance with 21 CFR §1306.11(d) • Delegating physician information & DEA# required • Only in specific situations
Texas Pharmacist Performing Drug Therapy Management (DTM)	No	No	No	No
Texas Therapeutic Optometrist (T)	No	No	No	No
Texas Therapeutic Optometrist-Optometric Glaucoma Specialist (TG)	No	No	No	No
Out-of-State[2] Physician, Dentist, Veterinarian, or Podiatrist	No Unless pharmacy has plan approved by TSBP	No Unless pharmacy has plan approved by TSBP: • Manual signature required	No Unless pharmacy has plan approved by TSBP: • Facsimile of a manually signed written (paper) Rx • Only in 3 situations described in 21 CFR §1306.11(e), (f), (g)	No Unless pharmacy has plan approved by TSBP: • Only for "emergency situations" in accordance with 21 CFR §1306.11(d)
Out-of-State[2] Nurse Practitioner or Physician Assistant	No	No	No	No
Canadian or Mexican Practitioner	No	No	No	No

[1] EPCS prescribing and pharmacy applications must meet the requirements of Title 21 Code of Federal Regulations (CFR) Chapter II Part 1311.

[2] Includes United States (excluding TX) and U.S. Territories (Puerto Rico, U.S. Virgin Islands, American Samoa, Guam, Northern Mariana Islands).

[3] Name of designated agent required on EPCS, faxed, and oral Rxs, if applicable. Statement indicating Rx has been "faxed" required for faxed Rxs.

[4] A pharmacist who receives a controlled substance prescription in a manner other than electronically is not required to verify that the prescription is exempt from the requirements for electronic transmission. A pharmacist may dispense a controlled substance pursuant to an otherwise valid written, oral, or telephonically communicated prescription consistent with the requirements in the Texas and Federal Controlled Substances Acts.

[5] In an "emergency situation," the practitioner may issue an oral prescription. Otherwise, a written prescription must be used if exempted from EPCS.

D. Miscellaneous Prescriber Issues

1. Scope of Practice.
    - **a.** Physician practitioners can legally prescribe drugs to treat any disease or illness in humans even if they have chosen to specialize in a certain type of practice.
    - **b.** For other practitioners, prescriptive authority is limited to their area of practice. This means that a prescription from a dentist must be to treat a dental issue, and a prescription from a podiatrist must be to treat an ailment related to the foot. Similarly, a veterinarian could not prescribe for a human.
    - **c.** APRNs and PAs can prescribe under a prescriptive authority agreement with a supervising physician or under a facility protocol and have limitations on prescribing controlled substances. *See IV. below.*
2. Self-Prescribing and Prescribing for Family Members.
    - **a.** There is nothing in federal or Texas law that strictly prohibits self-prescribing or prescribing for family members for either dangerous drugs or controlled substances.
    - **b.** However, Texas Medical Board rules state that inappropriate prescribing by physicians includes prescribing dangerous drugs or controlled substances for oneself, family members, or others in which there is a close personal relationship.
    - **c.** The Texas Medical Board does permit prescribing of controlled substances to such individuals to meet immediate needs which is defined as no more than a 72-hour supply.
3. Prescriptions for "Office Use."
    - **a.** There is no such thing as a prescription for office use.
    - **b.** If prescribers wish to purchase dangerous drugs or controlled substances for their "office use," they should order the drugs from a manufacturer, wholesaler, or pharmacy using an invoice or DEA Form 222 for a Schedule II controlled substance.
4. What happens to prescriptions with refills when the prescriber dies? There are no specific laws or rules regarding this situation. However, both the Texas State Board of Pharmacy and the Texas Medical Board have agreed by policy that it is an acceptable practice for a pharmacist to provide a

30-day supply of the medication and inform the patient that he or she needs to find a new practitioner.

III. Miscellaneous Provisions in the TDDA and Other Texas Laws

A. Pharmacists cannot possess dangerous drugs unless acting as an agent of a licensed pharmacy (e.g., when delivering a prescription to a patient's home).

B. Nurses of Home and Community Support Agencies may purchase, store, or transport the following drugs (in a portable sealed container) without being in violation of the Texas Dangerous Drug Act:

1. Sterile water for injection and irrigation.
2. Sterile saline for injection and irrigation.
3. Hepatitis B vaccine.
4. Influenza vaccine.
5. Tuberculin purified protein derivative for TB testing.
6. No more than 5 dosage units of:
    - **a.** Heparin sodium lock flush—10 units/ml or 100 units/ml.
    - **b.** Epinephrine 1:1000.
    - **c.** Diphenhydramine 50 mg/ml.
    - **d.** Methylprednisolone 125 mg/2 ml.
    - **e.** Naloxone 1 mg/ml in a 2 ml vial.
    - **f.** Promethazine 25 mg/ml.
    - **g.** Glucagon injection 1 mg/ml.
    - **h.** Furosemide 10 mg/ml.
    - **i.** Lidocaine 2.5% and prilocaine 2.5% in a 5 gm tube.
    - **j.** Lidocaine solution 1% in a 2 ml vial.

C. Opioid Antagonists (TSBP Rule 295.14)

1. A pharmacist may dispense an opioid antagonist under a valid prescription, including a prescription issued by a standing order, to:
    - **a.** A person at risk of experiencing an opioid-related drug overdose; or
    - **b.** A family member, friend, or other person in a position to assist a person at risk of experiencing an opioid-related drug overdose.
2. A prescription dispensed under this section is considered as dispensed for a legitimate medical purpose in the usual course of professional practice.
3. A pharmacist who, acting in good faith and with reasonable care, dispenses or does not dispense an opioid antagonist

under a valid prescription is not subject to any criminal or civil liability or any professional disciplinary action for:

a. Dispensing or failing to dispense the opioid antagonist; or
b. If the pharmacist chooses to dispense an opioid antagonist, any outcome resulting from the eventual administration of the opioid antagonist.

STUDY TIP: A pharmacy must have a standing order with a physician to dispense an opioid antagonist such as naloxone without an individual prescription. Many chain pharmacies have standing orders that cover all their pharmacies in Texas. The Texas Pharmacy Association also has a standing order that members can access after they complete training.

D. OTC Sales of Dextromethorphan
   1. Texas Health and Safety Code Chapter 488 prohibits over-the-counter sales of products containing dextromethorphan to customers under 18 years of age.
   2. Business establishments (including pharmacies) must require identification that indicates a customer is 18 years of age or older before providing a product containing dextromethorphan.
   3. These provisions of the law do not apply to products dispensed pursuant to a valid prescription.

STUDY TIP: The MPJE Competencies include knowing any restrictions related to the selling of dextromethorphan products.

IV. Prescribing by Mid-Level Practitioners—Advanced Practice Registered Nurses (APRNs) and Physician Assistants (PAs)

A. General Requirements
   1. May prescribe under a Prescriptive Authority Agreement with a supervising physician that identifies the locations and types or categories of drugs that may be prescribed.
   2. In a hospital or long-term care facility, prescriptive authority may be delegated to APRNs and PAs through a facility protocol. Freestanding clinics or other medical practices owned or operated by a hospital or long-term care facility are not considered facility-based practices.

3. For prescriptions for a child less than 2 years of age, the APRN/PA must consult with the delegating physician, and the consultation must be noted in the patient's chart.
4. A physician may not supervise more than 7 APRNs or PAs, except in medically underserved areas or in a facility-based practice in a hospital or long-term care facility.
5. Written prescriptions must contain the name, address, telephone number, and identifying number of the supervising physician as well as the APRN or PA.

STUDY TIP: Previously, the prescription label also had to contain the name of the APRN/PA and the name of the supervising physician. The name of the supervising physician is not required. The label is only required to list the prescribing APRN/PA.

B. Controlled Substance Prescribing by Texas APRNS and PAs

1. Prescribing of Schedule II controlled substances by APRNs and PAs is not generally permitted except in a hospital-based practice under policies approved by the medical staff. Patients must be admitted to the hospital for an intended length of stay of 24 hours or greater or be receiving care in the emergency department or have a terminal illness and be under hospice care.

STUDY TIP: APRNs and PAs in any practice setting may have prescriptive authority for Schedule III–V controlled substances. Schedule II prescriptive authority is limited to APRNs and PAs in hospital-based practices or for terminally ill patients receiving hospice care from a qualified hospice provider in any setting.

---

2. Schedule III, IV, and V prescriptions may be prescribed by an APRN/PA in any practice setting, but the total quantity prescribed, including any refills, may not exceed a 90-day supply.

STUDY TIP: Remember, this 90-day supply limit only applies to APRNs and PAs. A physician or other practitioner with full independent prescriptive authority can prescribe more than a 90-day supply except for opioids for acute pain.

---

3. The APRN/PA must be registered with DEA as a mid-level practitioner.
4. The DEA number of the APRN/PA and the supervising physician must be on the prescription.

STUDY TIP: Prescriptions from out-of-state APRNs or PAs for controlled substances are not valid in Texas even if these practitioners are registered with DEA and have prescriptive authority for controlled substances in the state where they are licensed.

V. Therapeutic Optometrists and Optometric Glaucoma Specialists

A. Therapeutic Optometrists (license ends in letter "T")

1. May prescribe dangerous drugs to treat the eye and adnexa (tissue surrounding the eye) but may not prescribe oral or parenteral drugs to treat glaucoma.
2. May not prescribe more than one 3-day supply of any controlled substance in Schedule III, IV, or V.
   Note: This implies Therapeutic Optometrists may not prescribe controlled substances in Schedule II.

B. Optometric Glaucoma Specialists (license ends in letters "TG")

1. Have all of the privileges of a Therapeutic Optometrist but may also administer and prescribe oral or parenteral drugs to treat glaucoma.
2. The law that allows Optometric Glaucoma Specialists to prescribe medication to treat glaucoma contains a number of restrictions and requirements. *See Texas Occupations Code § 351.3581 for more information.*

C. Cocaine Eye Drops for Diagnostic Purposes

1. Therapeutic Optometrists and Optometric Glaucoma Specialists may possess and administer no greater than a 10% solution of cocaine eye drops in prepackaged liquid form (solution cannot be compounded). However, they may not dispense cocaine solutions.
2. Must have a DEA registration to possess and store cocaine eye drops and cannot store more than two vials.

CHAPTER FOUR

Texas Pharmacy Act (TPA) and Selected Rules

CHAPTER FOUR

Texas Pharmacy Act (TPA) and Selected Rules

I. Introduction, Definitions, and Texas State Board of Pharmacy

A. The Texas Pharmacy Act is the primary law governing the practice of pharmacy in Texas. The Act establishes the Texas State Board of Pharmacy (TSBP) and provides the Board with certain authorities and responsibilities in regulating the practice of pharmacy. The purpose of the Act and of TSBP is to promote, preserve, and protect the public health, safety, and welfare of Texans.

B. Definitions (TPA Section 551.003)

STUDY TIP: When studying laws and rules, it is important to read the definition section usually found at the beginning of a new section.

Many definitions are consistent in different acts such as "controlled substance," "dangerous drug," "designated agent," "practice of pharmacy," and "practitioner." Over 40 terms are defined in TPA Section 551.003, and some are listed below:

1. Class A* Pharmacy License—Community Pharmacy.
2. Class B Pharmacy License—Nuclear Pharmacy.
3. Class C* Pharmacy License—Institutional (hospital) Pharmacy.
4. Class D Pharmacy License—Clinic Pharmacy.
5. Class E* Pharmacy License—Nonresident Pharmacy.

*Class A, C, and E pharmacies that compound sterile products must be licensed as Class A-S, C-S, and E-S pharmacies. This allows the Board to know which pharmacies are compounding sterile products.

Note: These classes of pharmacy are found in the law so they are defined here, but TSBP has also created additional classes (Class F and G pharmacies) by TSBP rule. These are specialized pharmacies that are defined and described in Chapter Seven in this book.

6. Medication Order—An order from a practitioner or practitioner's designated agent for administration of a drug or device.
7. Pharmacy—A facility at which a prescription drug or medication order is received, processed, or dispensed.

8. Prescription Drug Order—An order from a practitioner or practitioner's designated agent to a pharmacist for a drug to be dispensed or an order from a physician assistant or advanced practice registered nurse.

STUDY TIP: Note that a medication order is for administration of a drug (inpatient setting) and a prescription drug order is for dispensing of a drug (outpatient setting). Orders in a nursing home are considered prescription drug orders, as those orders are dispensed by a pharmacy and sent to the nursing home. However, TSBP rules allow for alternative labeling for prescriptions in nursing homes that are similar to medication orders since they are administered. *See TSBP Rule 291.33(c)(7)(D) or TFPDL pages G.22–23.*

C. Texas State Board of Pharmacy (TPA Chapter 552)

1. The Texas State Board of Pharmacy (TSBP) is composed of 11 members:
   a. 7 pharmacists.
   b. 1 pharmacy technician.
   c. 3 public members.
2. Qualifications.
   a. TSBP must include representation for pharmacists employed in both Class A and Class C pharmacies.
   b. Pharmacist members must be:
      (1) A resident of Texas.
      (2) Licensed for 5 years preceding appointment.
      (3) In good standing with TSBP.
      (4) Actively practicing pharmacy.
   c. Pharmacist members (and members' spouses) cannot be:
      (1) A lobbyist on behalf of a profession regulated by the Board.
      (2) An officer, employee, or paid consultant to a Texas trade association in the healthcare field.
   d. Public members (and members' spouses) cannot be:
      (1) Registered, certified, or licensed by an occupational regulatory agency (e.g., nurse, physician).
      (2) Employed by or participate in the management of a business or other entity regulated by the Board or receiving funds from the Board.
      (3) An owner or person who controls more than a 10% interest in a business or other entity regulated by the Board or receiving funds from the Board.

(4) An officer, employee, or paid consultant to a Texas trade association in the healthcare field.

3. Appointment and Terms of Office.
    a. Appointed by the governor with advice and consent of the Senate.
    b. Appointed for a 6-year term.
    c. May not serve more than 2 consecutive full terms.

D. Board Powers and Duties; Rulemaking Authority (*See TPA Chapter 554 or TFPDL pages D.10–20 for details.*)
1. Administering and enforcing the Texas Pharmacy Act and rules and other laws related to the practice of pharmacy.
2. Regulating the practice of pharmacy by:
    a. Issuing and renewing licenses.
    b. Determining and issuing standards for recognizing and approving degree requirements of colleges of pharmacy.
    c. Specifying and enforcing the requirements for practical training including internship.
    d. Regulating the training, qualifications, and employment of pharmacist interns and pharmacy technicians.

STUDY TIP: Unlike some states, TSBP does not regulate drug wholesalers. They are regulated by the Texas Department of State Health Services. TSBP also does not have the authority to regulate pharmaceutical manufacturers' representatives.

II. Licensing

A. Licensing of Pharmacists (TPA Chapter 558)
1. It is unlawful to practice in Texas without a license or to fraudulently obtain a license.

STUDY TIP: There is no grace period when renewing a pharmacist license. If you fail to renew your license on time, you cannot legally practice.

---

2. A person may not use the title "Registered Pharmacist" or "R.Ph." or similar words unless the person is licensed to practice pharmacy in Texas.
3. Licensure by Examination.
    a. Qualifications.
        (1) At least 18 years old.
        (2) Completed internship.

(3) Graduated and received professional practice degree.
(4) Passed NAPLEX and MPJE.
(5) Has not had pharmacist license in another state restricted, suspended, revoked, or surrendered.

Note: A person who is enrolled or plans to enroll in school to become a pharmacist (or a pharmacy technician) or prior to taking an examination for licensure who has reason to believe he or she may be ineligible due to a conviction or deferred adjudication for a felony or misdemeanor offense may request a criminal history evaluation letter. See TSBP Rule 281.12 or TFPDL pages D.21–22.

b. Examination retake.
   (1) If an applicant fails the NAPLEX or MPJE, he or she may retake each examination 4 additional times (5 total).
   (2) After 5 attempts, an applicant must meet additional requirements, including additional coursework, before being allowed to take the exams again. *See TSBP Rule 283.11 or TFPDL page D.24.*

4. Licensure by Reciprocity.
   a. Must provide proof of initial licensure by examination and that current license or any other licenses have not been suspended, revoked, cancelled, surrendered, or otherwise restricted.
   b. Must pass the Texas MPJE (score of 75 is passing).
   c. Texas allows a pharmacist to reciprocate his or her license from a state where a pharmacist obtained a license by examination or reciprocity.
5. Special rules apply for licenses for military service members, military veterans, and military spouses. *See TSBP Rule 283.12.*
6. Internship.
   a. Pharmacist intern—A student intern, a resident intern, or an extended intern who is participating in a Board-approved internship program.
   b. Student intern—An individual registered with the Board who is enrolled in the professional sequence of a college/school of pharmacy and is participating in a Board-approved internship program. Student intern designation expires if the person:

(1) Ceases enrollment at an accredited college/school.
(2) Fails NAPLEX and/or Texas MPJE.
(3) Fails to take NAPLEX and/or Texas MPJE within 6 calendar months after graduation.

c. Resident intern—An individual registered with the Board who has graduated from a college/school of pharmacy and is completing an accredited residency program.

d. Extended intern—An individual registered with the Board who is no longer a student intern and other individuals in specific circumstances such as foreign pharmacy graduates or those seeking reissuance of a pharmacist license.

e. Goal and objectives of internship—The goal of internship is for the pharmacist intern to attain the knowledge, skills, and abilities to safely, efficiently, and effectively provide pharmacist-delivered patient care to a diverse patient population and practice pharmacy under the laws and regulations of Texas. Some of the objectives are as follows:
(1) Providing drug products.
(2) Communicating with patients about prescription drugs.
(3) Communicating with patients about non-prescription drugs, devices, dietary supplements, diet, nutrition, traditional nondrug therapy, complementary and alternative therapies, and diagnostic aids.
(4) Communicating with healthcare professionals.
(5) Practicing as part of the patient's interdisciplinary healthcare team.
(6) Maintaining professional ethical standards.
(7) Compounding.
(8) Retrieving and evaluating drug information.
(9) Managing general pharmacy operations.
(10) Participating in public health, community service, or professional activities.
(11) Demonstrating scientific inquiry.

Note: The details of the objectives of internship can be found in TSBP Rule 283.4 or TFPDL pages D.27–28.

f. Intern duties (TSBP Rule 283.5 or TFPDL page D.31).

(1) Pharmacist interns may perform any duty of a pharmacist provided they are working under the supervision of a pharmacist registered as a preceptor or a healthcare professional preceptor.
Note: A healthcare professional preceptor may be a physician, dentist, podiatrist, veterinarian, advanced practice registered nurse, or physician assistant in Texas or another state; or a pharmacist in a state other than Texas but not licensed in Texas who is serving as an instructor for a Texas college/school-based internship program and who is recognized by a Texas college/school of pharmacy to supervise and be responsible for the activities and functions of a pharmacist intern.

(2) Interns may not present themselves as a pharmacist, sign documents that require a pharmacist to sign (such as controlled substance invoices), or supervise technicians.

(3) When not working under the supervision of a preceptor, an intern functions as a pharmacy technician (must have completed the pharmacy's technician training program) but does not count in any ratio of pharmacy technicians to pharmacists.

STUDY TIP: Be familiar with the duties an intern can perform that a technician cannot, such as patient counseling and receiving new prescriptions.

---

g. Hour requirements.

(1) Board rules dictate the number of hours required by ACPE, which is currently 300 hours of Introductory Pharmacy Practice Experience (IPPE) and 1440 hours of Advanced Pharmacy Practice Experience (APPE).

(2) An intern cannot receive credit for more than 50 hours per week.

h. Preceptors (TSBP Rule 283.6 or TFPDL pages D.31–32).

(1) Must have a current, active pharmacist license.

(2) Must have at least 1 year of experience or 6 months of residency training.

(3) Must have completed 3 hours of preceptor training through an ACPE course.
(4) Must complete 3 hours of preceptor training every 2 years.
(5) Must have a license that has not been disciplined.
(6) In addition to pharmacist preceptors, preceptors may also be healthcare professionals (physicians, dentists, veterinarians, or pharmacists licensed in other states serving as an instructor for a Texas college/school of pharmacy).
(7) A preceptor may only supervise one intern. However, the 1:1 ratio does not apply to student interns who are part of a Texas college/school of pharmacy program. In such a program, supervision must be direct for dispensing activities and general supervision for other activities.

STUDY TIP: There is no ratio for preceptors supervising pharmacist interns as a part of a Texas college/school of pharmacy program.

B. License Renewal (TPA Chapter 559)

1. Licenses shall be renewed annually or biennially. (TSBP now renews biennially.)
2. Licenses expire on the last day of the assigned month (birth month).
3. "Timely receipt" of renewal application and fee means received in the Board's office on the last day of the expiration month. There is no grace period. Most people now renew online.
4. If a license is expired for less than 90 days, the licensee may renew the license by paying a renewal fee that is equal to one and one-half times the renewal fee and report the required hours of continuing education (CE).
5. If a license is expired for more than 90 days but less than one year, the licensee may pay a renewal fee equal to two times the renewal fee and report the required number of CE hours. *Remember: You cannot practice if your license is expired.*
6. After one year, the license cannot be renewed, but see TSBP Rule 283.10 or TFPDL pages D.38–39 for alternatives to reexamination.

7. Inactive Status (TSBP Rule 295.9 or TFPDL pages D.47–48). Pharmacists not actively practicing pharmacy can place their license in inactive status.

STUDY TIP: You cannot practice while your license is inactive, and you must still pay the license renewal fee. To activate your license, you must pay a fee and meet specific CE requirements.

C. Continuing Education (CE)

1. To renew a pharmacist license, a pharmacist must complete at least 30 contact hours of CE (3.0 CEUs) during the preceding license period (2 years).
   - **a.** At least 1 contact hour (0.1 CEU) must be related to Texas pharmacy laws and rules.
   - **b.** For renewals received after August 31, 2021, and before September 1, 2023, at least 1 contact hour (0.1 CEU) annually for a total of 2 contact hours (0.2 CEUs) must be related to best practices, alternative treatment options, and multi-modal approaches to pain management. *Note: This must be 1 contact hour annually and cannot be a single 2-hour course during the renewal period.*
   - **c.** At least 2 contact hours (0.2 CEUs) must be related to approved procedures of prescribing and monitoring controlled substances. This one-time requirement had to be completed by September 1, 2021, and must be reported on the next license renewal after September 1, 2021. *Note: It may seem strange to require a CE course on "prescribing" controlled substances for pharmacists, but this is a statutory requirement for anyone who has access to the Prescription Monitoring Program.*
   - **d.** For renewals received after August 31, 2020, and before September 1, 2022, a pharmacist must have completed a human trafficking prevention course approved by the Texas Health and Human Services Commission. A list of approved courses is posted on the commission's website. *Note: This is a one-time requirement for all licensed healthcare professionals and is not part of the 30 contact hours requirement. Such a course would only count toward the general CE requirements if it is also an ACPE accredited course.*

e. For renewals received after August 31, 2021, and before September 1, 2023, at least one contact hour (0.1 CEU) shall be related to mental health awareness.
Note: This is a one-time requirement

2. Methods of Obtaining CE.
   a. Any Accreditation Council for Pharmacy Education (ACPE) accredited course.

STUDY TIP: ACPE uses Continuing Education Units (CEUs) to accredit courses, but TSBP (and nearly every organization) refers to Continuing Education contact hours. Be sure you know that one contact hour equals 0.1 CEU (1 hour = 0.1 CEU).

   b. Successfully completing during the preceding license period a one credit hour course for each year of his or her license period, which is part of the professional degree program (accredited by ACPE) in a college of pharmacy. (This would include people in a nontraditional Pharm.D. program.)
   c. Taking and passing the standardized pharmacy examination (NAPLEX) as a pharmacist during the preceding license period, which shall be equivalent to 30 contact hours of continuing education.
   d. In addition to ACPE accredited courses, TSBP allows other methods for obtaining CE that can be found under Approved Programs in TSBP Rule 295.8 or TFPDL pages D.43–45. These include:
      (1) Completing courses that are part of the professional degree program of a college of pharmacy.
      (2) Completing a cardiopulmonary resuscitation (CPR) course (1 hour).
      (3) Completing Advanced Cardiac Life Support courses leading to initial certification (12 hours).
      (4) Completing Advanced Cardiac Life Support courses leading to recertification (4 hours).
      (5) Attending a Texas State Board of Pharmacy meeting (3 hours).
      (6) Participating in a Texas State Board of Pharmacy appointed Task Force (3 hours).
      (7) Attending programs presented by the Texas State Board of Pharmacy.

(8) Completing an Institute for Safe Medication Practices Medication Safety Self-Assessment (3 hours).

(9) Passing a certain Board of Pharmaceutical Specialties certification examination administered by the Board of Pharmaceutical Specialties (3 hours).

(10) Completing programs accredited by Accreditation Council for Continuing Medical Education as Category 1 Continuing Medical Education (CME).

e. Must keep CE records for 3 years.

STUDY TIP: CE records are the only records that TSBP requires to be kept for 3 years. Most other records are required to be kept for 2 years.

---

3. CPE Monitoring Service.
   a. The CPE Monitoring Service is a joint effort of ACPE and NABP which allows pharmacists to electronically track pharmacist continuing education from ACPE accredited providers.
   b. Pharmacists should set up an NABP e-profile at NABP's CPE Monitor website and obtain an e-profile ID. The CPE Monitor e-profile ID should be provided when obtaining continuing education from an ACPE accredited provider.

D. Licensing of Pharmacies (TPA Chapter 560)
1. The use of the term "Pharmacy" or "Apothecary" in a business that would lead the public to believe that the business is a pharmacy is not permitted unless the business is a licensed pharmacy.
2. A separate license is required for each location.
3. Only one license may be issued to a location. If a hospital is operating a Class A pharmacy under its Class C license, it is not required to have a Class A license. However, it must follow Class A rules for the outpatient pharmacy including the Class A ratio of pharmacy technicians to pharmacists.
4. There are detailed qualifications and requirements for a pharmacy license application that can be found in TPA Section 560.052 and 560.0521 and TSBP Rule 291.1 or TFPDL pages D.49–52. Some of the requirements include the signature of the pharmacist-in-charge, notarized signature of the owner, an approved credit application from a primary drug wholesaler, a sworn disclosure statement, and

business formation documents. Certain pharmacy classes and business types may be exempt from some of the requirements. An onsite inspection is also required prior to issuing a license. However, TSBP can waive that requirement if the applicant holds another active pharmacy license in the state or for another good reason.

5. Any pharmacy that compounds sterile products cannot be licensed by TSBP until the pharmacy has been inspected by TSBP.
6. A pharmacy that fails to engage in the business as described in the application for a license within 6 months of the date of issuance of the license is subject to disciplinary action. *See TSBP Rule 291.11 or TFPDL page F.14.*
7. A pharmacy license is not transferable. If there is a change of location or change of name, the pharmacy must file a new application and return the old license. TSBP actually issues an amended license (the previous license number does not change). For a change of location, TSBP must be notified in writing at least 30 days before the change.
8. TSBP is prohibited by law from adopting rules regarding ratios of pharmacy technicians to pharmacists in Class C pharmacies.

III. Generic Drug Substitution and Interchangeable Biological Products (Texas Pharmacy Act Chapter 562 Subchapter A and Board of Pharmacy Rule 309)

A. Definitions

1. Generically Equivalent—A drug that is pharmaceutically equivalent and therapeutically equivalent.
2. Pharmaceutically Equivalent—Drug products having identical amounts of the same active chemical ingredient in the same dosage form.
3. Therapeutically Equivalent—Pharmaceutically equivalent drugs that when administered in the same amounts will provide the same therapeutic effect, identical in duration and intensity.
4. Interchangeable—A biological product that is designated as biosimilar and therapeutically equivalent to another product approved by the FDA.

   Note: The Texas statute refers to biological product designation as equivalent in the FDA Orange Book, but the publication FDA uses for therapeutic equivalency evaluations for biologicals is the FDA Purple Book.

B. Permissive Substitution—A pharmacist may dispense a generically equivalent drug or interchangeable biological product if:

1. The product costs less than the brand name prescribed.
2. The patient does not refuse the substitution.
3. The prescriber has not prohibited substitution by a dispensing directive.

C. Dispensing Directive

1. Written Prescriptions.
    - **a.** A practitioner may prohibit the substitution of a generically equivalent drug or interchangeable biological product by writing across the face of the prescription, in the practitioner's own handwriting, the phrase "brand necessary" or "brand medically necessary."
    - **b.** Two-line prescription forms, check boxes, or other notations on an original prescription drug order which indicate "substitution instructions" are not valid methods to prohibit substitution, and a pharmacist may substitute on these types of prescriptions.
    - **c.** The dispensing directive may not be preprinted, rubber-stamped, or otherwise reproduced on the prescription.
2. Verbal Prescriptions.
    - **a.** A practitioner may prohibit the substitution of a generically equivalent drug or interchangeable biological product by specifying "brand necessary" or "brand medically necessary."
    - **b.** On a verbal prescription for a Medicaid patient, the practitioner must also mail or fax a written prescription with the written dispensing directive to the pharmacy within 30 days.
3. Electronic Prescriptions.
    - **a.** A practitioner may prohibit the substitution of a generically equivalent drug or interchangeable biological product by noting "brand necessary" or "brand medically necessary" on the electronic prescription.
    - **b.** On an electronic prescription for a Medicaid patient, the practitioner must also mail or fax a written prescription with the written dispensing directive to the pharmacy within 30 days.

4. Out-of-State Prescriptions. For out-of-state, Canadian, or Mexican practitioners or practitioners in federal facilities, the prescription must authorize substitution (rather than prohibit it).

D. Pharmacist's Responsibilities

1. Patient Notification. Must inform patient that a less expensive generically equivalent drug or interchangeable biological is available for the brand prescribed. In addition, the pharmacist or his or her agent must ask the patient or the patient's agent to choose between the generically equivalent drug/interchangeable biological product and the brand prescribed.
2. Communication With Prescriber. No later than 3 days after dispensing a biological product, the dispensing pharmacist or designee shall communicate to the prescribing practitioner the specific product provided to the patient, including the name of the product and the manufacturer or NDC number. This can be done making an entry into a medical records system or prescription claim system that is accessible to the prescriber.
   Note: The physician notification is only required if the biological product dispensed has been substituted for the prescribed product.
3. Selection of Drug Products. The determination of the drug or biological product to be dispensed is the professional responsibility of the pharmacist. For drugs listed in *Approved Drug Products with Therapeutic Equivalents* (the FDA Orange Book), the pharmacist may only substitute "A" rated drugs. For drugs not listed in the FDA Orange Book, the pharmacist may use professional discretion. Biological products must be listed as interchangeable in the FDA Purple Book.
   Note: On July 28, 2021, FDA approved the first interchangeable biosimilar biological product, Semglee (insulin glargine-yfgn), which can be substituted for its reference product, Lantus® (insulin glargine), a long-acting insulin analog.
4. Labeling. The prescription label must include "Substituted for Brand Prescribed" or "Substituted for 'Brand Name'" where 'Brand Name' is the name of the actual product prescribed.

E. Substitution of Dosage Form

1. A pharmacist may dispense, with the patient's consent and notification to the prescriber, a dosage form of a drug

product different from that prescribed, such as a tablet instead of a capsule or a liquid instead of tablets.

2. Requirements.
    a. Must contain the identical amount of the active ingredient as the dosage prescribed.
    b. Is not an enteric-coated or timed-release product.
    c. Does not alter clinical outcomes.

IV. Other Provisions of Texas Pharmacy Act

A. Display of Pharmacy License (TPA Section 562.103)

1. Pharmacies shall display their pharmacy license in public view.

    Note: Pharmacists and pharmacy technicians are no longer required to post their licenses or renewal certificates.

2. Class A and C pharmacies must display the word "pharmacy" or a similar word or symbol in front of the pharmacy if they serve the general public.
3. A pharmacy shall make available to the public on request proof that each pharmacist, pharmacist intern, pharmacy technician, and pharmacy technician trainee holds the appropriate license or registration.

STUDY TIP: You cannot copy your original license or renewal certificate, but you may copy your "pocket license" card.

B. Emergency Refills (TPA Section 562.054 and TSBP Rule 291.34(b)(8)(D) and (E) or TFPDL pages G.41–43)—A pharmacist may exercise professional judgment in refilling a prescription for a drug, other than a Schedule II controlled substance, without authorization of the prescriber if:

1. Failure to refill the prescription might result in an interruption of a therapeutic regimen or create patient suffering.
2. Either a natural or manmade disaster has occurred that prohibits the pharmacist from being able to contact the prescriber or the pharmacist is unable to contact the prescriber after reasonable effort.
3. The quantity of the prescription drug dispensed does not exceed a 72-hour supply.
4. If the governor declares a disaster and if notified by TSBP, the pharmacist may dispense a 30-day supply.

5. By policy, TSBP permits dispensing the entire unit-of-use products such as oral contraceptives, inhalers, and ophthalmic solutions.
6. The pharmacist informs the patient at the time of dispensing that the refill is being provided without the prescriber's authorization and that the authorization of the prescriber is required for future refills, and
   a. The pharmacist informs the practitioner of the emergency refill at the earliest reasonable time.
   b. The pharmacist maintains a record of the emergency refill containing the information required to be maintained on a prescription.
   c. The pharmacist labels the refill as a prescription.

STUDY TIP: Remember that the emergency refill rules apply to Schedule III–V drugs also. Since DEA has not issued an opinion on this rule under federal law, pharmacists should exercise professional judgment applying the emergency refill rules to Schedule III–V controlled substances. For purposes of exam preparation, since Texas rules specifically allow this, the rules can be applied to emergency refills for Schedule III–V prescriptions.

C. Auto-Refill Programs
   1. Pharmacies may use a program that automatically refills prescriptions that have existing refills available to improve patient compliance with and adherence to prescribed medication therapy.
   2. Patients must affirmatively indicate that they wish to enroll in such a program, and the pharmacy shall document such indication.
   3. Patients must have the option to withdraw from such a program at any time.
   4. Auto-refill programs may be used for refills of dangerous drugs and Schedule IV and V controlled substances. Schedule II and III controlled substances may not be dispensed by an auto-refill program.

STUDY TIP: It makes sense that auto-refills for Schedule II prescriptions are not allowed, but this rule also prohibits auto-refills of Schedule III prescriptions.

D. Accelerated Refills and 90-Day Supply—A pharmacist may dispense up to a 90-day supply of a dangerous drug (no controlled substances) from a prescription that specifies for a lesser amount if:

1. The total quantity dispensed does not exceed the total prescribed (including refills).
2. The patient consents to the dispensing.
3. The physician has been notified electronically or by telephone.
4. The drug is not a psychotropic drug.
5. The patient is at least 18 years of age.

STUDY TIP: Prior to this law, a pharmacist could not advance refills on a prescription without calling the prescriber to change the quantity. If all the conditions are met, a pharmacist can now do this and then notify the prescriber afterward.

E. Bioterrorism, Epidemic, or Pandemic Disease Reporting

1. A pharmacist shall report to the Texas Department of State Health Services any unusual or increased prescription rates or trends that may be caused by bioterrorism, epidemic, or pandemic disease.
2. These include an increase in the number of prescriptions (including antibiotics) to treat respiratory or gastrointestinal complaints and sales of over-the-counter products to treat respiratory or gastrointestinal complaints or fever.

F. Administration of Epinephrine

1. A pharmacist may administer epinephrine through an auto-injector in an emergency.
2. The law also provides liability protection for a pharmacist who in good faith administers epinephrine in accordance with this section.
3. Immediately after administering the epinephrine, the pharmacist shall ensure that 911 is called and the patient is evaluated by emergency medical personnel.
4. A pharmacist must report such administration to the patient's primary care physician within 72 hours from the time of administration.

G. Prescriptions for Epinephrine Auto-Injector and Asthma Medication for Various Entities

1. Pharmacies are allowed to dispense epinephrine auto-injectors (and in some cases asthma medication) to

various entities based on prescriptions without requiring a patient name.

2. A physician or person who has been delegated prescriptive authority (APRN or PA) may issue an order for an epinephrine auto-injector to be stored at specific types of entities. Such an order must contain:
    a. The name and signature of the prescribing physician or other person;
    b. The name of the entity to which the order is issued;
    c. The quantity of epinephrine auto-injectors to be obtained and maintained under the order; and
    d. The date the order was issued.
3. Prescriptions for epinephrine auto-injectors may be dispensed by a pharmacy pursuant to a valid prescription without requiring the name or any other identifying information of the user for:
    a. Law enforcement agencies;
    b. Day care centers;
    c. Child care facilities;
    d. Day camps or youth camps;
    e. Private or independent institutions of higher education;
    f. Amusement parks;
    g. Restaurants;
    h. Sports venues;
    i. Youth centers; and
    j. Any other entity designated by rule of the Texas Health and Human Services Commission.

    See HB 1849, HB 4260, and SB 1827 from 86th Texas Legislature of 2019.
4. Prescriptions for epinephrine auto-injectors and asthma medication may be dispensed by a pharmacy pursuant to a valid prescription without requiring the name or any other identifying information of the user for:
    a. A school district;
    b. An open-enrollment charter school; and
    c. A private school.

    See HB 2243 from 86th Texas Legislature of 2019.

H. Required Notifications to TSBP

Required Report	Who Reports	Time Frame	Source
Change of pharmacist name or address	Pharmacist	Within 10 days	Rule 295.1
Change of pharmacist employment	Pharmacist	Within 10 days	Rule 291.3(e)
Permanent closing of pharmacy	Pharmacy	Within 10 days after closing	TPA 562.106 and Rule 291.5
Change of pharmacy ownership	Pharmacy	Within 10 days and new license required	TPA 562.106 and Rule 291.3(d)
Change of pharmacy location	Pharmacy	New license filed 30 days prior to change	TPA 562.106 and Rule 291.3(a)
Change of pharmacy name	Pharmacy	New license filed 10 days prior to change	Rule 291.3(b)
Change of managing officers or partnership/corporation	Pharmacy	Within 10 days	Rule 291.3(c)
Change of pharmacist-in-charge (PIC)	Incoming PIC	Within 10 days	TPA 562.106 and Rule 291.3(e)(2)
Sale or transfer of drugs as a result of closing or change of ownership	Pharmacy	Within 10 days	TPA 562.106
Fire or other disaster, accident, or emergency that may affect the strength, purity, or labeling of a drug or medical device	Pharmacy/ PIC	Within 10 days	TPA 562.106 and Rule 291.3(g)
Significant loss or theft of controlled substances or dangerous drugs	Pharmacy	Immediately upon discovery	Rule 291.3(f)
Significant loss of data from pharmacy computer system	Pharmacy	Within 10 days	Records requirements are in each Class of Pharmacy rules
A licensee or registrant obtaining dangerous drugs or controlled substances from a forged prescription	Pharmacy	Immediately upon discovery	Rule 291.3(i)
A final order against the pharmacy license holder or pharmacist-in-charge by the regulatory or licensing agency of the state in which the pharmacy is located if in another state.	Pharmacy	Within 10 days	TPA 561.106 and Rule 291.3(j)

I. Administration and Provision of Dangerous Drugs by Physicians (TPA Chapter 563 or TFPDL pages D.82-83)

1. Texas generally does not permit physician dispensing.
2. Exceptions.
    a. A physician may provide a 72-hour supply of dangerous drugs (no controlled substances) to a patient in the physician's office to meet the patient's immediate therapeutic needs.
    b. Physicians in certain rural areas and where there is no pharmacy may dispense dangerous drugs to patients and be reimbursed for the cost.
    c. Veterinarians are allowed to dispense to their own patients without being licensed as a pharmacy.

J. Impaired Pharmacists/Pharmacy Students Program and Peer Review Program (TPA Chapter 564 or TFPDL pages D.83–86)

1. Impaired Pharmacists/Pharmacy Students Program.
    a. Pharmacists and pharmacy students who have an alcohol or drug impairment can enter into treatment and monitoring through the Professional Recovery Network (PRN).
    b. Individuals who enter the program voluntarily are not reported to TSBP as long as they follow through with PRN's recommendations.
    c. Pharmacists and technicians may also be placed into the PRN program as part of the disciplinary process by TSBP.
    d. Any Board order by TSBP related to impairment is confidential.
    e. The program is partially funded by a surcharge on all pharmacy and pharmacist licenses. However, the funds only pay for evaluation of participants. They do not cover the cost for treatment.
2. Peer Review Program.
    a. A peer review committee may be set up by pharmacy owners or pharmacy associations to evaluate the quality of care in pharmacies by reviewing errors or near errors or other quality issues.
    b. In an effort to encourage pharmacies to establish these committees, the statute provides legal protection of peer review documents in civil litigation.

c. Setting up a peer review committee is voluntary. However, some pharmacies may be mandated to establish a committee as part of the disciplinary action against the pharmacy license (usually as a result of a medication error).

K. Reporting Professional Liability Claims (TSBP Rule 281.18 or TFPDL pages D.90–101)

1. An insurer who provides professional liability insurance to pharmacists, pharmacy technicians, or pharmacies must report to TSBP any claim filed against a pharmacist, pharmacy technician, or pharmacy related to care that results in injury or death.
2. If a pharmacist, pharmacy technician, or pharmacy does not have professional liability insurance and receives such a legal claim, the individual or pharmacy must report the claim to TSBP.
3. The initial report is required within 30 days of receiving the claim notice. A follow-up report is required within 105 days after disposition (settlement, dismissal, judgment, etc.) of the claim.

V. Pharmacy Technicians and Pharmacy Technician Trainees (TPA Chapter 568)

A. Registration Required (TSBP Rule 297.3 or TFPDL pages D.88–90)

1. Must be registered as a pharmacy technician or pharmacy technician trainee prior to beginning work in a pharmacy.
2. Pharmacy technician trainee registration is valid for 2 years and is not renewable.
3. Initial registration as a pharmacy technician requires passing a Board-approved certification examination, but maintaining certification is not required for renewal of registration.
4. Renewal of registration requires 20 hours of continuing education (every 2 years) including 1 hour of Texas law. *See TSBP Rule 297.8 or TFPDL pages D.92–97.*

B. Ratios

1. Ratio of pharmacists to pharmacy technicians and pharmacy technician trainees in a Class A pharmacy is 1:6 as long as a maximum number of pharmacy technician trainees is 3. If all are pharmacy technician trainees, the ratio is 1:3.
2. There is no ratio in Class C and Class G pharmacies.

C. Training
   1. Pharmacy technicians and pharmacy technician trainees must complete training conducted by the pharmacist-in-charge as outlined in a pharmacy technician training manual.
   2. Specific requirements for the training manual can be found in TSBP Rule 297.6 or TFPDL pages D.91–92.
   3. The pharmacist-in-charge must document such training.

D. Continuing Education (CE)
   1. Pharmacy technicians (but not trainees) are required to complete 20 contact hours of continuing education every 2 years to renew their registration.
   2. At least one hour must be related to Texas pharmacy laws and rules.
   3. Acceptable forms of CE are the same as those for pharmacists and also include pharmacy-related courses as part of a pharmacy technician training program.
   4. Pharmacy technicians who maintain their certification are considered to have met CE requirements and are not subject to audit by TSBP.
   5. For renewals received after August 31, 2020, and before September 1, 2022, a pharmacy technician must have completed a human trafficking prevention course approved by the Texas Health and Human Services Commission. A list of approved courses is posted on the Commission's website.

VI. Miscellaneous Texas Pharmacy Act Provisions and TSBP Rules

A. Immunizations and Vaccinations (TSBP Rule 295.15 or TFPDL pages D.16–19)

Note: Under the federal Public Readiness and Emergency Preparedness (PREP) Act, pharmacy technicians with appropriate training were given authority to administer COVID-19 vaccinations irrespective of state laws and regulations. This authority was extended for flu vaccines provided to adults 19 years of age or older in 2021. These authorities under the PREP act are temporary unless state law is changed. Despite some bills being introduced in 2021, Texas law was not amended to make these authorities permanent. It is unlikely that the MPJE would include questions based on temporary rules.

   1. Requires written protocol with a physician.
   2. Services to patients under age 14 may be provided only if referred by a physician except that a pharmacist may

administer an influenza vaccination to a patient over the age of 7 without an established physician-patient relationship.

3. May only be given at a pharmacy or location provided in the protocol; cannot be provided where patient resides except for nursing homes or hospitals.
4. Pharmacist certification requires an ACPE-approved course which includes:
   a. Basic Cardiac Life Support Certification.
   b. 20 hours of CDC training.
   c. 3 hours of CE every 2 years relating to disease states, drugs, and administration of immunizations or vaccines.
5. Notifications.
   a. Pharmacist must notify physician who issued the protocol within 24 hours of administration; and
   b. The primary care physician of the patient must be notified within 14 days of administration.

B. Drug Therapy Management (DTM) Under Protocol (TSBP Rule 295.13 or TFPDL pages E.2–5)

1. Pharmacists may perform drug therapy management as authorized by a physician under a written protocol.
2. Drug therapy management may include:
   a. Collecting and reviewing patient drug use histories.
   b. Ordering or performing routine drug therapy related patient assessment procedures such as temperature, pulse, and respiration.
   c. Ordering drug therapy related laboratory tests.
   d. Implementing or modifying drug therapy following diagnosis, initial patient assessment, and ordering of drug therapy by a physician as detailed in the protocol.
   e. Signing a prescription drug order for a dangerous drug (no controlled substances) if:
      (1) The delegation follows a diagnosis, initial patient assessment, and drug therapy order by the physician;
      (2) The pharmacist practices in a federally qualified health center (FQHC), hospital, hospital-based clinic, or an academic healthcare institution; and
      (3) The federally qualified health center, hospital, hospital-based clinic, or academic healthcare institution in which the pharmacist practices has bylaws and a medical staff policy that permit a physician

to delegate to a pharmacist the management of a patient's drug therapy.

Note: A prescription drug order "signed" by a pharmacist may be faxed to a pharmacy but may not be issued verbally. See Quick Reference Guide Chart on pages 123–125 above.

STUDY TIP: Drug therapy management can take place at any location, but the signing of a prescription drug order by a pharmacist under drug therapy management is restricted to specific sites, as indicated in e. above.

   - **f.** Any other drug therapy related act delegated by a physician.

3. Written Protocol.
   - **a.** Must identify the supervising physician and the pharmacist authorized to perform DTM.
   - **b.** Must identify types of DTM decisions the pharmacist is authorized to make.
   - **c.** Must state activities the pharmacist shall follow in performing DTM.
   - **d.** Must state mechanisms and time schedule for pharmacist to report to physician.

4. Notification and CE Requirements.
   - **a.** Must notify TSBP prior to engaging in DTM.
   - **b.** Must complete at least 6 hours of CE annually related to drug therapy.

5. Supervision.
   - **a.** Physician must review protocol and any deviations from protocol at least annually.
   - **b.** Physician must have physician-patient relationship with each patient.
   - **c.** Physician must be geographically located to be physically present daily.
   - **d.** Physician must receive periodic status reports on a schedule defined in the protocol.
   - **e.** Physician must be available through telecommunication for consultation.

STUDY TIP: There is no limit to the number of physicians for whom a pharmacist may perform drug therapy management, and there is no limit to the number of pharmacists with whom a physician can enter into a protocol.

6. Records.
    a. Must be kept for 2 years.
    b. Must keep a copy of the written protocol and any patient-specific deviations from the protocol.
    c. Must document all interventions.
    d. Must review protocol annually.

C. Inventory Requirements (TSBP Rule 291.17 or TFPDL pages E.16–18)
1. General Requirements.
    a. PIC is responsible for ensuring all inventories are taken.
    b. Inventories must be maintained in pharmacy, filed separately from other records, and be available for inspection for 2 years.
    c. Inventories include all stock "on hand" of controlled substances (including expired drugs).
    d. Persons taking inventory and PIC shall sign and date the inventory and indicate the time inventory was taken.
    e. The signature of the PIC and date of the inventory shall be notarized within 72 hours or 3 working days for all inventories except for the initial inventory and change in PIC inventory.
    f. The PIC is responsible for making an exact count of all Schedule II controlled substances.
    g. The PIC is also responsible for making an estimated count of Schedule III–V controlled substances provided the container has fewer than 1000 tablets or capsules.
    h. Schedule II controlled substances shall be listed separately.
    i. If a pharmacy maintains a perpetual inventory, it must be reconciled on the date of the annual inventory.
2. Required Inventories.
    a. Initial inventory—If on the opening day of business there are no controlled substances, then the pharmacist should record zero.
    b. Annual inventory—An annual inventory of controlled substances is required in Texas in contrast to the DEA every two-year inventory requirement.
    c. Change of ownership of Class A, A-S, C, C-S, or F pharmacy.
        (1) Inventory shall be taken on the date of change of ownership.

        (2) Constitutes the closing inventory for seller and the initial inventory for buyer.
    d. Change of PIC of Class A, A-S, C, C-S, or F pharmacy.
3. Perpetual Inventories.
    a. Class C and C-S pharmacies must maintain a perpetual inventory for Schedule II controlled substances.
    b. Class C Ambulatory Care Facility pharmacies and Class F (Freestanding Emergency Medical Center) pharmacies must maintain a perpetual inventory for all controlled substances.
    c. All pharmacies must maintain a perpetual inventory of any controlled substances stored at a remote location.

STUDY TIP: Although many Class A and A-S pharmacies maintain a perpetual inventory of all controlled substances, it is important to know that they are not required (other than for those stored in remote pharmacy locations). Similarly, many Class C and C-S pharmacies keep a perpetual inventory of all controlled substances but are only required to do so for Schedule II drugs.

D. Closing a Pharmacy (TSBP Rule 291.5 or TFPDL pages E.10–12)

STUDY TIP: This rule applies when closing a pharmacy and no further pharmacy activities will take place at the location. If a pharmacy is being sold and pharmacy activities will continue at the location, the rules for change of ownership should be followed. Those rules include applying for a new pharmacy license as well as DEA notification, inventory, and transfer requirements.

---

1. Prior to Closing. At least 14 days prior to closing, the PIC must:
    a. Notify DEA.
    b. Post a closing notice informing patients of the name, address, and telephone number of the pharmacy acquiring the records.
2. Closing Day. The PIC must:
    a. Take a closing inventory.
    b. Transfer prescription drug order files and patient medication records.
    c. Remove all signs that indicate the location is a pharmacy.
3. After Closing.
    a. Within 10 days after closing, the PIC must provide to TSBP a written notice of the actual date of closing, the pharmacy license, a statement that an inventory was

conducted according to TSBP Rule 291.17, the manner in which dangerous drugs and controlled substances were transferred or disposed of, and the name and address of the pharmacy to which records were transferred.

b. If the pharmacy is registered to possess controlled substances, a notification must be sent to a DEA divisional office explaining that the pharmacy has closed, along with the DEA registration certificate and any unused DEA Forms 222 which have been voided.

E. Remote Pharmacy Services (TSBP Rule 291.121 or TFPDL pages D.74–81)

TSBP rules recognize four types of remote pharmacy practices in which drugs may be stored and/or dispensed from locations where a pharmacist is not present. These four types of remote pharmacy practices include Emergency Medication Kits at nursing homes, Automated Pharmacy Systems for routine dispensing of drugs at certain healthcare facilities including nursing homes, Telepharmacy Systems used for dispensing drugs at remote dispensing sites and certain remote healthcare sites, and Automated Dispensing and Delivery Systems at locations outside a pharmacy.

1. Summary of TSBP Rule 291.121(b) Remote Pharmacy Services Using an Emergency Medication Kit.

a. This rule allows a Class A or C pharmacy or a Class E pharmacy located within 20 miles of a facility to provide pharmacy services to facilities licensed under Health and Safety Code Chapter 242 (Convalescent Homes, Nursing Homes, and Related Institutions) or Chapter 252 (Intermediate Care Facilities for the Mentally Retarded) using an Emergency Medication Kit as outlined in Section 562.108 of the Texas Pharmacy Act. It also allows a U.S. Department of Veterans Affairs pharmacy or other federally operated pharmacy to provide pharmacy services using an Emergency Medical Kit at an institution licensed under Chapter 242 that is a Texas State Veterans Home.

b. An application to TSBP is required before providing these services.

c. DEA Rule 1301.27(b) requires automated dispensing systems in long-term care facilities to be registered with DEA. However, if the automated system is being used solely as an emergency kit and not for routine dispensing of controlled substances, a DEA registration is not required.

d. Access to the Emergency Medication Kit is limited to pharmacists and healthcare personnel employed by the facility.

e. Contents of the Emergency Medication Kit shall be determined by the consultant pharmacist, pharmacist-in-charge of the provider pharmacy, medical director, and director of nursing and shall be limited to those drugs necessary to meet the resident's emergency medication needs. This refers to a situation in which a drug cannot be supplied by a pharmacy within a reasonable time.

STUDY TIP: Texas laws and rules do not have specific quantity limits or a list of specific drugs that can be stored in an Emergency Medication Kit.

---

f. Stocking of drugs in an automated pharmacy system must be done by a pharmacist, pharmacy technician, or pharmacy technician trainee unless the system uses bar-coding, microchip, or other technologies to ensure that the containers or unit-dose drugs are accurately loaded and other specific requirements are met.

g. A record must be maintained of all drugs sent to and returned from the remote location and should be kept separate from the records of the provider pharmacy and from other remote site records.

h. A perpetual inventory of all controlled substances must be maintained for each remote location, and each remote location's controlled substances must be inventoried on the same day as the provider pharmacy's inventory.

2. Summary of TSBP Rule 291.121(a) Remote Pharmacy Services Using Automated Pharmacy Systems (primarily in nursing homes).

   a. This rule allows a Class A or C pharmacy to provide pharmacy services to facilities licensed under Health and Safety Code Chapter 142 (Home and Community Support Service Agencies including hospices), Chapter 242 (Convalescent Homes, Nursing Homes, and Related Institutions), Chapter 247 (Assisted Living Facilities), and Chapter 252 (Intermediate Care Facilities for the Mentally Retarded), as well as jails or prisons operated by the State of Texas or local government.

b. Drugs may only be maintained in an automated pharmacy system.

c. If controlled substances are to be stored and dispensed from the automated system at the remote location, a DEA registration must be obtained for the remote location in the name of the pharmacy providing the remote pharmacy services.

d. An application to TSBP is required prior to providing these services.

e. A pharmacist may supervise operation of the system electronically, and a pharmacist shall control all operations of the automated pharmacy system and approve the release of the initial dose after receiving a valid prescription drug order.

f. Drugs dispensed using the automated pharmacy system must meet the labeling requirements or alternative labeling requirements found in TSBP Rule 291.33E. *See TFPDL page G.24.*

g. Drugs used in the automated pharmacy system must be in the original manufacturer's container or be prepackaged in the provider pharmacy.

h. Stocking of drugs in an automated pharmacy system must be done by a pharmacist, pharmacy technician, or pharmacy technician trainee unless the system uses removable cartridges or containers and other specific requirements are met.

i. A record must be maintained of all drugs sent to and returned from the remote location and should be kept separate from the records of the provider pharmacy and from other remote site records.

j. A perpetual inventory of all controlled substances must be maintained for each remote location, and each remote location's controlled substances must be inventoried on the same day as the provider pharmacy's inventory.

3. Summary of TSBP Rule 291.121(c) Remote Pharmacy Services Using Telepharmacy Systems.

   a. A telepharmacy system is a system that monitors the dispensing of prescription drugs and provides for related drug use regimen and patient counseling services by an electronic method which includes the use of audio and video, still image capture, and store and forward.

b. There are two types of remote sites that may use a telepharmacy system—remote healthcare sites and remote dispensing sites. The rules for each type are slightly different.

c. Remote Healthcare Sites.

(1) A Class A or C pharmacy may provide pharmacy services using a telepharmacy system at the following remote healthcare sites:

(a) Rural health clinics regulated under 42 U.S.C. Section 1395x(aa);

(b) Health centers as defined by 42 U.S.C. Section 254b (serving medically underserved populations);

(c) Federally qualified health centers as defined by 42 U.S.C. 1396d(1)(2)(B); or

(d) Healthcare facilities located in a medically underserved area or health professions shortage area as defined by HHS.

(2) A pharmacy may not provide remote pharmacy services at a remote healthcare site if a Class A or Class C pharmacy that dispenses prescription drug orders to outpatients is located in the same community (as defined in the rule). This rule does not apply to telepharmacy systems at federally qualified health centers.

Note: Community is defined by Board rule as within 10 miles if not in a metropolitan statistical area. This is applicable to telepharmacy systems in healthcare sites or clinics. Remote dispensing sites have more restrictive rules (i.e., within 22 miles).

d. Remote Dispensing Sites.

(1) A Class A pharmacy (but not a Class C pharmacy) may provide telepharmacy services at remote dispensing sites staffed by a pharmacy technician. Telepharmacy systems at remote dispensing sites have the following additional requirements that are not required for telepharmacy systems at remote healthcare sites.

(a) A remote dispensing site is defined as a location licensed as a telepharmacy that is authorized by a provider pharmacy through a telepharmacy system to store and dispense drugs and devices including dangerous drugs and controlled substances.

(b) A remote dispensing site must be staffed by an onsite pharmacy technician who is under the continuous supervision of a pharmacist employed by the provider pharmacy.

(c) Pharmacy technicians at a remote dispensing site must have worked at least 1 year at a retail pharmacy during the past 3 years and must complete a Board-approved training program on the proper use of a telepharmacy system.

(d) Pharmacy technicians at a remote dispensing site are included in the pharmacist-pharmacy technician ratio of the provider pharmacy. They may not perform extemporaneous sterile or nonsterile compounding but may prepare commercially available medications for dispensing, including reconstitution of orally administered powder antibiotics.

(e) Only a Class A pharmacy may serve as a provider pharmacy for a remote dispensing site.

(f) A provider pharmacy may provide pharmacy services at no more than 2 remote dispensing sites.

(2) A remote dispensing site may not be located within 22 road miles of a Class A pharmacy. If a Class A pharmacy opens within that mileage restriction after a remote dispensing site is operating, the remote dispensing site may continue to operate.

(3) A remote dispensing site may not dispense Schedule II controlled substances.

(4) If a remote dispensing site dispenses an average of more than 125 prescriptions each day the site is open (calculated annually), it must apply for a Class A license.

(5) A pharmacist employed by a provider pharmacy must make at least monthly onsite visits to a remote dispensing site and must reconcile the perpetual inventory of controlled substances to the on-hand count at the remote dispensing site.

SUMMARY OF DIFFERENCES PROVIDING TELEPHARMACY SERVICES BASED ON LOCATION

Remote Healthcare Sites	Remote Dispensing Sites
Provider pharmacy may be a Class A or Class C pharmacy.	Provider pharmacy must be a Class A pharmacy.
Provider pharmacy may not supervise more than two remote sites.	Provider pharmacy may not supervise more than two remote sites.
No restriction on drug classes.	May not dispense Schedule II controlled substances.
Does not require a pharmacy technician.	Must be staffed by a pharmacy technician.
Except for federally qualified health centers, may not be located if a Class A or Class C pharmacy dispensing to outpatients is within 10 miles (if not located in a metropolitan statistical area).	May not be located if a Class A pharmacy is within 22 road miles.
A DEA Registration is required for controlled substances.	A DEA Registration is required for controlled substances.
Perpetual inventory of controlled substances is required.	Perpetual inventory of controlled substances is required.
No special training for pharmacy technicians (if used).	Pharmacy technicians must have one year of retail experience and training on a telepharmacy system.
No requirement for pharmacist visits or reconciliation of controlled substances.	Pharmacist employed by a provider pharmacy must make at least monthly onsite visits to a remote dispensing site and must reconcile the perpetual inventory of controlled substances to the on-hand count.
No limit on prescriptions dispensed.	If a remote dispensing site dispenses an average of more than 125 prescriptions each day the site is open (calculated annually), it must apply for a Class A license.

e. The following rules apply to telepharmacy systems at both remote healthcare sites and remote dispensing sites.

(1) If controlled substances are to be stored at the remote location, a DEA registration must be obtained for the remote location.

(2) Drugs dispensed at a remote site through a telepharmacy system may only be delivered to the patient at the remote site.

(3) A provider pharmacy may not supervise more than 2 remote sites.
(4) An application to TSBP is required before providing these services.
(5) A perpetual inventory of all controlled substances must be maintained for each remote location. Each remote location's controlled substances must be inventoried on the same day as the provider pharmacy's inventory.
(6) Original prescription records shall be kept at the remote site, and the provider pharmacy shall have electronic access to those records.

f. The chart on the previous page provides a summary and comparison of the two types of "remote sites" where telepharmacy is allowed.

4. Summary of TSBP Rule 291.121(d) Remote Pharmacy Services Using Automated Dispensing and Delivery Systems

a. This rule allows a Class A or Class C pharmacy to provide pharmacy services using an automated dispensing and delivery system at a remote delivery site.

b. An automated dispensing and delivery system is a mechanical system that dispenses and delivers prescription drugs to patients at a remote delivery site and maintains related transaction information.
Note: These systems may provide prescriptions that have already been labeled, packaged, and dispensed by the provider pharmacy, or they may store bulk prescription drugs with the system doing the actual packaging, dispensing, and delivery.

c. A provider pharmacy may only provide remote pharmacy services using an automated dispensing and delivery system at Board-approved remote delivery sites. An application for approval to provide such services must be submitted to the Board and be renewed every two years with the provider pharmacy's pharmacy license.

d. A provider pharmacy shall comply with appropriate controlled substance registrations for each remote delivery site if dispensed controlled substances are maintained within an automated dispensing and delivery system.
Note: Pharmacists should be cautious about providing controlled substance prescriptions using an automated

dispensing and delivery system at a location that is not registered with DEA or should seek confirmation from DEA that this is allowed.

e. Patients obtaining their prescriptions from an automated dispensing and delivery system shall receive counseling via direct link to audio or video communication by a Texas licensed pharmacist who has access to the complete patient medication records (patient profile) maintained by the provider pharmacy prior to release of any new prescription.

Note: Counseling is not required for refill prescriptions.

f. A pharmacist must be accessible at all times to respond to patients' or other healthcare professionals' questions and needs pertaining to drugs delivered through the use of the system.

g. An automated dispensing and delivery system must be locked by key, combination, or other mechanical or electronic means to prohibit access by unauthorized personnel. There must also be a security system including security camera(s) that records a digital image of the individual accessing the system to pick up a prescription.

h. Access to an automated dispensing and delivery system is limited to pharmacists and pharmacy technicians or pharmacy technician trainees under the direct supervision of a pharmacist. Stocking of dispensed prescriptions must be completed under the supervision of a pharmacist.

i. A pharmacy providing services through an automated dispensing and delivery system at a remote delivery site shall operate according to a written program of quality assurance and written policies and procedures which:

(1) Requires continuous supervision of the automated dispensing and delivery system; and

(2) Establishes mechanisms and procedures to routinely test the accuracy of the automated dispensing and delivery system at a minimum of every six months and whenever any upgrade or change is made to the system and documents each such activity.

F. Destruction and Disposal of Dangerous Drugs and Controlled Substances (TSBP Rule Chapter 303 or TFPDL pages E.30–33)

Note: This process is not the same as a transfer of controlled substances to a DEA registered reverse distributor for destruction.

1. Destruction of Dispensed Drugs.
   a. Drugs dispensed to patients in healthcare facilities or institutions (nursing homes).
      (1) Destruction of dangerous drugs by consultant pharmacist.
         (a) Inventory is required.
         (b) Drugs must be destroyed in a manner to render the drugs unfit for human consumption and disposed of in compliance with all applicable state and federal requirements.
         (c) Destruction is witnessed by a peace officer or agent of the Board, Texas Department of Health and Human Services, or Texas Department of State Health Services, or two of the following persons from the facility: the facility administrator, the director of nursing, or a licensed nurse.
      (2) Destruction of dangerous drugs by a waste disposal service.
         (a) Inventory is required.
         (b) Drugs are placed in a sealed container in presence of a witness (same list as in (1)(c) above).
         (c) Drugs must be destroyed in a manner to render the drugs unfit for human consumption and disposed of in compliance with all applicable state and federal requirements.
         (d) Waste disposal service provides the facility with proof of destruction of the sealed container.
      (3) Controlled substances—Must follow DEA rules for destruction. *See Chapter Two in this book.*
   b. Drugs returned to a pharmacy.
      (1) Dangerous drugs.
         (a) Drugs must be destroyed in a manner to render the drugs unfit for human consumption and disposed of in compliance with all applicable state and federal requirements.
         (b) Document date of destruction, name and address of dispensing pharmacy, prescription number, name and strength of drug, and signature of pharmacist.
      (2) Controlled substances—Pharmacy must be a collector under DEA destruction rules.

2. Destruction of Stock Drugs.
   a. Stock dangerous drugs.
      (1) Pharmacists licensed by the Texas State Board of Pharmacy may destroy stock dangerous drugs if the drugs are destroyed in a manner to render the drugs unfit for human consumption (i.e., destroyed beyond reclamation) and disposed of in compliance with all applicable state and federal requirements.
      (2) Records of destruction are not required.
   b. Stock controlled substances. *See DEA destruction rules in Chapter Two in this book.*

G. Other TSBP Rules
   1. Drug Recalls (TSBP Rule 291.7 or TFPDL page E.12). Requires the PIC to have policies and procedures for handling prescription drug recalls, including ensuring that a recalled drug has been removed from inventory within 24 hours of notice of the recall.
   2. Return of Prescription Drugs (TSBP Rule 291.8 or TFPDL pages E.12–14). It is unlawful to accept prescription drugs that have been dispensed for purposes of resale. There is an exception for certain prescriptions dispensed to nursing home patients.
      Note: There is also a separate rule for returning undelivered prescriptions or prescriptions from a "will call" bin to stock. See Chapter Six, II.G. in this book.
   3. Prescription Pick Up Locations (TSBP Rule 291.9 or TFPDL page E.14).
      a. No person, firm, or business establishment may participate in an arrangement whereby prescriptions are solicited, collected, picked up, or advertised to be picked up from any location other than a pharmacy licensed by the Board.

STUDY TIP: An exception to this rule is use of an Automated Dispensing and Delivery System as provided in the Remote Pharmacy rules above.

---

      b. A pharmacy may, at the request of a patient, pick up prescription orders at the office or home of the prescriber, the residence or place of employment of the patient, or a hospital or medical care facility where the patient is receiving treatment.

c. A pharmacy may deliver prescription drugs (labeled for a specific patient) to the:
   (1) Office of the prescriber if the prescription is for a dangerous drug or for a single dose of a controlled substance that is for administration to the patient in the prescriber's office;
   Note: Federal law is more restrictive and only allows a pharmacy to deliver a controlled substance prescription for a specific patient to a prescriber's office if it is to be administered by injection or implant for maintenance or detoxification treatment. TSBP may need to modify this rule to match the federal law.
   (2) Residence of the patient;
   (3) Place of employment of the patient if the person is present to accept delivery; or
   (4) Hospital or medical care facility where the patient is receiving treatment.

4. Pharmacy Balance Registration/Inspection (TSBP Rule 291.10 or TFPDL pages E.14–15).
   a. Balance is required if a pharmacy performs nonsterile compounding.
   b. Balance must be registered with TSBP and shall be inspected for accuracy by the Board.
5. Pilot or Demonstration Projects (TSBP Rule 291.23 or TFPDL pages D.13–15). Specifies procedures to be followed to apply for approval of a research or demonstration project for innovative applications in the practice of pharmacy. TSBP may waive a rule to allow the pilot project but cannot waive a law.
6. Professional Responsibility of Pharmacists and the Practice of Telemedicine (TSBP Rule 291.29 or TFPDL pages E.20–23).
   a. Requires a pharmacist to exercise sound professional judgment with respect to the accuracy and authenticity of any prescription dispensed and to verify the order if there are any questions.
   b. The rule expands the concept of a pharmacist's corresponding responsibility to ensure that controlled substances are issued for a legitimate medical purpose by a practitioner in the usual course of medical practice to all prescriptions including dangerous drugs and not just controlled substances.

c. The rule indicates that a pharmacist may not dispense a prescription that was issued by means of the internet unless it is pursuant to a valid prescription written for a legitimate medical purpose without at least one in-person medical examination. However, the practice of telemedicine is now legal in Texas, so prescriptions issued based on telephonic or internet-based consultations are now allowed in Texas except for abortifacients or other drugs or devices that terminate a pregnancy and treatment of chronic pain with controlled substances. *See TFPDL page D.81 and also Telemedicine Frequently Asked Questions on the TSBP website.*

d. Nontherapeutic dispensing.

   (1) A pharmacist may not dispense a prescription if the pharmacist has reason to suspect that the prescription drug order was issued in the absence of a valid patient-practitioner relationship.

   (2) A valid patient-practitioner relationship is not required for the treatment of sexually transmitted diseases for partners of a physician's established patient or a patient's family member if the patient has an illness determined to be a pandemic by the Centers for Disease Control, the World Health Organization, or the Governor's office.
   Note: A standing order for naloxone may be another exception although it is not included in this rule.

   (3) See TSBP Rule 291.29 or TFPDL pages E.20–23 for a list of factors relevant to preventing nontherapeutic dispensing.

e. A pharmacist shall not dispense a prescription drug if the pharmacist knows or should know the prescription is fraudulent or forged.

7. Centralized Prescription Dispensing (TSBP Rule 291.125 or TFPDL pages E.23–24). Allows Class A or Class C pharmacies (the outsourcing pharmacy) to outsource prescription drug order dispensing to another Class A or C pharmacy or a Class E pharmacy (the central fill pharmacy) under certain conditions.

   a. Must be under common ownership or have a written contract or agreement.

    b. Must share a common database or have other technology to allow access to information.
    c. Must provide notice to patients (one-time written notification) or a sign in the pharmacy.
    d. The prescription label should include the name of the outsourcing pharmacy and some unique identifier of the central fill pharmacy.
    e. DEA does not allow a central fill pharmacy to deliver controlled substance prescriptions directly to a patient, but TSBP does allow a central fill pharmacy to deliver dangerous drug prescriptions directly to a patient.

8. Centralized Prescription Drug or Medication Order Processing (TSBP Rule 291.123 or TFPDL pages E.24–25). Allows Class A, Class C, and Class E pharmacies to outsource prescription or medication order processing (data entry, drug regimen review, adjudication, etc.) to another Class A, C, or E pharmacy.
    a. Must be under common ownership or have a written contract or agreement.
    b. Must share a common database or have other technology to allow access to information.
    c. Must provide notice to patients of Class A and E pharmacies that Central Processing is being used to fill their prescriptions. One-time notification or sign is required.
9. Satellite Pharmacy (TSBP Rule 291.129 or TFPDL pages E.25–30).
    a. This pharmacy is not what is typically considered to be a satellite pharmacy of a hospital pharmacy.
    b. This rule allows a Class A or C pharmacy to operate a satellite location that is not separately licensed.
    c. Prescriptions are dropped off at the satellite location and then sent to the Class A or C pharmacy to be filled. The filled prescriptions are then sent back to the satellite location where the patient picks up the prescription and counseling is provided as required.
    d. Detailed requirements can be found in TSBP Rule 291.129 or TFPDL pages E.25–30.
    e. This rule is an exception to the prohibition on prescription pickup locations.
    f. No bulk prescription drugs are allowed to be stored in a satellite pharmacy.

CHAPTER FIVE

Complaints, Inspections, Disciplinary Actions, Penalties, and Procedures

CHAPTER FIVE

Complaints, Inspections, Disciplinary Actions, Penalties, and Procedures

I. Notifications to the Public, Complaints, and Inspections

A. Notifications (TSBP Rule 291.3(h)(1) or TFPDL pages F.2–4)

1. Pharmacies must post a sign notifying patients how they can file complaints with TSBP. Rule also allows for an electronic messaging system.
2. If a pharmacy delivers prescriptions to patients, a written notification must be provided with the delivery.
3. Pharmacies that maintain internet sites must include the following information on the pharmacy's initial home page and on the page where a sale of a prescription drug occurs:
    - **a.** Information on the ownership of the pharmacy.
    - **b.** The internet address and toll-free telephone number that a consumer may use to report medication/device problems to the pharmacy and to report business compliance problems.
    - **c.** Information about each pharmacy that dispenses prescriptions for the website including the pharmacy name, address, telephone number; the name of the pharmacist responsible for the operation of the pharmacy; the Texas pharmacy license number; a link to the internet site of the Texas State Board of Pharmacy; and the names of all other states in which the pharmacy is located, including the license number in that state and a link to the internet site of the entity that regulates pharmacies in that state if available.
    - **d.** Pharmacies whose internet site has been verified by the National Association of Boards of Pharmacy to be in compliance with the laws of Texas, as well as all other states the pharmacy is licensed in, are considered compliant with the notification requirements.
4. Pharmacists not working in a pharmacy also must provide the notice to patients, either posting a sign in the practice location or providing written notice to each patient when services are provided. *See TSBP Rule 295.11 or TFPDL pages F.3–4.*

B. Complaints

1. TSBP must adopt policies and procedures concerning the investigation of complaints filed with the Board.
2. Confidentiality—The identity of any person who files a complaint with the Board is considered confidential information and is not subject to the Texas Open Records Act.
3. Immunity—A person who files a complaint in good faith to the Board is immune from civil liability.

C. Inspections and Investigations

1. Before entering a facility for an inspection, the person authorized to represent the Board must state the purpose for the inspection and provide the owner, pharmacist, or agent the appropriate credentials and a written notice of inspection authority.
2. A search warrant is not required.
3. The Board may inspect and copy documents; inspect a facility's storage, equipment, security, prescription drugs or devices, components used in compounding, finished and unfinished products, and records; and may perform an inventory and take samples of products.
4. The Board may inspect financial records only in relation to a specific complaint. Any financial data, sales data, or pricing data obtained by the Board during an inspection or investigation is confidential and not subject to the Texas Open Records Act.

STUDY TIP: DEA does not have the authority to inspect financial, sales, or pricing records unless the pharmacy consents to the inspection.

---

5. As a result of a compliance inspection, an agent of the Board may issue a written warning notice listing specific violations and providing a reasonable amount of time to comply with the laws and rules. TSBP considers a reasonable time to be no fewer than 10 days unless there is an imminent danger to the public health and safety.
6. A compliance officer may recommend the institution of disciplinary action against a licensee if he or she determines that:
   - **a.** Previously cited violations are continuing to occur; or
   - **b.** Violations observed are of a nature that a written warning notice would not be in the best interest of the public.

II. Grounds for Discipline

A. Applicant for or Holder of a Pharmacist License (TPA Section 565.001)

1. Violation of the TPA or any TSBP rule.
2. Unprofessional Conduct. *See TSBP Rule 281.7(a) or TFPDL pages F.9–11 for complete list.*
    - **a.** Dispensing fraudulent prescriptions or prescriptions based on orders not issued for a legitimate medical purpose.
    - **b.** Delivering or offering to deliver a prescription drug in violation of law.
    - **c.** Sharing or offering to share with a practitioner compensation received from an individual who was provided pharmacy services by a pharmacist.
    - **d.** Refusing an inspection.
    - **e.** Engaging in conduct that subverts or attempts to subvert any examination (NAPLEX, MPJE) required for a license to practice pharmacy.
    - **f.** Failing to practice pharmacy in an acceptable manner consistent with the public health and welfare.
    - **g.** Obstructing a Board employee in the lawful performance of his or her duties.
    - **h.** Demonstrating abusive, intimidating, or threatening behavior toward a Board member or employee during the performance of such person's lawful duties.
    - **i.** Failing to maintain effective controls to prevent the diversion or loss of controlled substances or dangerous drugs.
    - **j.** Dispensing a prescription drug while not acting in the usual course of professional pharmacy practice.
    - **k.** Failing to correct the issues identified in a warning notice by the specified time.
3. Gross Immorality (TSBP Rule 281.7(b) or TFPDL page F.12).
    - **a.** Demonstrating conduct which is willful, flagrant, and shameless and which shows moral indifference to community standards.
    - **b.** Engaging in an act which is a felony.
    - **c.** Engaging in an act that constitutes sexually deviant behavior.
    - **d.** Being required to register as a sex offender.
4. Incapacity.

STUDY TIP: Incapacity means that the practicing pharmacist has a mental or physical condition that may cause harm to the public if he or she continues to practice.

5. Fraud, Deceit, or Misrepresentation (TSBP Rule 281.7(c) or TFPDL page F.12).

STUDY TIP: One of the most common violations of this rule involves providing inaccurate information on an application for a license or renewal of a license.

6. Convicted or placed on deferred adjudication community supervision or deferred disposition or the applicable federal equivalent for a misdemeanor involving moral turpitude or a misdemeanor under the Texas Dangerous Drug Act, Texas or Federal Controlled Substances Act, or any felony.
7. Used alcohol or drugs in an intemperate manner.
8. Failed to keep and maintain records.
9. Violated the Controlled Substances Act or rules and Dangerous Drug Act or rules.
10. Aided or abetted an unlicensed individual to practice pharmacy.
11. Refused entry into a pharmacy for an authorized inspection.
12. Violated pharmacy or drug laws of this state or any other state.
13. Been negligent in the practice of pharmacy.
14. Failed to submit to a mental or physical exam as required.
15. Dispensed prescription drugs outside the usual course of professional practice.
16. Been disciplined by the regulatory board of another state.
17. Violated a disciplinary order including a confidential order or contract under the program to aid impaired pharmacists and pharmacy students.
18. Failed to adequately supervise a task delegated to a pharmacy technician.
19. Inappropriately delegated a task to a pharmacy technician.
20. Been responsible for a drug audit shortage.
21. Been convicted or adjudicated of a criminal offense that requires registration as a sex offender.

B. Grounds for Discipline of Pharmacy Technicians and Pharmacy Technician Trainees (TSBP Rule 281.9 or TFPDL pages F.16–17)

1. The grounds for discipline of pharmacy technicians are substantially similar to the grounds for discipline of pharmacists.

2. An additional ground for discipline of pharmacy technicians is performing duties that only a pharmacist may perform.

C. Grounds for Discipline of an Applicant for or Holder of a Pharmacy License *See TPA Section 565.002 or TFPDL pages F.13–15 for complete list.*

1. Been convicted of or placed on deferred adjudication for a misdemeanor involving moral turpitude or a violation of the FCSA or any felony.
2. Advertised prescription drugs or devices in a deceitful, misleading, or fraudulent manner.
3. Sold prescription drugs without legal authorization.
4. Allowed an employee who is not a pharmacist to practice pharmacy.
5. Sold an adulterated or misbranded drug.
6. Failed to engage in the business described in the application for license within 6 months of the date of issuance of the license.
7. Ceased to engage in the business described in the application for a license for a period of 30 days or longer. Upon discovery that a pharmacy has ceased to operate for 30 days, the Board must notify the pharmacy that the pharmacy license will be revoked. *See TPA Section 565.0591 or TFPDL pages F.24–25.*

D. Grounds for Discipline of a Pharmacy License *See TSBP Rule 281.8 or TFPDL page F.15–16 for a complete list.*

1. Failed to establish and maintain adequate controls to prevent diversion of prescription drugs.
2. Employed a pharmacist, intern, or pharmacy technician whose license has been revoked, cancelled, retired, surrendered, denied, or suspended.
3. Possessed or engaged in the sale of prescription drug samples.
4. Waived, discounted, or reduced a patient copay or deductible for a compounded drug in the absence of a legitimate documented financial hardship of the patient or evidence of a good faith effort to collect the copayment or deductible from the patient.

III. Penalties and Procedures (Applies to pharmacists, pharmacy technicians, pharmacy technician trainees, and pharmacies) *See TFPDL pages F.20–39.*

A. Penalties (Discipline authorized)

1. Reprimand—Public and formal censure of license.

2. Restriction—Limit, confine, or restrain a license with certain terms or conditions.
3. Suspension—License not in effect for a specified amount of time.
4. Probation—Placing a license under a period of supervision by the Board for a term and under conditions as determined by the Board, including a probation fee.
5. Refuse to issue or renew a license.
6. Revocation—License is void and no longer in effect.
7. Retire—License is withdrawn and no longer in effect.
8. Administrative Penalty—A fine; may be included with other sanctions above.
    a. Cannot exceed $5,000 per violation, but every day a violation occurs is a separate violation.
    b. Civil penalties for license violations and unlawful practice can be as much as $1,000 per day.

B. Rules of Procedure (How TSBP initiates formal disciplinary action against a licensee)
1. Preliminary Notice Letter.
    a. When TSBP initiates disciplinary action against an applicant or licensee, it sends a Preliminary Notice Letter.
    b. If a Preliminary Notice Letter is ignored, it could result in a default judgment against the license.
    c. The Preliminary Notice Letter will offer an opportunity for the licensee/registrant to attend a non-public, informal conference.
    d. Most cases are voluntarily settled through the informal conference as described in 2. below. If a settlement cannot be reached through an informal process or if the licensee chooses not to go through the informal process, a formal conference is held as described in 3. below.
2. Informal Conference (Non-public).
    a. This is a voluntary settlement conference where the licensee or applicant and/or his or her attorney meet with a TSBP panel consisting of one Board member, the Executive Director, and the Director of Enforcement.
    b. TSBP is represented at the informal conference by the Board's general counsel.
    c. The Board's attorney presents the allegations from the Preliminary Notice Letter, and the licensee and/or his

or her attorney are given an opportunity to show compliance with the law. If compliance with the law can be demonstrated, the charges are dismissed.

   d. If the charges are not dismissed, the Board panel then deliberates and makes a recommendation to resolve the case by proposing an Agreed Board Order (ABO).
   e. The licensee can accept or reject the ABO. If it is accepted, it is presented to the full Board for approval. If it is rejected, the matter goes through the formal disciplinary process.
   f. Once an ABO has been approved, it cannot be appealed.
3. Formal Conference (Public hearing).
   a. A hearing (like a trial) is conducted in front of an Administrative Law Judge (ALJ).
   b. The ALJ issues findings of facts and conclusions of law and recommends sanctions to the Board in a Board Order (BO).
   c. The Board accepts, denies, or modifies the Board Order.
   d. A Board Order can be appealed to a Texas district court, but a motion for a rehearing must first be filed with TSBP.
4. Reissuance or Removal of Restriction on License. Before requesting the reissuing of a license that has been revoked or removing a restriction that has been placed on a license, the licensee must wait a minimum of 12 months.
5. Other Disciplinary Issues.
   a. Subpoena authority—The Board may issue subpoenas to compel attendance of witnesses or to compel the production of documents or records.
   b. Temporary suspension—A 3-member disciplinary panel appointed by the Board president may temporarily suspend or restrict a license if continued practice or operation of a pharmacy would constitute a continuing threat to the public welfare. A temporary suspension can take place immediately without notice if a hearing is scheduled no later than 14 days after the suspension or restriction.
   c. Remedial plan—The Board may enter into a remedial plan to resolve a complaint unless the complaint involves a death, hospitalization, commission of a felony, unlicensed practice, audit shortages, diversion of controlled

substances, impairment, unauthorized dispensing, gross immorality, fraud, deceit, misrepresentation, or disciplinary action by a board of pharmacy in another state. Remedial plans are not considered formal disciplinary action but are public documents. Remedial plans are removed from a licensee's record after 5 years.

d. Alternative dispute resolution—The Board and a licensee can agree to mediate a disciplinary case through this process following an informal conference (when an agreement could not be reached) and before a formal disciplinary hearing is conducted.

e. Mental or physical exam—The Board may request or require an applicant, licensee, or registrant to submit to a mental or physical exam upon a finding of probable cause that identifies a mental or physical incapacity that would prevent him or her from practicing with a level of skill and competence that ensures the public health, safety, and welfare.

f. Automatic denial or revocation—The Board shall deny an application for licensure as a pharmacist or immediately revoke a pharmacist license of a person who is required to register as a sex offender or who has been previously convicted of or placed on adjudication involving the use or threat of force; or has been previously convicted or placed on deferred adjudication community supervision of an offense committed while a licensed pharmacist in the course of providing services to a person who was a patient of the applicant or pharmacist. *See TSBP Rule 281.69 or TFPDL pages F.38–39.*

CHAPTER SIX

Class A (Community) Pharmacy Rules

CHAPTER SIX

Class A (Community) Pharmacy Rules

Note: All Class A pharmacies that compound sterile products must have a Class A-S license. This provides the Board the ability to identify which pharmacies are engaged in this activity. In addition to the sterile compounding rules, Class A-S pharmacies must also follow all rules for Class A pharmacies.

I. Personnel

A. Pharmacist-in-Charge (PIC)

1. Each Class A pharmacy shall have one PIC who is employed full time.
2. Generally, the PIC may only be a PIC of one Class A pharmacy unless the additional Class A is not open at the same time. During an emergency, the PIC may serve as the PIC for 2 Class A pharmacies open at the same time if he or she works at least 10 hours per week in each pharmacy for no more than 30 consecutive days.
3. Responsibilities of PIC.
   - **a.** The legal operation of the pharmacy.
   - **b.** Educating and training pharmacy technicians.

   See TSBP Rule 291.32 or TFPDL pages G.5–6 for complete list.

B. Owner

1. Has responsibility for all administrative and operational functions of the pharmacy.
2. If not a pharmacist, must consult with the PIC or another pharmacist for establishing policies and procedures.

C. Pharmacists

1. Responsible for supervising pharmacy technicians and pharmacy technician trainees. Supervision may be done electronically if the pharmacist has the ability to immediately communicate directly with the pharmacy technician or pharmacy technician trainee and other conditions are met. *See TSBP Rule 291.32 or TFPDL pages G.6–8.*
2. The dispensing pharmacist (defined as the pharmacist who performs the final check) is responsible for ensuring that drugs are dispensed safely and accurately as prescribed unless the pharmacy's computer system can identify each pharmacist involved in different steps of the dispensing

process such as drug regimen review, verification of data entry, labeling, etc.

3. Duties which may be performed only by a pharmacist:
   a. Receiving verbal prescription drug orders for controlled substances and reducing these orders to writing.

STUDY TIP: Only a pharmacist may receive verbal prescription drug orders for controlled substances. Pharmacy technicians may receive verbal prescription drug orders for dangerous drugs.

---

   b. Interpreting prescription drug orders.
   c. Selecting drug products (this is referring to generic drug product selection).
   d. Performing the final check of a dispensed prescription.
   e. Patient counseling.
   f. Assuring that a reasonable effort is made to obtain, record, and maintain patient medication records.
   g. Interpreting patient medication records and performing drug regimen reviews.
   h. Performing drug therapy management under protocol.
   i. Verifying that controlled substances listed on invoices are received by initialing and dating invoices.
   j. Transferring or receiving a transfer of a controlled substance prescription.
   k. Administering immunizations.
   Note: Under the federal Public Readiness and Emergency Preparedness (PREP) Act, pharmacy technicians with appropriate training were given authority to administer COVID-19 vaccinations irrespective of state laws and regulations. This authority was extended to flu vaccines to adults 19 years of age or older in 2021. These authorities under the PREP act are temporary unless state law is changed. Despite some bills being introduced in 2021, Texas law was not amended to make these permanent. It is unlikely that the MPJE would include questions based on temporary rules.

STUDY TIP: Be sure to know the duties that only a pharmacist (and an intern supervised by a preceptor) can perform. These are the duties a pharmacy technician or pharmacy technician trainee cannot perform.

D. Pharmacy Technicians and Pharmacy Technician Trainees

1. Individuals working in pharmacies whose responsibilities are to provide nonjudgmental, technical services associated with the dispensing of a prescription drug order.
2. Duties may include:
    - **a.** Initiating and receiving refill authorization requests.
    - **b.** Initiating electronic transfer requests between pharmacies sharing a common database.
    - **c.** Entering prescription data into a computer system.
    - **d.** Taking a stock bottle from the shelf for a prescription.
    - **e.** Preparing and packaging prescription drug orders.
    - **f.** Affixing prescription labels and auxiliary labels to a prescription.
    - **g.** Reconstituting medications.
    - **h.** Loading bulk drugs into an automated counting or dispensing device provided a pharmacist verifies that the device is properly loaded prior to use.
    - **i.** Loading prepackaged containers previously verified by a pharmacist or manufacturer's unit-of-use packages into an automated dispensing machine.
    - **j.** Bulk compounding.
    - **k.** Compounding nonsterile prescription drug orders after appropriate training.
    - **l.** In a Class A-S pharmacy, compounding sterile preparations after appropriate training.
    - **m.** Receiving oral prescription drug orders for dangerous drugs and reducing these orders to writing either manually or electronically.
    - **n.** Transferring or receiving a transfer of original prescription information for a dangerous drug on behalf of a patient.
    - **o.** Contacting a prescriber for information regarding an existing prescription.

    Note: The duties in m., n., and o. above were added in rules adopted in late 2020.

STUDY TIP: In a Class A pharmacy there are no differences between the duties of a pharmacy technician and a pharmacy technician trainee.

---

3. Ratio—The ratio of onsite pharmacists to pharmacy technicians and pharmacy technician trainees in a Class A

pharmacy may be 1:6 as long as the maximum number of pharmacy technician trainees is 3.

II. Operational Standards

A. Environment

1. Orderly and clean.
2. Sink with hot and cold running water, exclusive of restrooms.
3. If serving the public, a patient counseling area shall be designed to maintain confidentiality.
4. Appropriate lighting and temperature.
5. No animals allowed.
6. Designated area for flammable materials.

B. Security (Only applies to pharmacies that possess drugs)

1. Prescription department must be locked by key, combination, or other mechanical or electronic means to prohibit unauthorized access.
2. The pharmacy's key, combination, or means of locking the pharmacy may not be duplicated.
3. At minimum, the pharmacy must have a basic alarm system with off-site monitoring and motion detectors.
4. The PIC or owner may authorize individuals to enter the prescription department to perform functions other than dispensing. However, the PIC or owner must maintain written documentation of authorized individuals other than individuals employed by the pharmacy who access the prescription department when a pharmacist is not on site.
5. The pharmacy must have written policies and procedures for security.

C. Temporary Absence of a Pharmacist

Note: This rule applies when there is only one pharmacist on duty in the pharmacy.

1. Pharmacist is On-Site (for breaks and meals without closing prescription department) (TSBP Rule 291.33(b)(3)(A) or TFPDL pages G.14–15).
   - **a.** At least one pharmacy technician (not a trainee) remains in the pharmacy.
   - **b.** Pharmacist must remain on the premises of the facility.
   - **c.** A notice must be posted that the pharmacist is on break.
   - **d.** During a break, pharmacy technicians may begin processing prescription drug orders or refills, but those

orders may not be delivered until the pharmacist returns and verifies the accuracy of the prescription. Upon return, the pharmacist must conduct a drug regimen review and verify all activities performed by the technician. Any pharmacist intern on duty may only act as a pharmacy technician while the pharmacist is absent.

e. Patients may pick up prescriptions that have already been filled and checked by the pharmacist.

STUDY TIP: This section causes much confusion. How can a patient pick up a new prescription where counseling is required if the pharmacist is on break? The rules allow you to treat that prescription the same way you would treat a new prescription that is delivered to the patient at his or her home. Counseling is provided by giving written information about the drug and a notice that the patient can call the pharmacist if the patient has any questions.

---

2. Pharmacist is Off-Site (prescription department is closed) (TSBP Rule 291.33(b)(3)(B) or TFPDL pages G.15–16).

a. If the pharmacist leaves the premises of the facility, the prescription department must be closed, and pharmacy technicians may not remain in the pharmacy. However, this rule allows delivery of filled prescriptions under certain conditions after the pharmacy department has closed (as follows in b.).

b. During short periods of time when a pharmacist is absent from the pharmacy, an agent of the pharmacist may deliver a previously verified prescription (new or refill) to a patient in the pharmacy provided the short periods of time do not exceed 2 consecutive hours in a 24-hour period.

STUDY TIP: This is a rule very unique to Texas and allows filled prescriptions to be delivered to patients in the pharmacy for up to 2 hours after the pharmacy department is closed. It may be useful in locations such as grocery stores or other locations where the prescription department is closed but the rest of the store remains open.

---

c. The pharmacy must maintain a record of the date of delivery, prescription number, patient's name and phone number, and signature of person picking up the prescription.

d. The pharmacy must also meet the same requirements of a prescription delivered to a patient at the patient's residence.

e. The pharmacy may also use an automated dispensing and delivery device to deliver prescriptions. This is not restricted to the 2-hour limitation in b. above. *See Summary of TSBP Rule 291.121(d) in Chapter Four in this book.*

D. Patient Counseling and Drug Regimen Review

1. Patient Counseling.

a. Mandatory patient counseling is required for new prescription drug orders.
Note: New prescription drug orders include prescriptions that have not been dispensed to the patient by the pharmacy in the same strength and dosage form within the past year.

b. Information must be provided which, in the pharmacist's professional judgment, the pharmacist deems significant.

c. Verbal and written information must be provided. Written information may be electronic (including email) if the patient has requested electronic communication and this request is documented.

d. The pharmacy must document initials or identification code of the pharmacist providing counseling either on the prescription or in the computer system.

e. If the prescription is delivered to the patient, the pharmacy must provide the following statement in English and Spanish: "Written information about this prescription has been provided for you. Please read this information before you take the medication. If you have any questions concerning this prescription, a pharmacist is available during normal business hours to answer those questions at (insert phone number)."

f. Only a pharmacist may verbally provide drug information to a patient and answer questions concerning prescription drugs. Non-pharmacist personnel and/or the pharmacy's computer system may not ask questions of a patient which are intended to screen or limit interaction with the pharmacist.

STUDY TIP: While a patient may refuse counseling, there is no such thing as an "offer to counsel" in Texas. Counseling is required for all new prescription drug orders. Any refusal of counseling by a patient or patient's agent must be documented.

2. Drug Regimen Review.
   a. Required for all prescriptions (new and refill).
   b. At a minimum, the pharmacist shall review and identify clinically significant:
      (1) Known allergies.
      (2) Rational therapy-contraindications.
      (3) Reasonable dose and route of administration.
      (4) Reasonable directions for use.
      (5) Duplication of therapy.
      (6) Drug-drug interactions.
      (7) Drug-food interactions.
      (8) Drug-disease interactions.
      (9) Adverse drug reactions.
      (10) Proper utilization including overutilization and underutilization.

E. Labeling Requirements for Dispensed Prescriptions

1. Name, address, and phone number of the pharmacy.
2. Prescription number (easily readable font no smaller than 10-point Times Roman).
3. Date dispensed.
4. Initials or identification code of the dispensing pharmacist (not required if maintained in the computer system).
5. Name of prescriber.
6. Name of pharmacist signing a prescription drug order (if applicable).
7. Name of patient. If for an animal, the species of the animal and name of owner.
8. Instructions for use (easily readable font no smaller than 10-point Times Roman).
9. Quantity dispensed.
10. Appropriate ancillary instructions.
11. If for a Schedule II–IV drug, the federal transfer statement "Caution: Federal law prohibits the transfer of this drug to any person other than the patient for whom it was prescribed."

STUDY TIP: The federal transfer caution is not required for Schedule V drugs or dangerous drugs even though many pharmacies comply by preprinting it on every label.

12. "Substituted for Brand Prescribed" or "Substituted for 'Brand Name'" if generic substitution has occurred.
13. Name and strength of drug dispensed unless otherwise directed by prescriber (easily readable font no smaller than 10-point Times Roman).
14. A beyond-use date that is not greater than one year from the date dispensed or the manufacturer's expiration date, whichever is shorter.
15. Either the prescription label or the written information accompanying the prescription shall contain the statement "Do not flush unused medications or pour down a sink or drain." A drug product on a list of medicines developed by the Federal Food and Drug Administration recommended for disposal by flushing is not required to bear this statement.

Note: The labeling requirements 1–15 above are not required to be met if the drug is for administration to an ultimate user who is institutionalized (hospital or nursing home patient) and no more than a 90-day supply is dispensed at one time. See TSBP Rule 291.33(c)(7)(D) or TFPDL pages G.22–23.

STUDY TIP: Although pharmacists rely on their computer system to print prescription labels, it is important to know the required elements on a label.

F. Notification on Safe Disposal of Schedule II Controlled Substances

1. Unless exempted by 4. or 5. below, a pharmacy that dispenses a Schedule II controlled substance prescription must provide the patient a notification on the safe disposal of controlled substances that includes information on locations at which Schedule II controlled substances are accepted for safe disposal.
2. In lieu of listing those locations, the notice may alternatively provide an address of an internet website specified by the Board that provides a searchable database of locations at which Schedule II controlled substances are accepted for safe disposal.
3. The written notice may be provided to the patient in an electronic format (such as by email) if the patient or patient's

agent requests the notice in an electronic format and the request is documented.

4. A pharmacy that is registered with DEA as an "authorized collector" of controlled substances and regularly accepts controlled substances for safe disposal does not have to provide the notice above.
5. A pharmacy that provides to the patient at the time of dispensing and at no cost to the patient either a mail-in pouch for surrendering unused controlled substances or chemicals to render any unused controlled substances unusable or non-retrievable does not have to provide the notice above.

G. Returning Undelivered Medication to Stock

1. Prescriptions that have not been picked up or delivered may be returned to the pharmacy's stock for dispensing.
2. Pharmacist must evaluate quality and safety of the returned prescriptions.
3. Returned prescriptions cannot be mixed in with manufacturer's containers and must be placed in a new container when dispensed unless the prescription is in the manufacturer's original container and the label from the undelivered prescription information is removed to prevent disclosure of patient information.

H. Equipment and Supplies

1. Data processing system (computer) including a printer.
2. Refrigerator.
3. Child-resistant, light-resistant, tight, and, if applicable, glass containers.
4. Prescription, poison, and other applicable labels.
5. Metric/apothecary weight and measure conversion charts.
6. Class A prescription balance if the pharmacy compounds prescription drug orders.

I. Library (May be hard copy or electronic)

1. Laws and Rules—Texas Pharmacy Act and rules, Texas Dangerous Drug Act and rules, Texas Controlled Substances Act and rules, and Federal Controlled Substances Act and rules.
2. At least one current general drug information reference which includes drug interaction information.
3. If the pharmacy dispenses veterinary prescriptions, a general reference on veterinary drugs.
4. Basic antidote information and phone number of the nearest regional poison control center.

J. Customized Patient Medication Packages (Med Paks)

1. A pharmacist may, with consent of the patient or the prescriber, provide a customized patient med pak, which is a container holding 2 or more prescribed solid oral dosage forms. The med pak container is designed so that each drug is labeled with the day and/or time each drug is to be taken.

2. Must have a prescription number for the med pak and a separate prescription number for each of the drugs within.

3. Must have a beyond-use date not exceeding one year from the date dispensed or the earliest manufacturer's expiration date for a drug in the med pak.

K. Automated Devices and Systems in a Class A Pharmacy—There are 3 types of automated devices and systems.

1. Automated Counting Devices.

a. Must be calibrated and verified on a routine basis.

b. Records of loading the device must be maintained.

c. Pharmacist must verify and sign that the system is properly loaded prior to use.

2. Automated Pharmacy Dispensing Systems.

a. System must have been tested and found to dispense accurately.

b. Must operate according to a written quality assurance program which requires continuous monitoring and tests accuracy at least every 12 months or when an upgrade or change is made to the system.

c. Must operate under written policies and procedures.

d. Must have a recovery plan for disasters or other interruptions.

e. System may be stocked or loaded by a pharmacist or a pharmacy technician or trainee under the supervision of a pharmacist.

f. Final check may be accomplished by:

(1) A pharmacist checking the final product after the automated system has completed the prescription and prior to delivery to the patient; or

(2) A pharmacist verifying that any bulk stock drugs have been accurately stocked and the pharmacist checks the accuracy of the data entry of each prescription entered into the system.
Note: With this method, the "final check" is being done prior to the prescription being processed.

Because this method does not require a pharmacist to check the bottle or the label at the end of the process, it requires that the system be fully automated from the time the pharmacist releases the prescription to the system until a completed, labeled prescription ready for delivery is produced. If this method is used, the system must be tested for accuracy monthly rather than every 12 months.

3. Automated Checking Device—A fully automated device which confirms, after dispensing but prior to delivery to the patient, that the correct drug and drug strength have been labeled with the correct label for the correct patient.

STUDY TIP: An automated checking device and automated pharmacy dispensing system both can be used to complete the final check of a prescription. However, in an automated pharmacy dispensing system, the system is actually filling the prescription while checking for accuracy. With an automated checking device, prescriptions are checked for accuracy after dispensing using technology such as barcoding.

III. Records

A. General Rules

1. All records shall be maintained for 2 years.
2. Schedule II records shall be maintained separately from other records.
3. Schedule III–V records, other than prescriptions, shall be maintained separately or be "readily retrievable" from other records. "Readily retrievable" means that the controlled substance records are asterisked, redlined, or in some other manner readily identifiable from other items in the record. *Note: Although Texas law allows imaging of original records for Schedule II–V controlled substances, DEA requires the hardcopy original records be kept for 2 years.*

B. Patient Medication Records (Required for all new patients)

1. Must provide for the immediate retrieval of information for the previous 12 months to conduct a drug regimen review.
2. PIC must assure that a reasonable effort is made to obtain and record at least the following information:
   - **a.** Name, address, and telephone number of patient.
   - **b.** Age and gender of patient.

c. Known allergies, drug reactions, idiosyncrasies, and chronic conditions or disease states.
d. Other drugs currently being used by the patient.
e. Pharmacist's comments relevant to drug therapy.
f. A list of all prescription drug orders dispensed (new and refill) to the patient by the pharmacy during the last 2 years.

C. Computer System
1. System must be backed up at least monthly.
2. Must maintain any information (records) purged from computer for 2 years from the date of final entry of data.
3. Must have capacity to produce a daily hardcopy printout consisting of:
   a. Prescription number.
   b. Date of dispensing.
   c. Patient name.
   d. Prescriber's name.
   e. Name and strength of the drug dispensed.
   f. Quantity dispensed.
   g. Initials or identification code of the dispensing pharmacist.
   h. Initials or identification code of pharmacy technician performing data entry, if applicable.
   i. If not immediately retrievable by computer display, must also include patient's address, prescriber's address, prescriber's DEA number if a controlled substance, quantity dispensed if different from quantity prescribed, date of issuance of prescription (if different from date of dispensing), and total refills dispensed to date.
   j. Any changes made to a record of dispensing.
4. Daily hardcopy printout shall be produced within 72 hours of the date the prescriptions were dispensed.
5. Each pharmacist who dispensed or refilled a prescription shall verify that the information is correct by signing and dating the hardcopy printout within 7 days from the date of dispensing.
6. Pharmacy may maintain a daily logbook that pharmacists must sign daily instead of the daily hardcopy printout in 3. above, but the computer system must be able to produce an "audit trail" consisting of 3.(a.-j.) above within 72 hours.
7. Each time a modification, change, or manipulation is made to a record of dispensing, documentation of such change

shall be recorded in the computer system. The documentation of any modification, change, or manipulation to a record of dispensing shall include the identification of the individual responsible for the alteration.

8. Pharmacies must maintain a log of the unique initials or identification codes which will identify each pharmacist, pharmacy technician, and pharmacy technician trainee who is involved in the dispensing process in the pharmacy's data processing system. The initials or identification code shall be unique to ensure that each individual can be identified (i.e., identical initials or identification code shall not be used). This log shall be maintained at the pharmacy for at least 7 years from the date of the transaction.

STUDY TIP: This is the only TSBP rule that requires a record be kept for 7 years.

D. Transfer of Prescription Drug Order Information

1. Transfers may be communicated verbally or via fax.
   Note: Pharmacy technicians cannot perform transfers of controlled substance prescriptions.
2. Transfers may also be conducted electronically as long as specific requirements are met.
3. Transfers of controlled substance prescriptions are allowed only one time unless the pharmacies share an electronic, real-time database.
4. DEA and TSBP rules do not generally permit a pharmacy to transfer a controlled substance prescription that has been received at a pharmacy but not yet filled at another pharmacy.
   Note: By policy DEA and TSBP allow a controlled substance prescription to be transferred or forwarded to another pharmacy if the original prescription was transmitted electronically and it can be forwarded electronically.
5. The prescription that is transferred must be voided in the computer system (or by writing "void" across the prescription if using a manual recordkeeping system).
6. An individual may not refuse to transfer a prescription, and transfers must be completed within 4 business hours of a request.
7. The electronic transfer of multiple or bulk prescription transfers is permitted.

CHAPTER SEVEN

Other Classes of Pharmacies

CHAPTER SEVEN
Other Classes of Pharmacies

I. Class C (Institutional) Pharmacy Rules

A. Personnel

1. Requirements for Pharmacist Services.

a. A facility with 101 beds or more shall be under the continuous on-site supervision of a pharmacist when the pharmacy department is open for services.

b. A facility with 100 beds or fewer shall have the services of a pharmacist at least part time or on a consulting basis, but the pharmacist must be on-site at least once every 7 days.

c. If an institution operates an outpatient pharmacy, there must be a pharmacist on-site when the outpatient pharmacy is open. The outpatient pharmacy must also meet all Class A rules, including the pharmacy technician to pharmacist ratio.

2. Pharmacist-in-Charge (PIC).

a. A pharmacist must be accessible in all Class C pharmacies at all times although this may be provided through a telephone service that is answered 24 hours a day, a paging service, or a list of phone numbers where a pharmacist may be reached.

b. Facilities with 101 beds or more must have one full-time PIC who can only be PIC for one such facility. This PIC may not serve as a PIC for a Class A or B pharmacy.

c. Facilities with 100 beds or fewer must have a PIC who may be employed or under contract as a consultant and may be part time. One pharmacist may be PIC of no more than 3 such facilities or 150 beds. A pharmacist may be the PIC of one facility with 101 beds or more and one facility with 100 beds or fewer as long as the total number of beds does not exceed 150.

d. PIC responsibilities.

(1) Assuring the legal operation of the pharmacy.

(2) Providing appropriate level of pharmaceutical care services.

(3) Ensuring drugs and/or devices are prepared and distributed safely and accurately as prescribed.
(4) Participating in development of a formulary for the facility.
(5) Supervising a system to ensure maintenance of effective controls against prescription drug diversion. *See complete list in TSBP Rule 291.73(b)(2) or TFPDL pages I.5–6.*

3. Pharmacists.
   a. Responsible for delegated acts performed by pharmacy technicians and pharmacy technician trainees.
   b. The distributing pharmacist (defined as the pharmacist who checks the medication prior to distribution) is responsible for ensuring that the drug is prepared for distribution safely and accurately as prescribed, unless the pharmacy's computer system can record and identify each pharmacist involved in the preparation process. This includes drug regimen review, verification of data entry, preparation, distribution, and labeling.
4. Pharmacy Technicians.
   a. In facilities with 101 beds or more, the following duties may be performed under physically present pharmacist supervision:
      (1) Prepackaging and labeling unit-dose and multiple-dose packages.
      (2) Preparing, packaging, compounding, or labeling prescription drugs pursuant to medication orders.
      (3) Compounding nonsterile pharmaceuticals after appropriate training.
      (4) Compounding sterile pharmaceuticals after appropriate training (Class C-S only).
      (5) Bulk compounding or batch preparation.
      (6) Distributing routine orders for stock supplies to patient care areas.
      (7) Entering medication orders and drug distribution information into a computer system.
      (8) Loading unlabeled drugs into an automated compounding or counting device.
      (9) Accessing automated medication supply systems.

b. In facilities with 100 beds or fewer, the following duties may be performed under physically present pharmacist supervision:
   (1) Prepackaging and labeling unit-dose and multiple-dose packages.
   (2) Bulk compounding or batch preparation.
   (3) Loading unlabeled drugs into an automated compounding or drug dispensing system.
   (4) Compounding medium-risk and high-risk sterile preparations after appropriate training (Class C-S only).

c. In facilities with 100 beds or fewer, the following duties must be performed under the physically present or electronic supervision of a pharmacist:
   (1) Preparing, packaging, compounding, or labeling prescription drugs pursuant to medication orders.
   (2) Distributing routine orders for stock supplies to patient care areas.
   (3) Entering medication orders and drug distribution information into a computer system.
   (4) Accessing automated supply systems.
   (5) Compounding nonsterile preparations.
   (6) Compounding low-risk sterile preparations after appropriate training (Class C-S only).

d. Ratio—There is no ratio of pharmacists to pharmacy technicians in a Class C pharmacy.

e. Special rules apply to rural hospitals. *See B. below.*

f. Tech-check-tech—A Class C pharmacy that has an ongoing clinical pharmacy program may allow a pharmacy technician (not a pharmacy technician trainee) to verify the work of another pharmacy technician (not a pharmacy technician trainee) relating to the filling of floor stock and unit-dose distribution systems if the patient's orders have been previously reviewed by a pharmacist. *See TPA Section 568.008 or TFPDL pages I.9–10.*

B. Rural Hospitals (75 beds or fewer and located in a county with a population fewer than 50,000 or designated as a critical access hospital, rural referral center, or sole community hospital)

1. If a practitioner orders a prescription drug or device for a patient in a rural hospital when the pharmacist is not on

duty or when the pharmacy is closed, a nurse or practitioner may withdraw the drug from the pharmacy in sufficient quantity to fulfill the order.

2. The hospital pharmacist must verify the withdrawal and perform a drug regimen review no later than 7 days after the withdrawal.
3. In a rural hospital when a pharmacist is not on duty, pharmacy technicians, but not pharmacy technician trainees, may perform the following duties without direct supervision of a pharmacist:
    a. Entering medication orders and drug distribution information into a computer system.
    b. Preparing, packaging, or labeling prescription drugs pursuant to medication orders if a licensed nurse practitioner or pharmacist verifies the accuracy by electronic supervision before administration to the patient.
    c. Filling medication carts used in the rural hospital.
    d. Distributing routine orders for stock supplies to patient care areas.
    e. Accessing and restocking automated medication supply cabinets.

    Note: A nurse or practitioner at the hospital or a pharmacist through electronic supervision must verify the accuracy of the pharmacy technician performing these duties.

C. Absence of a Pharmacist
  1. In facilities with a full-time pharmacist when the pharmacy is closed:
      a. A designated licensed nurse or practitioner may remove drugs for the patient's immediate therapeutic needs.
      b. A record of the withdrawal must be made containing:
          (1) Name of patient.
          (2) Name, strength, and dosage form of device or drug.
          (3) Dose prescribed.
          (4) Quantity taken.
          (5) Time and date taken.
          (6) Signature.
      c. A pharmacist must verify withdrawal as soon as possible but no more than 72 hours after withdrawal.

2. In facilities with a part-time or consultant pharmacist when the pharmacy is closed:
    a. A designated licensed nurse or practitioner may remove drugs and devices for the patient's immediate therapeutic needs.
    b. A pharmacist shall verify the withdrawal of the drugs from the pharmacy after a reasonable interval but in no event may the interval exceed 7 days.
    c. The pharmacist shall perform a drug regimen review within 96 hours if the facility has an average daily census above 10 and within 7 days if the facility has an average daily census of 10 or fewer.
    d. If using a floor stock system of distribution, the same rules apply, and the pharmacist must verify withdrawal no later than 7 days after withdrawal.

D. Library Requirements (Either electronic or hard copy)
1. Current copies of Texas Pharmacy Act and rules, Texas Dangerous Drug Act and rules, Texas Controlled Substances Act and rules, and Federal Controlled Substances Act and rules.
2. Drug interaction reference.
3. General drug information reference.
4. Injectable drug products reference.
5. Basic antidote information and phone number of the nearest regional poison control center.
6. Metric/apothecary weight and measure conversion chart.

E. Operational Standards
1. Formulary is required.
2. Prepackaging of drugs is allowed for distribution within the facility or for distribution to other Class C pharmacies under common ownership. Specific recordkeeping requirements must be met.
3. Written policies and procedures of a drug distribution system are required. *See TSBP Rule 291.74(f)(5)(B) or TFPDL pages I.19–20 for detailed requirements.*
4. Drug regimen review must be conducted on a prospective basis when a pharmacist is on duty and on a retrospective basis when a pharmacist is not on duty. The retrospective review must be conducted within 72 hours if the hospital has a full-time pharmacist. If the hospital has a part-time pharmacist, the drug regimen review must be conducted within 96 hours if the facility has an average daily census above 10

and within 7 days if the facility has an average daily census of 10 or fewer.

5. Floor stock records must be reviewed by a pharmacist at least every 30 days.
6. A perpetual inventory of Schedule II controlled substances is required.

F. Emergency Rooms

1. When a pharmacist is on duty in the facility, any drugs dispensed for outpatient use, including to emergency room patients, must be dispensed by a pharmacist.
2. When a pharmacist is not on duty, dangerous drugs and controlled substances may be supplied to patients admitted to the emergency room under the following conditions:
   - **a.** Only drugs on an emergency room drug list may be provided.
   - **b.** Drugs are supplied in prepackaged quantities not to exceed a 72-hour supply.
   - **c.** Drugs are prepackaged by the pharmacy department, and at time of delivery the label is completed by the practitioner or nurse with:
     - **(1)** Name, address, and telephone number of the facility.
     - **(2)** Date supplied.
     - **(3)** Name of practitioner.
     - **(4)** Name of patient.
     - **(5)** Directions for use.
     - **(6)** Unique identification number (prescription number).
     - **(7)** Brand name or generic name and strength of the drug used.
     - **(8)** Quantity supplied.
   - **d.** Pharmacist shall verify the contents of the emergency room drug list records at least once every 7 days.

G. Automated Devices and Systems

1. Automated Compounding or Counting Devices.
   - **a.** Must be calibrated and tested for accuracy.
   - **b.** May be loaded by a pharmacy technician but must be verified by a pharmacist prior to use.
2. Automated Medication Supply Systems.
   - **a.** Include robotic systems and nursing unit-based storage systems such as Pyxis®.
   - **b.** Must be tested and verified for accuracy.

c. Must operate according to a written quality assurance program which requires continuous monitoring and tests accuracy at least every 6 months or when an upgrade or change is made to the system.
d. Must operate under written policies and procedures.
e. May be restocked by a pharmacy technician provided the medication has been checked by a pharmacist prior to restocking or system uses machine-readable product identifiers such as barcodes.
f. Pharmacy must have a written plan for recovery from a disaster or other situation that disrupts the automated system.

H. Records
1. All records must be maintained for 2 years and must be supplied within 72 hours upon request.
2. Schedule II records must be maintained separately from other records.
3. Schedule III–V records must be maintained separately or be "readily retrievable."
4. Outpatient pharmacy records must be maintained under Class A rules.
5. Patient medication records must be maintained for each patient.
6. Computer system must be able to produce a hardcopy printout of an audit trail of all drugs distributed in the facility, including specific information such as patient's name and room number or identification number; prescribing physician; drug name, strength, and dosage form; and quantity. Any audit trail requested must be provided within 72 hours.

I. Class C Pharmacies in a Freestanding Ambulatory Surgical Center (C-ASC)
1. If the facility has a full-time pharmacist, drugs withdrawn from a Class C-ASC pharmacy must be reviewed by a pharmacist within 72 hours for controlled substances and at a reasonable interval but at least once per calendar week for dangerous drugs.
2. If the facility has a part-time or consultant pharmacist, the pharmacist shall verify withdrawal of all drugs (controlled substances and dangerous drugs) at a reasonable interval, but such verification must occur at least once every calendar week the pharmacy is open.

3. Class C-ASC pharmacies must maintain a perpetual inventory of all controlled substances.
4. Invoices of dangerous drugs and controlled substances in a Class C-ASC pharmacy must be dated and initialed by the person receiving the drugs, and a pharmacist must verify that the controlled substances were entered into the perpetual inventory with his or her initials.
5. A pharmacist must conduct an audit by randomly comparing the distribution records with the medication orders at least every 30 days.
6. Postoperative drugs may only be supplied to patients admitted to the ASC from the approved drug list.
7. Drugs may only be supplied in prepackaged quantities not to exceed a 72-hour supply.

II. Class B (Nuclear) Pharmacy Rules

- **A.** Also regulated by the Texas Department of State Health Services through its Radiation Control Program (Radioactive Material License).
- **B.** Authorized Nuclear Pharmacists
  1. Must be a Board of Pharmaceutical Specialties (BPS) Certified Nuclear Pharmacist; or
  2. Must complete 700 hours of a structured education program:
     - **a.** 200 hours of didactic training approved by the TDSHS Radiation Control Program; and
     - **b.** 500 hours of supervised experience.
- **C.** Nuclear Pharmacist to Pharmacy Technician Ratio—No more than 1:6 as long as the maximum number of pharmacy technician trainees is 3.
- **D.** Policy and procedure manual is required.
- **E.** Federal Department of Transportation (DOT) regulations must be met.
- **F.** Outer Container Labeling Requirement
  1. Name, address, and phone number of the pharmacy.
  2. Date dispensed.
  3. Directions for use.
  4. Prescription number.
  5. Name of the patient if known or "for physician use" if the name of the patient is not known.
  6. Radiation symbol.

7. The words “Caution—Radioactive Material” or “Danger—Radioactive Material.”
8. The name of the radiopharmaceutical or its abbreviation.
9. Amount of radioactivity in millicuries or microcuries or bequerels and the corresponding time that applies to this activity if different from the requested calibration date and time.
10. Initials or identification code of the person preparing and the nuclear pharmacist checking the product.
11. If a liquid, volume in milliliters.
12. Requested calibration date and time.
13. Expiration date and time.

G. Inner Container Label

1. Standard radiation symbol.
2. “Caution—Radioactive Material” or “Danger—Radioactive Material.”
3. Name of radiopharmaceutical or its abbreviation.
4. Prescription number.

H. Refills of radioactive prescriptions are not allowed.

I. Preparation of sterile radiopharmaceuticals must meet requirements of sterile compounding rules which contain special exemptions and exceptions for certain provisions that cannot be met in nuclear pharmacies.

III. Class D (Clinic) Pharmacy Rules

A. Definitions and Personnel

1. Clinic—A facility/location other than a physician's office where limited types of dangerous drugs or devices restricted to those listed in and approved for the clinic's formulary are stored, administered, provided, or dispensed only to outpatients of the clinic.
2. License—A copy of the Class D pharmacy's policy and procedure manual and formulary is required as part of the license application.
3. Pharmacist-in-Charge.
   - **a.** Employed or under a written agreement as a consultant to the facility.
   - **b.** May be the PIC for any number of clinics.
   - **c.** Responsibilities include:
     - **(1)** Continuous supervision (not on-site) of nurses, physician assistants, and others carrying out pharmacy-related aspects of the provision of drugs.

(2) Documented on-site visits.

(3) Development of a formulary.

See TSBP Rule 291.92 or TFPDL page J.10 for complete list.

4. Supportive Personnel—Responsible for provision of drugs according to written policies and procedures and completion of the drug label.

B. Formulary

1. May include:
   - **a.** Anti-infective drugs.
   - **b.** Musculoskeletal drugs.
   - **c.** Vitamins.
   - **d.** Obstetrical and gynecological drugs.
   - **e.** Topical drugs.
   - **f.** Serums, toxoids, and vaccines.
2. May not include:
   - **a.** Nalbuphine (Nubain®).
   - **b.** Drugs to treat erectile dysfunction.
   - **c.** Controlled substances.

C. Expanded Formulary

1. May petition TSBP for an expanded formulary if serving at least 80% indigent patients.
2. An expanded formulary may provide for other drugs based upon the documented objectives of the clinic but not those listed in B.2. above.
3. Additional requirements if using an expanded formulary:
   - **a.** Supportive personnel providing drugs must be licensed nurses or practitioners.
   - **b.** Must have policies and procedures for drugs on the formulary that require special monitoring.
   - **c.** Retrospective drug regimen reviews of a random sample of clinic patients must be done on a quarterly basis.
   - **d.** If the pharmacy provides antipsychotic drugs, the therapy must be initiated by a physician of the clinic. A practitioner shall monitor ongoing therapy, and the patient shall be physically examined by a physician at least yearly.

D. Provision of Drugs

1. Drugs are prepackaged and labeled with the name and address of the clinic, name and strength of the drug, quantity, lot number and expiration date, directions for use (may be incomplete), and appropriate ancillary labels.

2. Drugs are provided to patients by designated supportive personnel who complete the label with the patient's name, any information necessary to complete directions for use, date of provision, and practitioner's name.
3. Patient counseling shall be provided at the time of provision.
4. If using an expanded formulary, only licensed nurses or physician assistants may provide drugs.
5. A Class D pharmacy may store and provide samples of dangerous drugs on the clinic's formulary that have been supplied to the clinic's practitioners from a manufacturer.

E. Dispensing of Drugs
Dangerous drugs may only be dispensed by a pharmacist in a Class D pharmacy pursuant to a prescription drug order.

STUDY TIP: Be sure you understand the difference between the dispensing of dangerous drugs and the provision of dangerous drugs in a Class D pharmacy.

F. Supervision
1. PIC, consultant pharmacist, or staff pharmacist must personally visit the clinic at least monthly.
2. Clinics operated by state or local governments or funded by government sources may petition TSBP for an alternative visitation schedule.

IV. Class E (Nonresident) Pharmacy Rules

A. Class E pharmacies are nonresident (not located in Texas) pharmacies whose primary business is to dispense a prescription drug or device under a prescription drug order and deliver the drug or device to patients in Texas, process a prescription drug order for a patient in Texas, or perform another pharmaceutical service as defined by Board rule.

STUDY TIP: A mail-order pharmacy that is located in Texas would not have a Class E license. It would have a Class A license. Class E licenses are only issued to out-of-state pharmacies.

B. Pharmacies must have a license in good standing in their home state.

C. Individual pharmacists working in the pharmacy do not have to have a Texas license, but the PIC of a Class E pharmacy must be a Texas licensed pharmacist.

D. Pharmacies must be able to provide dispensing records within 72 hours of TSBP request.
E. Unless compliance would violate the pharmacy or drug laws or rules in the state in which the pharmacy is located, Class E pharmacies are required to comply with the provisions of TSBP Rules 291.101–291.105 relating to purpose, definitions, personnel, operational standards, and records.
F. Patient counseling is required for all new prescription drug orders. Since prescriptions filled by Class E pharmacies are mailed to patients, they are treated as delivered prescriptions. A Class E pharmacy may meet the counseling requirements by providing written information regarding the prescription drug, along with a statement that a pharmacist is available via a toll-free telephone number for counseling.
G. A Class E pharmacy that compounds sterile products must register with TSBP as a Class E-S pharmacy.

V. Class F (Freestanding Emergency Medical Care Facility) Pharmacy Rules

A. Definitions and Personnel
   1. A Freestanding Emergency Medical Care Facility (FEMCF) is a freestanding facility that is licensed by the Texas Department of State Health Services to provide emergency care to patients.
   2. An FEMCF must have one pharmacist-in-charge who is employed or contracted at least on a consulting or part-time basis.

B. Operational Standards
   1. The pharmacy and storage area for prescription drugs must be enclosed and capable of being locked.
   2. Only individuals authorized by the PIC may enter the pharmacy or have access to storage areas for prescription drugs.
   3. The pharmacy shall have locked storage for Schedule II controlled substances.
   4. In the absence of a pharmacist, only a designated licensed nurse or practitioner may remove drugs from the pharmacy in sufficient quantities for the immediate therapeutic needs of a patient.
   5. In Class F pharmacies with a full-time pharmacist, the pharmacist shall verify the withdrawal of controlled substances from the pharmacy as soon as practical but no more than

72 hours from the time of such withdrawal and at a reasonable interval for dangerous drugs, but at least once in every calendar week.

6. In Class F pharmacies with a part-time or consultant pharmacist, the pharmacist shall verify withdrawals of all drugs (controlled substances and dangerous drugs) at a reasonable interval, but such verification must occur at least once in every calendar week that the pharmacy is open.
7. A Class F pharmacy must maintain a perpetual inventory of all controlled substances which shall be verified for completeness and reconciled at least once in every calendar week that the pharmacy is open.
8. Invoices of dangerous drugs and controlled substances must be dated and initialed or signed by the person receiving the drugs. A pharmacist shall verify that the controlled drugs listed on the invoices were added to the pharmacy's perpetual inventory by clearly recording his or her initials and the date of review of the perpetual inventory.
9. Drugs on an approved outpatient drug list may be supplied for outpatient use only in prepackaged quantities not to exceed a 72-hour supply if prelabeled by the pharmacy. At the time of delivery of the drug, the practitioner or licensed nurse under the practitioner's supervision must complete the label.
10. A retrospective random drug regimen review must be conducted at least every 31 days to verify proper usage of drugs.

VI. Class G (Central Prescription Drug Order or Medication Order Processing) Pharmacy Rules

A. A Class G pharmacy license is issued to a facility established for the primary purpose of processing prescription drug or medication drug orders on behalf of another pharmacy, a healthcare provider, or a payor.

B. A Class G pharmacy cannot possess, store, or dispense drugs but may perform the following:
   1. Receiving, interpreting, or clarifying prescription drug or medication drug orders.
   2. Data entering and transferring of prescription drug or medication order information.
   3. Performing a drug regimen review.
   4. Obtaining refill and substitution authorizations.

5. Verifying accurate prescription data entry.
6. Interpreting clinical data for prior authorization for dispensing.
7. Performing therapeutic interventions.
8. Providing drug information concerning a patient's prescription.

C. Class G pharmacies do not have a maximum ratio of pharmacists to technicians.

CHAPTER EIGHT

Compounding Laws and Rules

CHAPTER EIGHT
Compounding Laws and Rules

See TFPDL Chapter H for complete rules with explanatory annotations.

I. Nonsterile Compounding (TSBP Rule 291.131 or TFPDL pages H.5–18)

A. Establishes requirements for:

1. Compounding of nonsterile preparations pursuant to a prescription or medication order for a patient from a practitioner in Class A (Community), Class C (Institutional), and Class E (Nonresident) pharmacies.

2. Compounding, dispensing, and delivering of a reasonable quantity of a compounded nonsterile preparation in a Class A (Community), Class C (Institutional), and Class E (Nonresident) pharmacy to a practitioner's office for office use by the practitioner.

3. Compounding and distribution of compounded nonsterile preparations by a Class A (Community) pharmacy for a Class C (Institutional) pharmacy.

4. Compounding of nonsterile preparations by a Class C (Institutional) pharmacy and the distribution of the compounded preparations to other Class C (Institutional) pharmacies under common ownership.

B. Nonsterile preparations may be compounded in anticipation of future prescription drug orders or medication orders based on routine, regularly observed prescribing patterns.

C. Commercially available products may be compounded if they are not reasonably available from normal distribution channels in a timely manner, the pharmacy maintains documentation of this, and the prescribing practitioner has requested that the drug be compounded.

D. A pharmacy cannot compound preparations that are essentially copies of commercially available products (e.g., slightly varying the strength) unless the prescribing practitioner specifically orders the strength or dosage form and specifies why the patient needs the product compounded.

E. A pharmacy may enter an agreement to compound and dispense for another pharmacy if the pharmacy complies with the centralized prescription dispensing rule. *See TSBP Rule 291.123.*

F. Pharmacists compounding nonsterile preparations must obtain continuing education appropriate for the type of compounding done by the pharmacist; inspect and approve all components, drug product containers, closures, labeling, and any other materials involved in the compounding process; review all compounding records for accuracy and conduct in-process and final checks to ensure that errors have not occurred in the compounding process; and be responsible for the proper maintenance, cleanliness, and use of all equipment used in the compounding process.

G. Compounding pharmacies must have a Class A prescription balance or analytical balance and weights which are subject to inspection by TSBP.

H. In addition to normal labeling requirements, a compounded prescription label must include the name(s) of the principal active ingredient(s) of the compounded preparation and a statement that the preparation has been compounded by the pharmacy.

I. All significant procedures performed in the compounding area shall be covered by written standard operating procedures (SOPs) designed to ensure accountability, accuracy, quality, safety, and uniformity in the compounding process.

J. All compounding pharmacies must have a documented quality assurance and quality control program.

K. Office use compounding for distribution to physicians, Class C pharmacies, or veterinarians requires a written agreement with the practitioner or pharmacy. In addition, there are specific recordkeeping requirements, recall procedures, and products that must be labeled "For Institutional or Office Use Only—Not for Resale" or "Compounded Product" for distribution to veterinarians.

Note: The provisions for office use compounding in the Texas Pharmacy Act should be read with the federal law on compounding including Sections 503A and 503B of the FDCA. There are concerns that the Texas law may conflict with the federal law. However, for the purpose of the MJPE, you should follow Texas law and rules.

L. Pharmacies may add flavoring to a prescription at the request of a patient provided certain conditions are met, including having documentation that the flavoring does not alter clinical outcomes. This is not allowed for an OTC drug unless a prescription for the OTC drug is provided by a practitioner.

M. DEA generally allows pharmacists to compound narcotic controlled substances in Schedules II–V so long as the concentration of the final solution, compound, or mixture is no greater than 20%.

II. Sterile Compounding (TSBP Rule 291.133 or TFPDL pages H.18–64)

A. General

1. The Texas sterile compounding rule is similar to the requirements of USP Chapter 797.
2. Sterile preparations may be compounded pursuant to a prescription or medication order for a patient from a practitioner; in anticipation of prescription drug or medication orders based on routine, regularly observed prescribing patterns; as an incident to research, teaching, or chemical analysis and not for sale or dispensing; in reasonable quantities for a practitioner's office for office use by the practitioner; by a Class A-S pharmacy for a Class C-S pharmacy; and by a Class C-S pharmacy for distribution to other Class C or Class C-S pharmacies under common ownership.
   Note: The provisions for office use compounding in the Texas Pharmacy Act should be read with the federal law on compounding including Sections 503A and 503B of the FDCA. There are concerns that the Texas law may conflict with the federal law. However, for the purpose of the MPJE, you should follow Texas law and rules.
3. Commercially available products may be compounded if a product is not reasonably available from normal distribution channels in a timely manner. In addition, the pharmacy must maintain documentation of the lack of availability of the product and that the prescribing practitioner has requested the drug be compounded.
4. A pharmacy cannot compound preparations that are essentially copies of commercially available products (e.g., slightly varying the strength) unless the prescribing practitioner specifically orders the strength or dosage form and specifies why the patient needs the product compounded.
5. A pharmacy may enter an agreement to compound and dispense for another pharmacy if the pharmacy complies with the centralized prescription dispensing rule.

B. Training Requirements

1. All compounding personnel must receive didactic and experiential training that includes:
   - **a.** Aseptic technique.
   - **b.** Critical area contamination factors.
   - **c.** Environmental monitoring.
   - **d.** Facilities.
   - **e.** Equipment and supplies.
   - **f.** Sterile preparation calculations and terminology.
   - **g.** Sterile preparation compounding documentation.
   - **h.** Quality assurance procedures.
   - **i.** Aseptic preparation procedures.
   - **j.** Handling of cytotoxic and hazardous drugs, if applicable.
   - **k.** General conduct in the clean room.
2. Initial Training and Continuing Education.
   - **a.** Pharmacists who compound sterile preparations or supervise personnel who compound sterile preparations must complete 20 hours of instruction through either a college of pharmacy or an ACPE-approved course and complete on-the-job training at the pharmacy which cannot be transferred to another pharmacy unless the pharmacies are under common ownership.
   - **b.** To renew a license, a pharmacist who engages in compounding sterile preparations shall complete 2 hours of CE related to compounding if engaged in compounding low- and medium-risk preparations or 4 hours if engaged in compounding high-risk preparations.
   - **c.** Pharmacy technicians and pharmacy technician trainees who compound sterile preparations must complete 40 hours of instruction through either an ACPE-approved course or a training program accredited by the American Society for Health-System Pharmacists and complete a structured, on-the-job training program at the pharmacy which provides 40 hours of instruction and experience.
   - **d.** To renew a registration, a pharmacy technician who engages in sterile compounding shall complete 2 hours of CE related to compounding if engaged in compounding low- and medium-risk preparations or 4 hours if engaged in compounding high-risk preparations.

3. Evaluation and Testing.
    a. All personnel must be trained and pass media-fill tests for assessing aseptic technique.
    b. All compounding personnel shall successfully complete an initial competency evaluation and glove fingertip sampling procedure no fewer than three times before initially being allowed to compound sterile preparations for patient use. Sampling of compounding personnel glove fingertips shall be performed for all risk-level compounding.
    c. All evaluation and testing must be conducted during orientation and training, whenever the quality assurance program yields unacceptable results, and at least annually for low- or medium-risk products and twice a year for high-risk products.
    d. Media-fill tests.
        (1) Media-fill tests must be conducted at each pharmacy where an individual compounds low- and medium-risk sterile preparations. If pharmacies are under common ownership and control, the media-fill testing may be conducted at only one of the pharmacies, provided each of the pharmacies is operated under equivalent policies and procedures and the testing is conducted under the most challenging or stressful conditions.
        (2) Media-fill tests must be conducted at each pharmacy where an individual compounds high-risk sterile preparations.
        (3) No preparation intended for patient use shall be compounded by an individual until the on-site media-fill tests indicate that the individual can competently perform aseptic procedures. An exception is a pharmacist may temporarily compound sterile preparations and supervise pharmacy technicians compounding sterile preparations without media-fill tests provided the pharmacist completes the on-site media-fill tests within 7 days of commencing work at the pharmacy.

C. Risk Levels for Sterile Compounding (USP Chapter 797)
1. Low Risk.
    a. Compounded with aseptic manipulations entirely within ISO Class 5 or better conditions.

b. Examples—Single transfers of sterile dosage forms from ampules, bottles, and vials using sterile syringes and needles, other administration devices, and other sterile containers; and manually measuring no more than 3 manufactured products to compound drug admixtures and nutritional solutions.
c. May be stored 48 hours at room temperature, 14 days if cold (refrigerated), or 45 days if frozen.

2. Medium Risk.
   a. Multiple individual or small doses of sterile products are combined to prepare a product administered to multiple patients or one patient on multiple occasions; or involves complex aseptic manipulations other than single volume transfer; or requires an unusually long compounding process.
   b. Examples—TPN fluids with multiple injections, detachments, and attachments of products to deliver to a final sterile container; filling reservoirs and infusion devices with multiple sterile products; and transfers of volumes from multiple ampules or vials into a single final sterile product.
   c. May be stored 30 hours at room temperature, 9 days if cold (refrigerated), or 45 days if frozen.
3. High Risk.
   a. Nonsterile ingredients are used to prepare a sterile product; or sterile ingredients or devices or components are exposed to air quality inferior to ISO Class 5 for more than one hour; or nonsterile water-containing preparations are exposed more than 6 hours before being sterilized.
   b. Example—Dissolving nonsterile bulk drug powders to make solutions which will be terminally sterilized.
   c. May be stored 24 hours at room temperature, 3 days if cold (refrigerated), or 45 days if frozen.

D. Environment
   1. Sterile preparations shall be compounded in a primary engineering control device which is capable of maintaining at least ISO Class 5 conditions. Primary engineering control devices include:

   a. Laminar air flow hoods—Must be certified at least every 6 months.
   b. Biological safety cabinets—If being used for hazardous sterile products, they must be a Class II or III vertical cabinet and be located in an ISO Class 7 area. If being used for nonhazardous preparations, they must be located in a buffer area.
   c. Compounding aseptic isolators—Must be placed in an ISO Class 7 buffer area unless certain conditions are met.
   d. Compounding aseptic containment isolator—If used for low- and medium-risk products, it must be placed in an ISO Class 7 buffer area unless specific conditions are met. If used for high-risk hazardous preparations, it must be placed in an area or room with at least ISO Class 8 conditions.
2. Low- and Medium-Risk Compounding—Must have a clean room meeting specific requirements including having an ante and buffer area. *See TSBP Rule 291.133(d)(6)(A) or TFPDL pages H.38–40 for details.*
3. High-Risk Compounding—In addition to the requirements for low- and medium-risk compounding, when high-risk preparations are compounded, the primary engineering device must be located in a buffer area that provides a physical separation through the use of walls, doors, and pass-throughs and has a minimum differential positive pressure of 0.02 to 0.05 inches water column.
4. Cleaning and Disinfecting of Sterile Compounding Area. *See detailed requirements in TSBP Rule 291.133(d)(6)(F) or TFPDL pages H.42–44.*
5. Labeling of Sterile Prescription Drug or Medication Orders—In addition to labeling requirements for the class of pharmacy (A, B, C, or E), the label must contain:
   a. The generic or official name of the principal active ingredients.
   b. A beyond-use date determined as outlined in USP Chapter 797. BUDs for CSPs that do not have stability information for the specific formulation (including drug, diluent, container, and closure) must limit the BUDs assigned to the following:

Category	Stored at controlled room temperature	Stored under refrigeration	Stored frozen
Immediate Use	1 hour	Not applicable	Not applicable
Low Risk Made in an SCA	12 hours	12 hours	Not applicable
Low Risk	48 hours	14 days	45 days
Medium Risk	30 hours	9 days	45 days
High Risk	24 hours	3 days	45 days

STUDY TIP: You should be familiar with different BUDs based on storage conditions and risk levels.

c. A statement for outpatient prescriptions (other than sterile radiopharmaceuticals) that the sterile preparation was compounded by the pharmacy.

E. Compounding Process

1. All significant procedures shall be covered in written standard operating procedures (SOPs).
2. Personnel Cleansing and Garbing. *See detailed requirements in TSBP Rule 291.133(d)(13)(C) or TFPDL pages H.51–53.*
3. Quality assurance program must include media-fill test procedures, filter integrity testing, finished preparation release and checks, and environmental monitoring.
4. Quality control program must include monitoring compounding environment and quality of compounded drug preparations including verification of compounding accuracy and sterility.

F. Immediate Use of Compounded Sterile Products—Provides an exemption from low-risk compounding requirements in an emergency or for immediate use where meeting the requirements would subject the patient to additional risk due to delay. Specific conditions must be met including that the preparation time does not exceed one hour and administration begins no later than one hour after compounding. Examples of immediate use of compounding sterile products are ERs, ICUs, etc.

G. Office use compounding and distribution to Class C pharmacies or veterinarians require a written agreement with the practitioner or pharmacy, specific recordkeeping requirements, recall procedures, and products that must be labeled "For Institutional or Office Use Only—Not for Resale" or "Compounded Product" for distribution to veterinarians.

H. USP Chapter 800—Handling Hazardous Drugs in Healthcare Settings

1. USP Chapter 800 details practice and quality standards for handling hazardous drugs in various healthcare settings from receipt, storage, compounding, dispensing, administration, and disposal.
2. It includes information on proper engineering controls and quality standards, personnel training, labeling, packaging, transport, and disposal of all hazardous drugs in various healthcare facilities.
3. The National Institute of Occupational Safety and Health (NIOSH) maintains a list of hazardous drugs and antineoplastic agents used in healthcare.
4. USP Chapter 800 became effective December 1, 2019, but it is currently informational only until the new versions of USP 795 and 797 are finalized. At the time of this book's publication, the Texas State Board of Pharmacy had not adopted rules that would require pharmacies to comply with USP Chapter 800.

CHAPTER NINE

Practice Questions

CHAPTER NINE
Practice Questions

The following questions are designed to test your knowledge of the material in this review guide. The author has no knowledge of specific questions on the Texas MPJE and has developed these questions independently. No representation is made that these questions are similar to actual questions on the MPJE. The Answer Key follows at the end of this section.

1. Which of the following duties may not be performed by a pharmacy technician in a Class A pharmacy? **Select all that apply.**
   - a. Entering prescription data into a pharmacy computer system
   - b. Receiving a new verbal prescription for a controlled substance
   - c. Interpreting patient medication records
   - d. Initiating refill authorization requests

2. Which individual is responsible for ensuring all inventories of controlled substances are taken?
   - a. Pharmacy manager
   - b. Pharmacist-in-charge
   - c. Pharmacist on duty on the day of the inventory
   - d. Pharmacy owner

3. Pharmacist Bill orders and receives a bottle of generic glipizide from his supplier. Bill notices the label of the bottle is crooked and some of the lettering on the label appears to have different fonts in the same word. Bill calls the supplier to verify the transaction data and learns that the lot number on the bottle is not a valid NDC number for that brand of glipizide. What is Bill required to do? **Select all that apply.**
   - a. Order a Class I recall of the drug.
   - b. Notify FDA and all trading partners of this illegitimate product.
   - c. Take steps to work with the manufacturer to prevent the illegitimate product from reaching patients.
   - d. Notify the DEA.

4. Which of the following are required on the label of an OTC product? **Select all that apply.**
   a. Adequate directions for safe and effective use
   b. Name and address of the manufacturer, packager, or distributor
   c. Inactive ingredients
   d. NDC number

5. A pharmacy in Texas must comply with a request from a patient for a copy of his or her prescription records within
   a. A reasonable time
   b. 10 days
   c. 15 days
   d. 30 days

6. Pharmacist Sally received a Preliminary Notice Letter from the Texas State Board of Pharmacy indicating that the Board intended to initiate disciplinary action against her license for allegedly making several dispensing errors. She was given an opportunity to attend an informal conference with a Board panel at which the Board offered to settle the case with a reprimand of her license and payment of an administrative penalty of $1500. Which of the following statements are true? **Select all that apply.**
   a. If Sally agrees to this settlement, she will sign an Agreed Board Order.
   b. This will not be considered disciplinary action against Sally's license.
   c. If Sally and the Board agree to this settlement, Sally cannot appeal the decision.
   d. The Board cannot discipline Sally's license for dispensing errors.

7. Which of the following prescriptions can be filled by a Class A pharmacy in Texas? **Select all that apply.**
   a. A written prescription for buprenorphine from a DATA-waived physician assistant licensed only in Florida
   b. A verbal prescription for Enbrel® (etanercept) from a Texas advanced practice registered nurse (APRN)
   c. A written prescription for Eliquis® (apixaban) from a medical doctor licensed only in Canada
   d. A written prescription for an estradiol transdermal patch from a Naturopath licensed only in California

8. Who is responsible for making a copy of DEA Form 222 when ordering Schedule II controlled substances?
   a. The supplier
   b. The purchaser
   c. DEA
   d. The PIC of the pharmacy

9. Which types of prescriptions are limited to a 10-day supply?
   a. Prescriptions for all Schedule II controlled substances
   b. Prescriptions for Schedule II controlled substances for acute pain
   c. Prescriptions for Schedule II opioids for acute pain
   d. Prescriptions for opioids for acute pain

10. Unless an exemption applies, pharmacists must check the Prescription Monitoring Program (PMP) before dispensing which of the following? **Select all that apply.**
   a. All Schedule II drugs
   b. Carisoprodol
   c. Benzodiazepines
   d. Opioids

11. Which of the following statements regarding dextromethorphan is true?
   a. Dextromethorphan is classified as a dangerous drug in Texas and requires a prescription.
   b. Dextromethorphan may not be sold to a patient under 18 years of age.
   c. Dextromethorphan is classified as a Schedule V controlled substance in Texas.
   d. Dextromethorphan prescriptions are limited to a 10-day supply.

12. A pharmacy may dispense epinephrine auto-injectors pursuant to a valid prescription that does not have a patient name to which of the following entities? **Select all that apply.**
   a. School districts
   b. Day care centers
   c. Law enforcement agencies
   d. Restaurants

13. Pharmacist Harry works at Community Health Services Clinic and has entered into a Drug Therapy Management Protocol with Dr. Patel that allows Harry to sign prescription drug orders for Dr. Patel's patients. Which of the following statements regarding this arrangement are true? **Select all that apply.**

   a. The prescriptions signed by Pharmacist Harry must be filled at the Community Health Services Clinic pharmacy.
   b. Community Health Services Clinic must be a federally qualified health center, hospital-based clinic, or academic healthcare institution for the prescriptions to be valid.
   c. The prescriptions must be issued in writing.
   d. The prescriptions may only be for dangerous drugs.

14. Which of the following statements regarding prescriptions that were filled but never picked up from a pharmacy are true?

   a. A prescription that has been filled but is not picked up by the patient within 30 days must be voided out and the drugs must be quarantined and sent for destruction.
   b. Prescriptions for dangerous drugs that were not picked up may be returned to stock, but prescriptions for controlled substances cannot be returned to stock and must be sent to a reverse distributor.
   c. Before returning prescription drugs that were not picked up into inventory, a pharmacist must evaluate the drugs for quality and safety.
   d. All prescriptions that have not been picked up from a pharmacy must be returned to stock after 21 days.

15. Which of the following statements accurately describe the legal status of marijuana?

   a. Medical marijuana is legal in Texas, but recreational marijuana is not.
   b. Both medical and recreational marijuana are legal in Texas.
   c. Neither medical marijuana nor recreational marijuana is legal in Texas.
   d. Medical marijuana is legal in Texas but may only be dispensed by practitioners, not by pharmacies.

16. Your pharmacy has been asked to provide an Emergency Medication Kit for a nursing home. Which of the following statements are true?
  a. A pharmacy may provide an Emergency Medication Kit to a nursing home, but the kit may not contain any controlled substances.
  b. A pharmacy may only provide an Emergency Medication Kit to a nursing home if the drugs are stored in an automated dispensing machine.
  c. Only Class C pharmacies may provide an Emergency Medication Kit to a nursing home.
  d. A pharmacy that provides an Emergency Medication Kit to a nursing home must maintain a perpetual inventory of any controlled substances in the emergency kit.

17. In a rural hospital, a pharmacy technician may perform which of the following duties without direct supervision of a pharmacist?
  a. Accessing and restocking automated supply systems
  b. Interpreting new medication orders
  c. Withdrawing medication from the pharmacy for new prescription drug orders
  d. Compounding sterile preparations

18. Outsourcing prescription drug dispensing to another pharmacy is legally known as
  a. Centralized prescription processing
  b. Centralized prescription dispensing
  c. Remote prescription processing
  d. Remote prescription dispensing

19. At which class of pharmacy are drugs not stored or dispensed?
  a. Class A
  b. Class B
  c. Class E
  d. Class G

20. A zero report must be sent to the Prescription Drug Monitoring Program if a pharmacy does not dispense any controlled substance prescriptions for how many consecutive days?
  a. 3 days
  b. 7 days
  c. 14 days
  d. 21 days

21. The daily sales purchase limit for pseudoephedrine products is
  - **a.** 0.6 grams of base product
  - **b.** 2.6 grams of base product
  - **c.** 3.6 grams of base product
  - **d.** 120 tablets

22. CMS requires that consultant pharmacists perform a medication regimen review for long-term care patients
  - **a.** When requested by the facility
  - **b.** At least weekly
  - **c.** At least every 30 days
  - **d.** When a medication error occurs

23. To qualify as an Authorized Nuclear Pharmacist, a pharmacist who does not hold a Board of Pharmaceutical Specialties certification as a Certified Nuclear Pharmacist must complete a structured educational program of how many hours?
  - **a.** 500 hours
  - **b.** 700 hours
  - **c.** 1000 hours
  - **d.** 1500 hours

24. The purpose of a peer review committee in a pharmacy is to
  - **a.** Assist pharmacists or pharmacy technicians who have an alcohol or drug impairment problem
  - **b.** Evaluate the quality of care in a pharmacy by reviewing errors or other quality issues
  - **c.** Determine the standard of care in a pharmacy
  - **d.** Establish the discipline that should be imposed on a pharmacist after making a medication error

25. Drugs R Us Pharmacy is located on the ground floor of a high-rise office building and offers delivery of prescriptions to the workers of the various companies in the building. Several of the companies have established a procedure to have the prescription delivered to the front desk of their offices, and employees are notified by the front desk clerk that their prescriptions are ready for pickup at the front desk. Which of the following statements regarding this arrangement are true? **Select all that apply.**

- **a.** This arrangement likely violates HIPAA privacy requirements.
- **b.** This arrangement is an added convenience for patients and acceptable and legal.
- **c.** This arrangement violates the prescription pickup rule because prescriptions delivered to a patient's place of employment are allowed only if the patient is present to accept delivery.
- **d.** This arrangement is valid for dangerous drugs but not for controlled substances.

26. Dr. Trang calls your pharmacy and asks if she can call in a prescription for Vicodin for Mr. Garcia, a cancer patient who is well known to you. Dr. Trang explains that her e-prescribing system is not working, that Mr. Garcia cannot get relief from any other pain medication, and that Mr. Garcia is unable to get to her office to pick up a written prescription. She asks if you can fill the prescription and deliver it to Mr. Garcia's house. Which of the following is true?

- **a.** You cannot take a verbal prescription for Vicodin under these circumstances because Mr. Garcia is not a hospice patient.
- **b.** You can take the verbal prescription, but Dr. Trang must send you an electronic prescription for the Vicodin within 7 days.
- **c.** You can take the verbal prescription and fill the prescription, but it can only be for a 72-hour supply.
- **d.** Both b and c

27. Which of the following must be included as part of a prospective drug regimen review? **Select all that apply.**

- **a.** Drug-drug interactions
- **b.** Underutilization
- **c.** Rational drug therapy combinations
- **d.** Reasonable dose and route of administration

28. Pharmacist Ann is the owner and pharmacist-in-charge at City Drug, a busy community pharmacy in Waco, Texas. In a routine audit, Ann discovers a shortage of 500 dosage units of phentermine. Ann questions her pharmacy technician, who admits to stealing the drugs. **Select all that apply.**

  a. If Ann determines that 500 dosage units is not a significant quantity, she does not have to report this to DEA or TSBP.
  b. Ann must report this to TSBP but not DEA as phentermine is not a controlled substance under federal law.
  c. Ann must report this to DEA and TSBP.
  d. The initial report to DEA must be made within one business day.

29. A busy mother comes to your pharmacy to pick up a prescription for clobetasol cream 0.1% for her 12-year-old son. The prescription was electronically transmitted from Dr. Turner's office to your pharmacy earlier that day, was filled by another pharmacist, and is now ready for pickup. When the mother arrives, she informs you that the prescription was supposed to be for clobetasol lotion 0.1%, even though the prescription was written by Dr. Turner for clobetasol cream 0.1%. Which of the following is true?

  a. Because the prescription is for a child, you must call Dr. Turner to have the prescription changed from a cream to a lotion.
  b. Because the prescription was filled by another pharmacist, you must call Dr. Turner to have the prescription changed from a cream to a lotion.
  c. You can substitute the lotion for the cream and then send notification of the change to Dr. Turner.
  d. You must send the mother back to Dr. Turner to get a new written prescription for the lotion.

30. Who is authorized to witness the destruction of dispensed dangerous drugs by a consultant pharmacist at a nursing home? **Select all that apply.**

  a. An agent of the Texas State Board of Pharmacy
  b. A peace officer
  c. Another licensed pharmacist
  d. A registered pharmacy technician

31. Which of the following drugs may be prescribed by a DATA-waived practitioner for treatment of narcotic addiction? **Select all that apply.**

- **a.** Buprenorphine
- **b.** Naloxone
- **c.** Buprenorphine/Naloxone combination
- **d.** Methadone

32. When a pharmacy requests a transfer of a prescription from another pharmacy, the pharmacy where the prescription is held must complete the transfer

- **a.** In a timely manner
- **b.** Within 4 business hours
- **c.** Within 24 hours
- **d.** Within 48 hours

33. Which of the following are true regarding balances in pharmacies? **Select all that apply.**

- **a.** All pharmacies must have a prescription balance.
- **b.** All pharmacy balances must be calibrated every 60 days.
- **c.** All pharmacies performing nonsterile compounding must have a prescription balance.
- **d.** Prescription balances must be registered with the Texas State Board of Pharmacy.

34. All partial dispensings of Schedule II controlled substances for a nursing home patient must be completed within

- **a.** 72 hours
- **b.** 7 days
- **c.** 30 days
- **d.** 60 days

35. Pharmacist Fred believes that customers would like to buy small quantities of nonprescription drugs and decides to repackage bottles of 100 ibuprofen 200 mg tablets into amber prescription vials of 10 tablets and then sells them to the public. The vials are labeled with the name of the drug, the manufacturer, the lot number, and the expiration date from the original bottles. Which of the following statements are true? **Select all that apply.**
   - **a.** Pharmacist Fred can repackage in this manner because it is for his own use in the pharmacy.
   - **b.** Pharmacist Fred has misbranded the ibuprofen.
   - **c.** The repackaging by Pharmacist Fred is considered compounding and within the practice of pharmacy.
   - **d.** The repackaging by Pharmacist Fred is considered manufacturing.

36. On November 30, 2022, Dr. Williams asks you to prepare a customized medication package (Med Pak) for a patient to assist with the patient's compliance. The patient takes the following three drugs every morning: Losartan 25 mg, Synthroid 0.125 mcg, and Hydrochlorothiazide 25 mg. The stock bottles of the drugs to be used in the Med Pak have the following expiration dates: Losartan—December 2024; Synthroid—November 2023; Hydrochlorothiazide—June 2023. What should be listed as the beyond-use date for the Med Pak?
   - **a.** November 30, 2023
   - **b.** May 31, 2023
   - **c.** June 30, 2023
   - **d.** December 31, 2024

37. A pharmacist receives prescriptions for 12 different patients from the same physician over a 3-hour period. All of the prescriptions are written for patients from out of state and for the same combination of Vicodin, Xanax, and Soma. Which of the following are true? **Select all that apply.**
   - **a.** If the pharmacist confirms that the physician has a valid license and DEA number, the prescriptions are likely valid and can be filled.
   - **b.** If the pharmacist calls the physician and the physician confirms that he or she wrote the prescriptions and saw the patients, the prescriptions are likely valid and can be filled.
   - **c.** The prescriptions are not likely to be valid because they appear to have not been issued for a legitimate medical purpose.
   - **d.** If the pharmacist fills the prescriptions, he or she could be subject to disciplinary action by TSBP.

38. Which of the following is likely to be outside the scope of practice for a dentist to prescribe?

a. Alprazolam
b. Amoxicillin
c. Oral contraceptives
d. Lidocaine gel

39. Dr. Smith sets up a new private practice near your pharmacy. Soon after, you begin to receive several prescriptions for methadone written by Dr. Smith. You call Dr. Smith and she explains to you that she is treating patients for opioid addiction. You should

a. Document this conversation and continue to fill the methadone prescriptions.
b. Ask Dr. Smith for her Drug Addiction Treatment Act (DATA) waiver identification code or "X" number and continue to fill the methadone prescriptions.
c. Explain to Dr. Smith that she cannot prescribe methadone to treat opioid addiction and that you must refuse to fill any further prescriptions for methadone from Dr. Smith.
d. Fill prescriptions for methadone 10 mg from Dr. Smith but refuse to fill prescriptions for methadone 40 mg.

40. Dr. Garcia is exempt from the mandatory electronic prescription requirements for controlled substances. On September 3, 2022, Dr. Garcia issues three prescriptions to Sally for Adderall. Each prescription is for a 30-day supply. The prescriptions are each written on separate official Texas prescription forms and all are dated September 3, 2022. Prescription #1 contains no additional instructions. On Prescription #2, Dr. Garcia writes "Do not fill before October 1, 2022." On prescription #3, Dr. Garcia writes "Do not fill before November 1, 2022." Which of the following is true?

a. Dr. Garcia cannot postdate Schedule II controlled substance prescriptions in this manner; therefore, Prescription #2 and Prescription #3 are not valid.
b. All the prescriptions are valid, but all must be dispensed by October 4, 2022.
c. Prescription #1 is valid and must be dispensed by October 4, 2022. Prescription #2 is valid and must be dispensed by November 2, 2022. Prescription #3 is valid and must be dispensed by December 2, 2022.
d. None of the prescriptions are valid because Adderall should not be written on an official Texas prescription form.

41. Which of the following products is required to be dispensed with the warning "Caution: Federal law prohibits the transfer of this drug to any person other than the patient for whom it was prescribed"?
   a. Buprenorphine
   b. Naloxone
   c. Robitussin A-C
   d. Lipitor
   e. All of the above

42. How many public members are appointed to the Texas State Board of Pharmacy?
   a. 1
   b. 2
   c. 3
   d. 5

43. A pharmacist received a bottle of generic tetracycline capsules from a wholesaler. The label stated that each capsule contained 500 mg of the drug when it only contained 250 mg of the drug. There was nothing about the drug that would indicate to the pharmacist that this problem existed. The pharmacist dispensed several prescriptions before the problem was detected. Which of the following statements is true regarding the tetracycline?
   a. It is adulterated only.
   b. It is misbranded only.
   c. It is both adulterated and misbranded.
   d. It is neither adulterated nor misbranded but is instead a minor technical violation of the potency requirements.
   e. It is in violation of the Poison Prevention Packaging Act.

44. Pharmacist Jessica works as the only pharmacist during the overnight shift at a hospital pharmacy in Beaumont, Texas. How many pharmacy technicians may Jessica supervise during her shift?
   a. Not more than 3
   b. Not more than 6 as long as there are no more than 3 pharmacy technician trainees
   c. Not more than 6 as long as only 3 technicians are involved in sterile compounding
   d. As many as required, as there is no limit

45. Pharmacist Vincent has some expired morphine tablets he would like to send to a reverse distributor for destruction. What documentation is required to accomplish this?

- **a.** DEA Form 41
- **b.** DEA Form 106
- **c.** DEA Form 222
- **d.** An invoice

46. A nonprescription bottle of 1¼ grain aspirin tablets cannot contain more than

- **a.** 24 tablets
- **b.** 36 tablets
- **c.** 50 tablets
- **d.** 100 tablets

47. Physician Assistant Nancy from Dallas, Texas, calls in a prescription for Billy, the six-year-old son of Mrs. Davidson, to Pharmacist Adam. The prescription is for a 30-day supply of phenobarbital with 2 refills. Pharmacist Adam fills the prescription, and Mrs. Davidson picks it up later that day. Which of the following is true?

- **a.** Pharmacist Adam filled an invalid prescription because a prescription for phenobarbital from a physician assistant is not legal.
- **b.** Pharmacist Adam filled an invalid prescription because a prescription from a physician assistant for a six-year-old child is not legal.
- **c.** Pharmacist Adam filled an invalid prescription because the prescription was not issued electronically, and Pharmacist Adam failed to confirm that an exception to the electronic prescribing requirement was met and that an emergency existed.
- **d.** Pharmacist Adam is not required to confirm that an exception to the electronic prescribing requirement applied or that an emergency existed.

48. Which of the following is not part of the transaction data required to be maintained by a pharmacy when it purchases most prescription drugs from a wholesaler or manufacturer?

- **a.** Transaction Information
- **b.** Transaction History
- **c.** Transaction Statement
- **d.** Transaction Certification

49. Under the iPLEDGE Risk Evaluation and Mitigation Strategy (REMS) for isotretinoin, the maximum quantity that can be dispensed is a

a. 7-day supply
b. 14-day supply
c. 30-day supply
d. 60-day supply

50. The Texas State Board of Pharmacy is composed of

a. 9 members consisting of 6 pharmacists and 3 public members
b. 10 members consisting of 6 pharmacists, 1 pharmacy technician, and 3 public members
c. 11 members consisting of 8 pharmacists and 3 public members
d. 11 members consisting of 7 pharmacists, 1 pharmacy technician, and 3 public members

51. Before requesting reinstatement of a license which was revoked or lifting of a restriction on a license, a pharmacist must wait

a. At least 6 months
b. At least 12 months
c. At least 2 years
d. At least 5 years

52. Which of the following products requires a prescription to be dispensed?

a. Humalog®
b. Humulin N®
c. Lantus®
d. Both a and c

53. Manuel is preparing a Total Parenteral Nutrition (TPN) sterile preparation for a single patient consisting of dextrose, amino acids, and various vitamins. The TPN is prepared in a USP 797–compliant area of the pharmacy department. Manuel does not have stability information for the formulation. What is the maximum beyond-use date (BUD) that can be assigned to the preparation if it is to be stored under refrigerated conditions?

a. 30 hours
b. 3 days
c. 9 days
d. 14 days

54. Which type of pharmacy may be in possession of prescription drug samples?

- **a.** A Freestanding Emergency Medical Care Center Pharmacy (Class F) clinic
- **b.** A Class D pharmacy owned by a charitable organization that is part of a healthcare entity providing care to indigent or low-income patients at no or reduced cost
- **c.** A Central Prescription Drug Order Processing Pharmacy (Class G)
- **d.** A Community Pharmacy (Class A) if located in a medically underserved area

55. How often must a Class A pharmacy conduct an inventory of controlled substances?

- **a.** Every six months
- **b.** Annually
- **c.** Biennially
- **d.** A perpetual inventory is required and must be reconciled annually.

56. During each 2-year license renewal cycle to maintain certification to administer vaccinations and immunizations, a pharmacist must obtain how many hours of continuing education relating to disease states, drugs, and administration of immunizations or vaccines?

- **a.** 3 hours
- **b.** 6 hours
- **c.** 20 hours
- **d.** 30 hours

57. To renew a pharmacist license, a pharmacist who engages in compounding sterile preparations shall complete

- **a.** 8 hours of continuing education related to sterile compounding
- **b.** 4 hours of continuing education related to sterile compounding if compounding high-risk products
- **c.** 2 hours of continuing education related to sterile compounding if compounding low- or medium-risk products
- **d.** Both b and c

58. How can a prescriber prohibit generic substitution on a written prescription?

a. By checking the "dispense as written" box
b. By writing the words "dispense as written"
c. By signing the prescription on the "dispense as written" signature line
d. By writing the words "medically necessary" or "brand medically necessary"

59. Records of withdrawal of drugs when the pharmacy department is closed in a Class C pharmacy that employs a full-time pharmacist-in-charge must be reviewed by the pharmacist

a. Within 24 hours
b. Within 48 hours
c. Within 72 hours
d. Within 7 days

60. How many continuing education units (CEUs) are required to renew a pharmacist license?

a. 20
b. 2.0
c. 30
d. 3.0

61. Which of the following is not considered disciplinary action on a pharmacist's license?

a. A reprimand
b. A suspension
c. A remedial plan
d. A revocation

62. If a supplier cannot provide the entire quantity of a Schedule II controlled substance ordered on a DEA Form 222, the remaining quantity must be sent

a. Within 72 hours
b. Within 7 days
c. Within 30 days
d. Within 60 days
e. None of the above

63. The Texas State Board of Pharmacy's policy regarding the filling or refilling of a prescription issued by a practitioner who subsequently dies is that a pharmacist
  a. May no longer fill such prescription under any circumstances
  b. May provide up to a 10-day supply and inform the patient to find a new practitioner
  c. May provide up to a 30-day supply and inform the patient to find a new practitioner
  d. May fill the initial prescription and all refills for up to one year

64. Which of the following is NOT a permissible use or disclosure of protected health information under HIPAA?
  a. Providing a list of all prescription medications to a patient's primary care physician
  b. Sending prescription information to a third-party insurance company for payment purposes
  c. Sending coupons for diapers to all pharmacy customers taking prenatal vitamins
  d. Providing a face-to-face recommendation of an OTC product to a patient based on the patient's symptoms and drug allergy profile

65. Which type of pharmacy may provide remote pharmacy services at a remote dispensing site through use of a telepharmacy system?
  a. Class A pharmacy
  b. Class B pharmacy
  c. Class C pharmacy
  d. Class D pharmacy
  e. Class E pharmacy

66. For which of the following prescriptions may a pharmacist accelerate or advance refills?
  a. A prescription for a quantity of 30 Lipitor with 2 refills
  b. A prescription for a quantity of 30 Valium with 3 refills
  c. A prescription for a quantity of 30 tetracycline with 2 refills for a 16-year-old patient
  d. A prescription for a quantity of 30 tablets of Effexor for a 30-year-old patient

67. Which of the following products or prescriptions is exempt from the Poison Prevention Packaging Act's requirement for child-resistant containers?

- **a.** A prescription for 50 Nitro-Bid 6.5 mg capsules
- **b.** A prescription for 100 Isosorbide 10 mg sublingual tablets
- **c.** A prescription for 20 Erythromycin stearate 500 mg tablets
- **d.** Ibuprofen 200 mg tablets in a 30-count bottle

68. A mail-service pharmacy located in El Paso, Texas, would obtain which type of pharmacy license?

- **a.** Class A
- **b.** Class C
- **c.** Class E
- **d.** Class F
- **e.** Class G

69. The pharmacist-in-charge of a pharmacy must have a policy and procedure to ensure that recalled drugs are removed from a pharmacy's inventory

- **a.** As soon as reasonably practical
- **b.** Within 24 hours
- **c.** Within 72 hours
- **d.** Within 7 days

70. Dr. Galloway issues a prescription for Percocet on July 7, 2022. What is the last day the prescription can be dispensed?

- **a.** July 14, 2022
- **b.** July 28, 2022
- **c.** August 6, 2022
- **d.** Technically there is no expiration date, but the pharmacist should use professional judgment.

71. For which class of recall is there a reasonable probability that the product could cause serious adverse effects or death?

- **a.** Class I
- **b.** Class II
- **c.** Class III
- **d.** Class IV

72. Which of the following are grounds for discipline of a pharmacist's license? **Select all that apply.**

- **a.** Refusing an inspection
- **b.** Failure to wear a lab coat while working
- **c.** Physically abusing a Board employee
- **d.** Failure to maintain required records

73. A nursing home patient who is prescribed estrogen must receive a copy of the patient package insert

- **a.** After one week of therapy
- **b.** Prior to the administration of the first dose and then every 30 days
- **c.** Annually
- **d.** If the doctor specifically requests it be given

74. When must a pharmacy electronically transmit the dispensing of a controlled substance prescription to the Texas State Board of Pharmacy?

- **a.** Immediately after the prescription was completely filled
- **b.** No later than the next business day after the date the prescription was completely filled
- **c.** No later than 7 days after the date the prescription was completely filled
- **d.** No later than 21 days after the date the prescription was completely filled

75. What is the maximum ratio of pharmacists to pharmacy technicians and pharmacy technician trainees in a Class A pharmacy?

- **a.** 1:6 as long as the maximum number of pharmacy technician trainees is 2
- **b.** 1:6 as long as the maximum number of pharmacy technician trainees is 3
- **c.** 1:4 as long as 1 of the technicians is registered (only 3 can be trainees)
- **d.** 1:4 as long as 2 of the technicians are registered (only 2 can be trainees)
- **e.** None of the above

76. A pharmacist receives a written prescription for Fentanyl from a practitioner who is exempt from the mandatory electronic prescription requirements. The pharmacist consults with the prescriber of the medication. After such consultation, which of the following pieces of information may not be changed on the prescription even if the prescriber authorizes the change?

- **a.** Patient's address
- **b.** Patient's name
- **c.** Drug strength
- **d.** Drug quantity
- **e.** Directions for use

77. Which of the following are required elements of a pharmacy library in a Class A pharmacy? **Select all that apply.**

- **a.** Texas pharmacy laws and rules
- **b.** General drug information reference
- **c.** Pharmacotherapy: A Pathophysiologic Approach
- **d.** Basic antidote information and phone number of the nearest regional poison control center

78. A DEA Form 41 is used to document

- **a.** Transfer of controlled substances to another registrant
- **b.** Transfer of controlled substances to a Narcotic Treatment Facility
- **c.** Loss or theft of controlled substances
- **d.** Destruction of controlled substances
- **e.** None of the above

79. Drugs dispensed for outpatient use in a Class F pharmacy may not exceed a

- **a.** 24-hour supply
- **b.** 48-hour supply
- **c.** 72-hour supply
- **d.** 7-day supply

80. In which location must a perpetual inventory be kept of all controlled substances?

- **a.** A Class A pharmacy
- **b.** A Class C pharmacy
- **c.** Any remote pharmacy location
- **d.** All of the above

81. The Texas Controlled Substance Prescription Monitoring program is administered by

- **a.** The Drug Enforcement Administration
- **b.** The Texas Department of Public Safety
- **c.** The Texas Department of State Health Services
- **d.** The Texas State Board of Pharmacy

82. Place the following in order from the least amount of time to the greatest amount of time.

- **a.** Time limit for filling a prescription for Xanax
- **b.** Time for a practitioner to provide an electronic prescription after authorizing an emergency verbal prescription for Percocet
- **c.** Days to provide the remaining quantity of a prescription for Ritalin that was partially filled because the pharmacy was unable to supply the full quantity (not for an LTCF patient)
- **d.** Number of days to provide notification to a patient's primary care physician that an immunization was provided in the pharmacy

83. If a pharmacist performs the final check after an automated pharmacy dispensing system has completed the prescription and prior to delivery to a patient, an automated pharmacy dispensing system in a Class A pharmacy must be tested for accuracy at least

- **a.** Monthly
- **b.** Quarterly
- **c.** Every six months
- **d.** Every 12 months

84. Anabolic steroids are classified under which schedule?

- **a.** Schedule II
- **b.** Schedule III
- **c.** Schedule IV
- **d.** Schedule V
- **e.** None of the above

85. Sterile preparations must be compounded in a primary engineering control device which is capable of maintaining at least

- **a.** ISO Class 3 conditions
- **b.** ISO Class 5 conditions
- **c.** ISO Class 7 conditions
- **d.** ISO Class 8 conditions

86. What must be provided prior to the first dose and every 30 days thereafter to a patient in an institutional setting who is taking an estrogen prescription?

  a. A safety data sheet
  b. A package insert
  c. A patient package insert
  d. A Medication Guide

87. Which inventory does not require the signature of the PIC to be notarized within 3 working days? **Select all that apply.**

  a. Change of ownership inventory
  b. Change of PIC inventory
  c. Initial inventory
  d. Annual inventory

88. Which of the following may not be on a Class D pharmacy's formulary even if it has been granted permission to have an expanded formulary?

  a. Amoxicillin
  b. Birth control pills
  c. Flexeril
  d. Cialis
  e. Both c and d

89. What is the maximum number of physicians a pharmacist may enter into a protocol to provide Drug Therapy Management services?

  a. No more than 3 physicians
  b. No more than 5 physicians
  c. No more than 7 physicians
  d. There is no maximum number

90. A physician issues a prescription for lidocaine in order to obtain a supply for the use in his or her office. What notation must the prescriber place on this prescription to make it a legitimate prescription that a pharmacist can fill?

  a. "Not for resale"
  b. "Own Use"
  c. "General Office Use Only"
  d. "Office Use"
  e. None of the above

91. A fire broke out in the front part of Debra's pharmacy, but the flames did not reach the prescription department. Can the drugs still be dispensed?

- **a.** Yes, as long as the containers are all closed
- **b.** Yes, unless the drugs are heat sensitive
- **c.** Yes, but only after notifying patients that their prescription may have been exposed to smoke
- **d.** No, the smoke from the fire may have adulterated the drugs

92. Pharmacist Kurt reconstitutes a pharmacy bulk package of vancomycin to make a batch of 10 IV bags for dispensing today. What is the risk level of the batch of preparations he is compounding?

- **a.** Immediate Use
- **b.** Low Risk
- **c.** Medium Risk
- **d.** High Risk

93. Which of the following disciplinary actions taken against a pharmacist's license means that a license is not in effect for a specified amount of time?

- **a.** Revocation
- **b.** Suspension
- **c.** Restriction
- **d.** Reprimand

94. What is the youngest age patient whom a pharmacist may provide a flu vaccine without a referral from a physician?

- **a.** Greater than age 7
- **b.** Greater than age 10
- **c.** Greater than age 14
- **d.** None of the above

95. A pharmacist compounding high-risk sterile products must pass media-fill tests at least

- **a.** Every month
- **b.** Every quarter
- **c.** Every six months
- **d.** Annually

96. Ms. Nguyen comes into the pharmacy to pick up her prescription while Pharmacist Marie is on a lunch break at Joe's Discount Pharmacy, but the prescription department is still open. The prescription was called in earlier in the day, and the prescription has already been filled and checked by Pharmacist Marie. The prescription is for methotrexate, and this is a drug that Ms. Nguyen has never taken before. Which of the following are true? **Select all that apply.**

a. Pharmacist Marie must return from her lunch break to counsel Ms. Nguyen.

b. The prescription can be given to Ms. Nguyen by the pharmacy technician as long as written information regarding the drug is provided along with a notice that a pharmacist is available during normal business hours to answer any questions she may have.

c. Pharmacist Marie cannot leave the facility for her lunch break.

d. The prescription department cannot remain open while Pharmacist Marie is on a lunch break.

97. A pharmacist's continuing education records must be maintained

a. For one year

b. For two years

c. For three years

d. Until the next renewal cycle

98. Which of the following may a pharmacy technician NOT perform?

a. Prescription data entry

b. Taking a new prescription for lefunamide over the phone

c. Overriding a drug interaction alert

d. Bulk compounding

e. None of the above

99. A pharmacy that plans to change location must notify TSBP at least how many days before the planned move?

a. 10 days

b. 14 days

c. 30 days

d. 60 days

100. A student intern designation expires if a student fails to take the NAPLEX/MPJE

a. Within 3 months after graduation

b. Within 6 months after graduation

c. Within one year of graduation

d. Within 18 months of graduation

ANSWER KEY TO PRACTICE QUESTIONS

1. B and C
2. B
3. B and C
4. A, B, and C
5. C
6. A and C
7. B and C
8. B
9. D
10. B, C, and D
11. B
12. A, B, C, and D
13. B and D
14. C
15. C
16. D
17. A
18. B
19. D
20. B
21. C
22. C
23. B
24. B
25. A and C
26. B
27. A, B, C, and D
28. C and D
29. C
30. A and B
31. A and C
32. B
33. C and D
34. D
35. B and D
36. C
37. C and D
38. C
39. C
40. C
41. A
42. C
43. C
44. D
45. C
46. B
47. D
48. D
49. C
50. D
51. B
52. D
53. C
54. B
55. B
56. A
57. D
58. D
59. C
60. D
61. C
62. D
63. C
64. C
65. A
66. A
67. B
68. A
69. B
70. C
71. A
72. A, C, and D
73. B
74. B
75. B
76. B
77. A, B, and D
78. D
79. C
80. C
81. D
82. C, B, D, and A
83. D
84. B
85. B
86. C
87. B and C
88. D
89. D
90. E
91. D
92. C
93. B
94. A
95. C
96. B and C
97. C
98. C
99. C
100. B

114490